Marketing Excellence

Marketing Excellence

Winning companies reveal the secrets of their success

Hugh Burkitt and John Zealley

John Wiley & Sons, Ltd

Other Wiley Editorial Offices

John Wiley & Sons Inc., 111 River Street, Hoboken, NJ 07030, USA
Jossey-Bass, 989 Market Street, San Francisco, CA 94103-1741, USA
Wiley-VCH Verlag GmbH, Boschstr. 12, D-69469 Weinheim, Germany
John Wiley & Sons Australia Ltd, 42 McDougall Street, Milton, Queensland 4064, Australia
John Wiley & Sons (Asia) Pte Ltd, 2 Clementi Loop #02-01, Jin Xing Distripark, Singapore 129809
John Wiley & Sons Canada Ltd, 6045 Freemont Blvd, Mississauga, ONT, L5R 4J3, Canada
Wiley also publishes its books in a variety of electronic formats. Some content that appears in print
may not be available in electronic books.

Library of Congress Cataloging-in-Publication Data

Burkitt, Hugh.
   Marketing excellence : winning companies reveal the secrets of their success / Hugh Burkitt and
John Zealley.
      p. cm.
   "Thirty-four success stories . . . selected from the last five years of the Marketing Society Awards
for Excellence"—Introd.
   Includes bibliographical references and index.
   ISBN-13: 978-0-470-06027-8 (HB : alk. paper)
   ISBN-10: 0-470-06027-1 (HB : alk. paper)
   1. Marketing—Great Britain—Case studies.   2. Success in business—Great Britain—Case
studies.   3. Business enterprises—Great Britain—Case studies.   I. Zealley, John.   II. Marketing
Society.   III. Title.
   HF5415.12.G7B87   2007
   658.8—dc22   2006033563

British Library Cataloguing in Publication Data

A catalogue record for this book is available from the British Library

ISBN 13 978-0-470-06027-8 (HB)

Typeset in 11/15pt Goudy by SNP Best-set Typesetter Ltd., Hong Kong
Printed and bound in Great Britain by TJ International Ltd, Padstow, Cornwall, UK
This book is printed on acid-free paper responsibly manufactured from sustainable forestry in which
at least two trees are planted for each one used for paper production.

Contents

Foreword

In a discipline known for its addiction to puffery and hyperbole, it becomes critical when introducing a book on "Marketing Excellence" to wrestle with some definitions. In a world where superlatives like "outstanding" and "perfect" have been debased through over-use, it behoves one to attempt to say what excellent really means in our world of marketing and commerce.

Well, to begin with, excellence has to be unusual and rare. My old football coach used to say about winning that if it was easy we'd all be doing it (true; not that it helped our team very much). The same goes for excellence – to excel is to outperform, not merely perform averagely or have tried really hard.

Secondly, excellence is linked to endurance and sustainability. In some walks of life one piece of brilliance can count as excellent. But in our world it is the execution of ideas over a long period of time which is a non-negotiable criterion for excellence. A great quarter does not a reputation make. This requirement for grinding out results is especially true in competitive markets, where, for every action, there is counter-reaction and the merit of what marketers do can only be judged by the tough laws of competition. Celebrating the internal beauty and logical consistency of the marketing plan is not the objective of this book – but rather, sustained success in the mess of the real world.

Finally, building on the theme of dealing with the real world and not the virtual reality of the plan, excellence is most certainly not the same as perfection. Perfectionists are usually the death of organisations in competitive markets. Perfectionists hate the grubbiness of compromise and trade-off, which sustained excellence usually requires if it is ever to be delivered. A former colleague of mine, George Sewell, who built the Quaker business in the UK over the last ten years, always liked to remind me that in his opinion "excellence is the continued delivery of 80% of the critical elements of one's business".

He was, and is, right, and his wisdom is worth its weight in gold. Marketing is about grappling with real life; that's why it's hard and challenging. Striving for perfection will kill you, but uniformly high and consistent standards will mark you out and usually result in success (if they are better than your competition).

This book captures the examples of excellence that meet these definitions. It's a book for practitioners, but will nonetheless inspire anybody for whom winning in the commercial world is important. The book is essential in itself for celebrating excellence, because excellence is a fragile concept that requires, demands and screams out for the oxygen of publicity. It's the kind of thing that, if it isn't celebrated and talked about, will diminish in quantity. As the 17th century poet Lyttleton said of it: "Where none admire 'tis useless to excel; where none are beaux 'tis useless to be belle".

So enjoy and learn from the book. Occasionally, especially if you are new to marketing, you may think that you are, for example, simply seeing examples of "common sense"; so Innocent and Green and Black's weren't geniuses to spot the demand for natural food, Tesco didn't need a PhD in human behaviour to spot the demand for home delivery, and Avon was hardly the pioneer of the idea that cause-related marketing can be enormously effective in these more civic-minded times. But this brings me back to definitions of excellence and the enduring insight of my old football coach, who used to say, "We live in a world where common sense is rarely common practice".

How true. Perhaps the best and most practical way to think about marketing excellence is when, for a time, common sense manifests itself as common practice – to the unbridled relief of the consumers and customers who reward us with their custom.

Martin Glenn, former President of PepsiCo UK and Ireland

Introduction: so what's the big idea?

The idea of this book is to inspire you through these examples of successful marketing. We are confident that you will find lessons from these thirty-four success stories which you can apply to the development of marketing programmes in your own company. They are all winners, selected from the last five years of the Marketing Society Awards for Excellence, and they reflect the different categories of entry, from *Customer Insight* through to *Developing Marketing Capabilities*.

The markets represented here are highly varied – from peanuts to world poverty – and the brands are equally diverse – from Innocent Drinks to Microsoft. But all these stories have one thing in common: they demonstrate the power of a good idea, consistently executed, with clear evidence of success.

The lessons in this book come in all shapes and sizes. There are lessons based on big unifying ideas that have helped re-energize the whole company, like Brains's "Positive Thinking" and Tesco's "Every Little Helps". There are lessons based on shrewd observation of the customer, like Heinz Ketchup's upside-down bottle and Specsavers' move from eyes to ears. There's a wonderful example of niche marketing from Silentnight Beds, which introduced a customised bed for children called "My First Bed". By contrast, *The Independent* and *The Times* newspapers describe their bids to reach out to a wider market by going compact.

The examples of both Dove and Waitrose demonstrate the impact of finding and backing an original advertising idea in a very competitive market, and Olivio, Nicorette and Famous Grouse prove that good ideas can travel across borders.

Toyota offers a multitude of ideas for increasing customer loyalty through its "*kaizen*" philosophy of continuous small improvements, and in the *Developing Marketing Capabilities* chapter, Vodafone describes a great idea for a system that will help you decide which of many possible new ideas you should prioritise and develop.

Some of the examples in this book are of ideas that have been so powerful that they have continued to provide the mainspring of brand success for over twenty years. Lynx first persuaded young men to get to grips with their personal hygiene in the early eighties by promising it would improve their chances of seduction, and has kept this eternally appealing promise fresh through different phases of advertising.

Stella Artois first positioned itself as "*Reassuringly expensive*" in the 1970s and has been reassuringly consistent in its premium positioning throughout its move into the mass market, although the case presented here also explains how the communication idea had to be subtly altered in the early nineties as the brand moved into television.

But if you don't have twenty years of success to build on, you will find cases here which fit any stage of development of your brand, from planning its launch, like The Number 118 118, through to fighting to maintain its customers' loyalty after the first flush of success, like O_2.

The cases all conclude at a particular point in time, and occasionally there have been further dramatic changes in the market since these stories were written, but nearly all of these winners have gone on to achieve even greater success.

To help draw out the lessons, we have also been fortunate to have the comments of a dozen leading marketing directors who have judged the awards over the past few years. They were chosen as judges because they are successful marketers themselves, and their comments clearly show that they found reading and judging these cases a rewarding exercise. We are sure that you will too, if you follow their example, and we encourage you to study and apply these lessons to your own marketing endeavours.

Hugh Burkitt and John Zealley

Acknowledgements

The authors would like to thank all the companies and agencies who have allowed us to publish their winning entries. We have occasionally been asked to omit some sensitive financial data, but in all of the cases which we have selected, the marketing problem, the solution and the success come across clearly. While we have used the original submissions as the basis for the case studies, we have reworked, edited, embellished and in some cases updated them to transform them into case studies suitable for the book. A complete list of winning companies and the awards won is included in the appendix.

The Marketing Society's partner throughout the past five years has been *Marketing* magazine, and we are grateful to Craig Smith, editor of *Marketing*, and all the team at Haymarket who have helped us build the scope and stature of the awards during that time.

We could not have put this book together without the support of Accenture, who, as headline sponsors of the awards for a number of years, have played a key role in helping us to ensure that the awards have been able to mature into the premier acknowledgement of successful marketing impact in the UK. In particular, as we have prepared this book, we must thank Peter Thomas, Accenture's UK Marketing Director, who has been a valued advisor, and Bridget Jackson, who has led the research project on marketing measurement which forms the first chapter of this book.

Unilever has also been a sponsor throughout this period, and we are grateful to the company for its sponsorship of this book. Keith Weed, Group Vice President Homecare, and President of the Marketing Society, and Roger Kirman, Head of Marketing Excellence, have been enthusiastic supporters.

Laura Mazur of Writers 4 Management has done a brilliant job in persuading the entrants to part with their material, chasing up the illustrations and editing the final manuscript in a timely and thoughtful manner. Claire Watson has kept us all to schedule and Claire Plimmer at publishers John Wiley & Sons has shown faith in this project from its conception.

Finally, the original "editors" of this book are, of course, the judges who choose the winners in each year. We are very grateful to all of them for the time they have given during the awards process each year, and especially so to those who have added their comments at the beginning of each chapter.

We would also like to thank all those who have entered the Marketing Society Awards in association with *Marketing* in the past five years. There have been many excellent cases written, which we have not had space to include. Without these entries there would have been no competition.

We also extend our thanks, in anticipation, to our readers. If you can draw lessons from these cases that help you develop your own marketing success story, then you will be helping us prove that marketing excellence is indeed the key driver of business growth.

About the authors

Hugh Burkitt is Chief Executive of the Marketing Society, which is the leading network for senior marketers in the UK. At the Society he was responsible for the launch of the Society's *Manifesto for Marketing*, introduced the *Marketing Leaders Programme* for potential marketing directors and established the *Panoramic Group*, which has created a new forum where all the UK's marketing organisations have agreed to work together to promote marketing.

He began his own marketing career as a Unilever trainee at Birds Eye Foods in 1967, and progressed via the Manchester Business School to Collett Dickenson Pearce in 1972. He spent the next thirty years in advertising, founding the agency Burkitt Weinreich Bryant Clients and Company in 1986, and leaving in 2002 as Chairman of Burkitt DDB.

Successes during this period included the launch of Piat d'Or, Malibu, Archers and Coors; the relaunch of Bailey's Irish Cream; gaining market leadership for Nestlé Purina's Bakers Complete; and being the first advertising agency to demonstrate to John Lewis that advertising works.

He is a council member of the Advertising Association, and has also served on the Advertising Standards Authority Council, the Institute of Practitioners in Advertising Council and the Complaints Panel of the Portman Group.

In February 2005 he completed a walk up Kilimanjaro to raise money for VSO projects in Tanzania – where he had been a volunteer teacher nearly forty years earlier.

John Zealley is a Managing Director within Accenture's Global Business Consulting Group, responsible for the Consumer Goods, Retail, Auto &

Industrial Equipment, Travel & Transportation and Pharmaceutical Industries. He works with senior executives of leading companies on growth generation and business reorganisation programmes.

As a consultant, initially with McKinsey & Co and latterly with Accenture, John has worked with consumer based businesses in such diverse sectors as financial services, food and drink, grocery and general retailing, leisure and healthcare and in markets across Europe, Africa, Asia Pacific and North America.

John began his career in industry in marketing with Procter & Gamble, where he worked on the Ariel business, was brand manager of Daz, responsible for the launch of the liquid product, and led the Republic of Ireland business.

John is a Fellow of the Marketing Society and sits on the Editorial Board of *Market Leader*, the Society's quarterly journal. He is a Liveryman of the Worshipful Company of Marketors.

In addition, he uses his marketing skills with a number of not-for-profit organisations, including Cancer Research UK, The Royal Shakespeare Company and the Institute for Citizenship.

1

Marketing measurement excellence

Introduction

The marketing function, especially in a large global company, faces enormous challenges. Competition is more intense in virtually every industry. The current marketing landscape is the most complex it's ever been. Media fragmentation and consumer segmentation demand more sophisticated and differentiated marketing strategies. And there's more data on both marketing activities and outcomes to sort through than ever before, making generating meaningful insights much more difficult.

To add to that, senior executives everywhere have ratcheted up their demands for demonstrable return on marketing investments. And marketing specialists need to rise to that challenge. As the Marketing Society's *Manifesto for Marketing* has noted, many chief executives believe that their marketers are not stepping up to the challenge and tend to see their marketing professionals as "lacking the discipline and capabilities to drive profitable growth". To address this, marketers must realign themselves to the priorities of the business, in part by measuring and articulating the value the function creates.

Long experience has shown that while marketers typically want to demonstrate their business value to the organisation, few have the range of capabilities needed to measure what has historically been more of an artistic than a scientific pursuit. In fact, effectively designing, deploying and using such measurement capabilities has posed a vexing challenge for many companies, and their inability to solve the measurement conundrum is preventing them from realising their full potential.

To shed light on the state of marketing measurement, Accenture and The Marketing Society joined forces to conduct a series of interviews with some of the UK's most pre-eminent marketing executives across all industries[1]. More specifically, the research sought to understand the importance of marketing measurement to these companies' business; the processes, systems and resources these organisations have in place to gauge marketing performance; and the impact that marketing measurement is having on overall business performance.

Defining high performance

The research found that high performers had three broad characteristics of marketing measurement:

1. **High performers live a measurement culture.** They place measurement at the centre of the organisation, with marketing measurement a boardroom agenda item; they accelerate their learning through a systematic process of "test and learn"; and they effectively share and utilise marketing measurement insights and best practices across the organisation.
2. **High performers invest in the right skills and capabilities.** They recruit and develop individuals to build a consistent base of marketing know-how, analytical skills and commercial perspective; support the marketing function through strategic partnerships with an extended team of finance and research specialists; and use appropriate technologies to help them analyse critical data.
3. **High performers measure intelligently and comprehensively.** They operate a clear measurement strategy aligned to business goals and outcomes; and they measure what matters – provided it's cost-effective and actionable.

[1] Jackson, B., Spooner, J. and Ingleton, R. (2006) *Measuring Up*, Accenture.

Each of these characteristics is explored in detail in this chapter, with examples and insights gleaned from conversations with the executives interviewed.

High performers live a measurement culture

In many companies, marketing still struggles to build real boardroom credibility – largely because marketing lacks accountability and is often unable to justify marketing spend when budgets come under pressure.

Conversely, in high performers, marketing and brand are part of the organisation's fabric. Marketing is championed from the top because it is central to building strong brands and driving business value. For example, at Procter & Gamble (P&G), the contribution of marketing is well understood because P&G is a marketing company at its core. A marketing mindset is so pervasive at the consumer-products giant that most P&G general managers rise in the organisation through marketing.

Along with such a marketing mindset comes a true measurement culture. The high performers in the research recognise that the best decisions are made using the best available evidence, and as a result see superior measurement as being at the heart of business success and competitive advantage.

Starting at the top

But how do these organisations ensure that measurement actually happens – and does so consistently and comprehensively? It all starts at the top. In all the high performers talked to, marketing measurement is actually part of the boardroom agenda, which ensures that the entire marketing organisation clearly understands how critical measurement is.

At Diageo, for example, there is regular board-level review of consumer response to what's put in the marketplace. A similar situation exists at Toyota; according to Paul Philpott, Toyota's Marketing Director: "While board members don't look at individual campaigns, they do receive the key performance indicators. The marketing team is empowered to do its job, but they know they are being watched."

One result of such boardroom interest is that metrics become "hard-wired" into marketing and business processes and fact-based thinking permeates the company from top to bottom. High performers use common metrics to measure and compare marketing activities and outcomes systematically. Through a commitment to continuous measurement and review, they build insights into what is working and what is not and learn how to improve future performance.

Toyota embodies "hard-wired metrics" through its application of the principles of *kaizen* – continuous improvement – to marketing, just as in every part of the business. (See the Toyota case studies in Chapters 3 and 8). That means employing a consistent approach to measuring marketing programmes against common key performance indicators, with a focus on interpretation and future actions. The Toyota way is to try new things, learn from mistakes and build on successes in order to evolve.

In fact, such a "test and learn" approach is common among all the high performers talked to during the research. These companies proactively identify the gaps in their knowledge and design clear experiments to provide the evidence they need to make decisions. "Test and learn" means start small and scale up. However, once a new concept is validated, clear evidence gives the confidence to move fast.

Importantly, high performers' experiments are judged against different goals and funded using specific budgets. In such an "acorn fund" approach, high performers prune the lowest performing investments among existing marketing activities and transfer that money into an innovation budget for which marketers compete to win funding for new ideas. Andy Fennel, European Marketing Director at Diageo, explained: "We rank activities and cut out the bottom 20%. This allows us to up-weight our top-performing activities and to invest in experiments. We're clear about what we want to do and assess rigorously. We manage the risk and don't bet the farm."

This helps high performers avoid the trap that other companies often fall into: focusing on using metrics simply to monitor and refine existing marketing activities through incremental optimisation of cost effectiveness while missing out on truly innovative and creative opportunities that lack a proven track record and, thus, are much harder to justify.

Sharing knowledge is key

But even the most measurement-driven company would struggle to understand the full impact of marketing without the ability to effectively share and leverage knowledge. Indeed, in many companies, different departments may track the same key performance indicators in separate spreadsheets, which results in multiple and often conflicting versions. While the latest structured data may be only a few clicks away in the company intranet, storage issues mean it is often difficult to obtain long runs of historical data. Furthermore, unstructured data and insights often are held locally without clear processes for sharing and learning.

High performers, however, excel in sharing measurement data, learnings, insights and best practices within and across brands and countries. In doing so, these companies strive to have "one version of the truth" throughout the organisation, investing more in connecting people and information. They are thus able to reduce the cost of measurement while increasing marketing effectiveness.

Furthermore, because it takes time to build up a useful knowledge base that supports meaningful analyses, high performers invest in creating unique knowledge assets over the long term. As just one example, P&G has systematically developed and grown a database of advertising copy pre-test scores. By combining this data with sales results by category and brand, P&G can create consistently high-performing copy and accurately predict the sales impact of its advertising.

High performers invest in the right skills and capabilities

Creating a culture of marketing measurement is not easy. Nor does it happen quickly or on its own. It requires a company to develop or acquire the right skills, data and technology, and to do so with an eye toward building a capability that can help the organisation grow and compete successfully over the long term.

Combining the right skills

In the past, the core skills of the marketer have centred on consumer understanding, brand insight and creative flair. However, this is no longer enough. The modern marketer must operate in a broader business constituency where an analytical mindset and commercial perspective are essential to making fact-based decisions aligned to business goals. Recognising this, high performers excel in hiring the right individuals and investing in their development through training that reinforces an evidence-driven culture.

At Diageo, for instance, analytical skills are a core part of the training for everyone in the marketing function, and a combination of on-the-job coaching and formal training ensures that the Diageo Way of Building Brands (DWBB) – which has marketing measurement at its centre – is instilled throughout the company. This includes a clear understanding of measurement and the role each function plays in improving performance.

Many companies find they do not have the right skills in the marketing department to carry out or understand all the required analysis. And business accountability can be held back by parochial and adversarial relationships between the marketing and finance functions. That's why high performers build an extended marketing team based on open strategic partnerships with either other functions in the organisation or with third parties that can bring deep expertise in key areas.

For instance, in high-performance companies, a key role of finance is decision-support and to work as a partner with marketing, bringing increased objectivity to commercial decisions. At P&G, all marketing teams have a finance resource embedded within them. And at AOL, the company's central marketing planning group is linked tightly with the strategic planning group that is part of the company's finance department.

High performers also strengthen marketing's capabilities by ensuring that the marketing function has deep relationships with key groups that can provide new or more sophisticated techniques for measurement and analysis – although marketing retains ultimate ownership of the process, responsibility for developing conclusions and acting on them.

Again, at Diageo, there is a discrete consumer planning function inside the marketing department. "Their job is to determine the truth when it comes to consumers," explained Andy Fennell. "They are market researchers with brains often sourced from the best ad agency planning departments." To reinforce this team's strategic contributions, Diageo now outsources lower-level activities that market research previously performed. At Toyota, marketing also teams with a separate group for specialised skills, but in this case it's an external agency.

Toyota relies on its agency's analysts to "dig into the data" and let Toyota know the return of various campaigns and how to improve future returns. "In an ideal world, the [analyst] capability would be in-house," said Paul Philpott, "but it's not realistic for us, so we develop in-depth relationships with a limited number of agencies. And to be most effective, agencies need to feel that they're part of our business and really understand what we're trying to accomplish."

Enabling the best decisions

Having the right people in place is one part of the battle. Another part is gathering the right data and using it effectively to make better decisions. In today's world, companies typically do not lack for data. In fact, marketers can feel overwhelmed by the bewildering range of often conflicting data that they are faced with. The instinct is to simplify or to "go with the gut", and it's easy to confuse detail with accuracy. As a result, marketers need a strong appreciation for the uses and limitations of the data and analysis they are presented with.

"We have an incredibly sophisticated level of data and analysis, and our analytical skill set is very strong," said AOL's UK Chief Executive Karen Thomson. "Our biggest challenge, in a fast-moving and complex market, is to think about the big picture and the overall direction. We spend a lot of time developing that business perspective in our people." The high performers in our research have the confidence to challenge and interpret the data. They stand back and consult their experience and, whether drawing on other facts or applying judgement, they make sense of the numbers by placing them in the context of an evolving picture of the business. Where others simplify, high performers distil the facts and take the holistic view.

"None of the [analysis and measurement] techniques is foolproof," said Gary Coombe, General Manager, P&G Fabric and Homecare New Business Development. "[ROI models] don't take account of everything. For example, they miss the value of scale. Although the ROI on one test might be higher than another, you have to take account of the overall size of the return. I find that part of my role is making sure people aren't viewing marketing as 'painting by numbers'." Of course, the need to navigate through such large amounts of data means companies are starting to invest in technology to enable more effective marketing measurement.

High performers measure intelligently and comprehensively

As the preceding section illustrates, most companies feel they spend heavily on data and analysis. They measure on multiple levels from micro to macro;

capture multiple metrics depending on the type of marketing activity; and look at multiple consumer, brand and financial outcomes. However, many companies lack clear measurement principles. Much of the data isn't fully used, many of the metrics can seem disconnected from the wider business, measurement can be ad hoc and inconsistent, and there is no line of sight between inputs and outcomes. When the objective is accountability and tracking, the focus may be on generating information instead of creating insight.

Focusing on outcomes

While they recognise the importance of managing and tracking inputs, high performers focus on key business outcomes and align their measurement architecture to a clear understanding of how their business works. A complete picture of the links between individual marketing activities and tangible business outcomes is still the "holy grail" which no-one has fully mastered. However, high performers have the confidence to make informed judgements about these relationships, and a relentless drive to quantify them.

For example, Toyota uses a number of metrics to gauge the effectiveness of its direct campaigns, but these ultimately are tied back into common key performance indicators that demonstrate prospects' active engagement with the brand: numbers of test drives taken and brochure requests made.

At Diageo, global brand teams seek to understand and codify the "growth drivers" of each brand. "We don't always start with all the evidence we need," Andy Fennell explained, "but it is better to have a framework and replace educated guesses with facts over time."

In addition to emphasising business outcomes, high performers measure comprehensively. They aim to measure all elements of the marketing mix and have an integrated approach that links execution, planning and strategy and the different domains of sales, marketing and innovation. These companies continuously look for new and better ways to measure both established and new media – including consumer touch points that may be hard to measure or that fall into the domain of other functions, such as sales.

For instance, in the consumer goods industry it is now recognised that the first "moment of truth" is at the point where the consumer interacts with the brand in-store. Therefore, leading UK companies are investing in virtual reality technology to accelerate their learning about how to maximise impact at the fixture. And in the US, www.Tremor.com was set up to measure the reach and value of word-of-mouth. The website acts as a focal point for a community of 250 000 "connector" teenagers, who were recruited to help companies such as P&G and Coca-Cola to learn how to generate a powerful "buzz".

The three golden rules of measurement

Regardless of the specific metrics used, the best companies follow three golden rules when constructing their measurement strategy.

1. **Measure what matters, not just what you can.** Sometimes it can seem that some things are measured to the "nth" degree while others are not measured at all. By targeting the evidence they need to make decisions, high performers can cut through the clutter and focus on the data that really matters. If the evidence doesn't exist, they design experiments or invest in new techniques to get what they need.
2. **Only measure if it's actionable.** There are many things that it would be interesting to know, but before investing in a new piece of data or analysis, the primary question should be "What decision will I be able to make as a result?" As Paul Philpott of Toyota said, "I haven't got time to be curious for its own sake. As business leaders, effectiveness is all that matters."
3. **Only measure if it's worth the candle.** Because measurement is expensive, high performers look at cost and benefit and always seek ways to do more for less. It's easy to get overwhelmed by the possibilities of everything that could be measured. By keeping the focus on business outcomes, high performers can ensure there is little wasted effort in their measurement activities.

Benefits of marketing measurement

High performers reap a number of substantial benefits by measuring their marketing activities. One of the most important of these is higher growth and profitability. By cultivating a superior understanding of today's complex marketing landscape, high performers use measurement more effectively to build brand differentiation and sustain product premiums. Furthermore, because they proactively seek the evidence to make decisions, high performers gain the confidence to move faster and make bigger bets than their competitors.

High performers also are much more adept at positioning for the future. Their ability to accelerate learning through a systematic cycle of test and learn, and willingness to champion marketing innovation through "acorn funds", keep them always a few steps ahead of the competition.

Finally, by measuring marketing, high performers enjoy a high level of consistency in their operations. They are able to reduce risk and improve predictability by filtering out failures and betting on winners. And, because they share and implement best practices, they don't repeat failures but, instead, build on past successes.

To be sure, even the high performers in this research are not immune to vagaries of their markets or the limitations of current measurement tools and approaches. There's always more to be done and more to learn. However, these companies have succeeded in substantially increasing marketing's business impact and value through their commitment to a disciplined, data-driven approach to measurement – which is a major differentiator in their quest for market leadership and profitable growth.

The case studies in the rest of this book illustrate the tangible impact that measurement effectiveness, as a key part of marketing excellence, can have on company performance.

2

Customer insight

Introduction

Classically, this is where all great marketing thinking begins. Finding those valuable nuggets of customer insight is one of marketing's great quests, because they can lead to innovation that has a measurable impact.

One of the problems with discussions of insight is that they tend to veer slightly to the over-glib. Real insight is hard to find and harder to put into practice. It goes beyond mere observation. The definition of insight is the capacity to gain an accurate and deep intuitive understanding of something. But it also has its roots in psychiatry, where it is defined as the clarity patients gain about themselves through treatment.

It is arguably most likely to be of value in product innovation, where something is developed which a consumer is truly looking for. Both of the case studies in this chapter from Heinz and Vodafone are compelling examples of this.

"Great innovation based on insight nearly always looks obvious after the fact. These case studies illustrate that successful innovation is usually the product of hard work and a disciplined approach.

A preparedness to get to the bottom of customers' issues and not to accept the status quo is clear in both cases. In Heinz's example, the status quo was a long-established industry norm. In its commitment to tackle consumers' issues head on, Vodafone was prepared to make a move in exactly the opposite direction to the prevailing trend of category development.

Both case studies highlight that innovation efforts are often most productive when they have a specific end in mind or issue to address. For Vodafone that led to a root and branch redesign of the product and service for a large segment of users.

And finally, both examples show the benefits of rigorous testing and post-implementation evaluation."

Phil Smith, Commercial and Operations Director, Camelot

Heinz Tomato Ketchup: turning a packaging icon on its head

Snapshot: Consumer insight and observation led to one of the biggest packaging changes in the famous brand's history.

Key insights

- Don't be afraid of pursuing a relatively straightforward idea, because it can add huge value.
- The valuable insight Heinz gained that consumers turned the bottle on its head to get the last drop helped make what was already a successful brand even more so.
- This was done without losing the brand's long heritage, and, indeed, capitalised on it.

Summary

Heinz is one of the largest food companies in the world, with a portfolio of powerful brands holding number-one and number-two market positions in more than 50 countries. The company's top-15 power brands account for two-thirds of annual sales.

The Heinz Tomato Ketchup bottle is one of the most well-known marketing symbols in the UK. Since the product's launch in 1896, Heinz has continually evolved the design and packaging of the sauce, with such innovations as the move from glass to plastic bottles in 1987.

By 2001, the company realised that it was time to make another significant shift. The subsequent design of the top-down (TD) format was based on the simple but compelling insight that consumers turned their bottles upside down to get the last drop. The first design of the top-down bottle was launched in the UK in July 2003, and within weeks was exceeding all expectations. More than seven million of the bottles were sold in the first 12 months: more than three times the base estimate of 2.2 million sales.

In early 2004, a second design came into play, making more of its iconic "57" varieties via embossing. This move ensured the brand's heritage and long-term values were maintained throughout the transition.

In October 2004, two additional sizes of the bottle launched, with two more added in March 2005. One glass format was retained for consumers loyal to the design. Heinz Tomato Ketchup's share of the market by value reached 77.5% by the end of December 2004, up from 72.8% in 2003.

The birth of a packaging icon

Heinz Tomato Ketchup was first launched in the US in 1876, taking its place alongside other Heinz products from the innovative Henry J. Heinz, purveyor of fine foods. Thick and spicy, ketchup was presented as a convenience food: "a blessed relief for mother and other women in the household."

By 1882, Heinz patented the first glass ketchup bottle, one of the most famous iconic symbols to be found across the globe. The brand was introduced to the UK in 1896 and quickly became the nation's favourite sauce. By 2005, Heinz Tomato Ketchup commanded a 66.5% volume share of the UK ketchup market and was recognised worldwide as the "defining ketchup".

In 1987, following extensive consumer research, the first plastic Heinz Tomato Ketchup bottle was launched. The insight driving this innovation was that consumers loved their Heinz Tomato Ketchup but didn't want to wait to get it out of the bottle. So the squeeze bottle was the perfect solution.

Delving more deeply

By 2003, 80% of the bottles of Heinz Tomato Ketchup sold in the UK were plastic, proving convenience to be a key consumer need. However, Heinz consumer contact data had also shown that while consumers loved Heinz Tomato Ketchup, they had one or two niggles about the bottle. Focus groups were thus run to review packaging and understand the issues.

The question was asked: "*What makes you mad, sad and glad about Heinz Tomato Ketchup?*" Some of the answers included:

- "The taste of the product!"
- "The ketchup sometimes makes a mess around the cap."
- "You have to turn the bottle upside down when it's nearly empty."

- "It is difficult and takes time to get the last of the ketchup out of the bottle."

Following these consistent messages fed back to Heinz by consumers, it was clear that the company needed to start the development of a bottle that would resolve these issues. This led to the biggest change brought about by the packaging development teams at Heinz.

The result was launched in the US after research showed that purchase intent of 77% prior to use rose to 90% after use, while the 40% who said they definitely would buy the products rose to 67% after use. These were the highest results any Heinz Ketchup had scored. And these results were repeated in the UK. Consumers felt the benefits of the new design were worth paying a higher price for. They liked the convenience, ease of use and the stay-clean cap.

One stock-keeping unit (sku) in the new top-down format (570 g) was launched in the UK in July 2003, and within weeks was exceeding all expectations (Figure 2.1). It surprised most consumers to the extent that the Heinz

The birth of Top-Down

- **June 2003**
  - 570g SKU launched
  - £10.8m sales in the first 12 months

Source: IRI, 12 w/e 31ˢᵗ Dec 2005

Figure 2.1

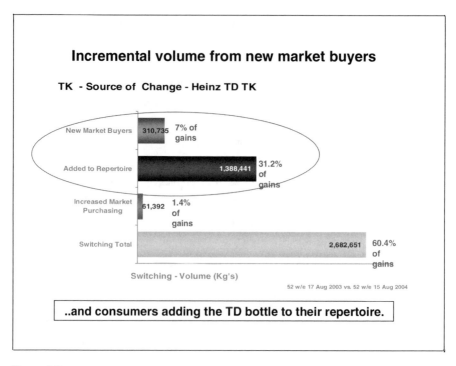

Figure 2.2

Consumer Careline received many calls from consumers congratulating the company on the new bottle format.

Obviously the potential threat was cannibalisation of the existing ketchup bottle formats. The predicted cannibalisation was 85%, but when the data came through it was even more encouraging, at a little over 60% (Figure 2.2).

A top-down revolution

The launch was rolled out into 14 countries across Europe, with similar results. After six months, it was clear the new top-down format was working and it could be the future of Heinz Tomato Ketchup.

So, by 2004, it was time for the next stage of research to see what consumers thought of more Heinz Tomato Ketchup being turned on its head. It

A new bottle design

- More icon cues

  - eyebrows
  - facets
  - 57

- More prominent than current bottle

Figure 2.3

was also clear that if top-down was going to be the future of Heinz Tomato Ketchup, then the bottle needed to reflect all the iconic values of the first Heinz Tomato Ketchup bottle that was patented in 1882.

This led to the symbol of Heinz Tomato Ketchup taking another evolutionary twist. The "eyebrows", facets and "57" embossing were all made more prominent than on the original top-down bottle, bringing it much closer in line with the glass shape (Figure 2.3).

Clear-cut results

A study was commissioned from Research International in three countries across Europe – the UK, Belgium and Sweden. The results were very clear:

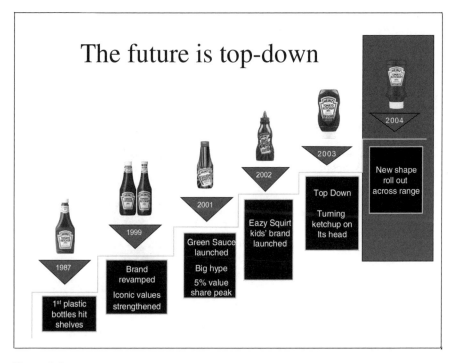

Figure 2.4

- consumers loved the new top-down bottle (Figure 2.4);
- once people had tried the bottle they significantly preferred it to other ketchup bottles;
- the company still had some consumers who were loyal to the glass bottle and they should not be alienated;
- consumers wanted to be reassured that only the packaging had changed and that it was still the same Heinz Tomato Ketchup they know and love inside.

Heinz Tomato Ketchup's share of the market by value reached 77.5% by the end of December 2004, up from 72.8% in 2003. Volume share also increased from 64.1% to 66.5%.

Figure 2.5

Extending the range

In October 2004, two further sizes of the new top-down bottle were launched in the UK, and the final two sizes were launched in March 2005 (Figure 2.5). One glass Heinz Tomato Ketchup bottle was retained for the loyal glass consumers.

All images appearing in this case study are reproduced by permission of Heinz.

Vodafone Simply: turning reluctant users into enthusiasts

Snapshot: Vodafone developed a powerful but simple proposition to reconnect with consumers alienated by the technologically-driven marketing of mobile phone companies.

Key insights

- Even a company as large and successful as Vodafone can reap dividends from basic research into a core consumer group.
- Its research showed that the needs of a substantial segment of the market were being ignored by mobile phone companies.
- It used this core understanding to develop a radical, consumer-oriented proposition – Vodafone Simply – to engage these consumers.

Summary

Vodafone Group provides a full range of mobile telecommunications services, including voice and data communications. Vodafone has equity interests in 27 countries and partner networks in a further 27 countries, with almost all the group's mobile subsidiaries operating principally under the brand name "Vodafone". Turnover for year-end March 2006 was £29.4 billion.

In 2003, Vodafone realised it had a problem with a certain segment of its target audience. These 31–55 year-olds, dubbed adult personal users (APUs), were characterised by low or no usage of their phones. The company realised that to grab the attention of these potentially profitable consumers, it had to become far more aware of their needs and behaviours.

Extensive research led to the development of Vodafone Simply, a radical new concept in mobile phone offering that was geared to overcoming the resistance APUs felt towards ever more complicated mobile technology.

The concept struck a chord with this audience, judging by the number of new customer acquisitions in the six months after it was launched in 16 markets, and the rising levels of customer satisfaction. In addition, APUs began to use their phones far more.

Background

The mobile phone market has been heavily driven by advances in technology. This has led to more technically advanced mobile phones with more and more features, capable of more advanced tasks. While this has been broadly welcomed in the market, particularly by the younger, technically confident consumer, not everyone has embraced these advances.

Vodafone recognised that a large group of consumers was being left behind by the mobile phenomenon. These were typically the adult personal users (or APUs: 31–55 year-olds, they own and pay for their mobile, mainly for personal use). Bucking the prevailing growth trend in the market, these consumers were clearly not engaging fully with their mobiles:

- their usage was low or non-existent;
- their usage was not growing;
- they were not using features beyond calling or text.

At Vodafone, the marketing team grasped two crucial insights about this substantial consumer group:

- their needs were clearly not being met by ever-advancing mobiles with more features;
- but their communication needs and behaviour meant that the mobile phone should be of far greater use and relevance in their lives.

A deeper investigation of this group led Vodafone to develop "Vodafone Simply" – a radical new concept in mobile phones to get APUs using their mobiles and embracing them as friends, not foes.

The challenge: rethinking the direction

Initial research revealed that APUs were not disengaged with their mobiles merely because they did not know how to use them. Instead, mobile phones lacked relevance and fit in their lives. A mobile phone was a necessary evil, or something others said they should have. The gulf between the mobile and the APU mindset is illustrated in Figure 2.6.

The big challenge was to find a way to change their mindsets and engage with them much more closely in the mobile world. This called for a radical

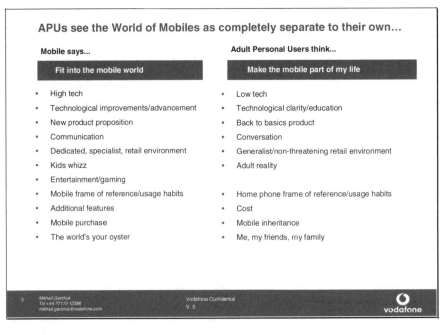

Figure 2.6

rethink within Vodafone, because not all consumers' needs and aspirations were going to be met via innovations led by technological advances. It meant that the company had to stop, re-evaluate its direction, and recognise that it was moving away from this group, not towards them.

It might seem to have been a relatively easy move in hindsight, but it was most certainly not so at the time. Vodafone needed to challenge prevailing market thinking and go down a consumer-led, rather than a technology-led, development path. Such a change in direction had to be rigorously supported every step of the way by consumer insight and robust research.

Getting to know you

Initial segmentation research in 2003 helped to define and provide a core understanding of mobile phone consumer segments, including APUs. Subsequent analysis of the Vodafone customer database revealed the extent of the opportunity if these customers could be further engaged (Figure 2.7).

During late 2003 and 2004, Vodafone embarked upon a programme of proposition and product development, informed by highly attuned research

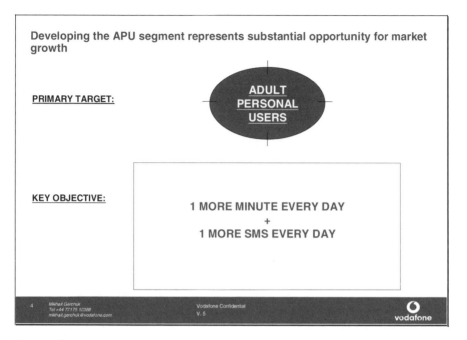

Developing the APU segment represents substantial opportunity for market growth

PRIMARY TARGET:

ADULT
PERSONAL
USERS

KEY OBJECTIVE:

1 MORE MINUTE EVERY DAY
+
1 MORE SMS EVERY DAY

4 | Mikhail Gerchuk
Tel +44 77175 12388
mikhail.gerchuk@vodafone.com | Vodafone Confidential
V. 5 | vodafone

Figure 2.7

which provided key consumer insights and direction. Each stage of the research delivered critical insights that were the basis of the development of the proposition and advanced it significantly. This was followed by validation to ensure that the design was on-track and truly consumer-led. The result was Vodafone Simply: a mobile proposition designed to meet the mobile needs of the APU consumer as fully as possible.

The particularly disengaged nature of APUs (and the developmental process itself) meant the company needed to employ particularly creative techniques to bring the proposition to life. These included:

• Three distinctive prototype handsets. It was imperative to get respondents to hold and feel each handset design in order to evaluate the tactile and ergonomic quality. This was particularly important in understanding the value of the shape, feel and finish of the handsets in overall appeal.
• An experiential, computer-based demonstration of how the features would look and what the user interface would deliver. Doing this resulted in an immediate lift in response. APUs visibly sat up and got interested.

- A testbed retail simulation to put the prospective handsets into a realistic competitive arena. It was important to see whether these handsets would have an impact and catch the eye.
- An interactive computer program to allow respondents to choose their own design by selecting differing colours/finishes for the front, back and buttons from an extensive palette. It was important to understand why differing solutions appealed, and not to end up with hundreds of different solutions.

Shaping the launch

A number of key consumer insights shaped the design and launch of Vodafone Simply.

1. **APUs felt disenfranchised and left behind by mobile phones: distant and disengaged.** Vodafone Simply was developed to be deliberately distinct and different from other mobiles, and was positioned as a phone designed to meet their mobile needs rather than offer new technology.
2. **APUs did not feel positive or comfortable about using their mobiles.** Vodafone Simply handsets were designed around APUs' aesthetic priorities: the curvy handset was smooth and sculpted to feel natural and comfortable in the hand. The straight handset was more highly designed and had more masculine lines. Colours, contrast and design lines for each were honed to APU aesthetic desires.
3. **APUs were disengaged with mobiles through lack of relevance more than low confidence.** Vodafone Simply was actively designed around the needs of APUs to build their confidence.
4. **APUs had trouble getting help when they had a problem, because there was no easy access to appropriate help when needed. And manuals were over-long/complex/not there, and with language that was too technical or scientific.** Vodafone Simply offered helpful tips on-screen, accessed through a single button push and written in easy, straightforward language. Help and specific advice were offered, geared specifically to the task or feature being used.

5. **APUs had differing design tastes**. Vodafone Simply was developed with a range of handset designs: initially two distinct and different bar designs, followed by a clam design launch.

6. **APUs found menus confusing and overly complicated. They got lost in them.** The design of Vodafone Simply focused on the most important APU features (identified through research), and provided three dedicated buttons giving instant access to them.

7. **For APUs, people came first: whom they were communicating with was of paramount importance.** Vodafone Simply's user interface was totally people-centric. The phone book showed the three most frequently called numbers at the top and the last time each person was contacted. If there was a message, the screen immediately showed the name of the person it was from (and only then whether voice or text).

8. **APUs cared about etiquette.** Because APUs worried about disturbing people with their phone ringing loudly or calling them accidentally, Vodafone added dedicated slider keys on the side of the handsets, to adjust the ringer setting and lock/unlock the keypad.

9. **APUs wanted things to be as clear and easy to read as possible**. Vodafone Simply was developed with higher resolution screens, uncluttered graphics, clear language and legible fonts. The information most important to them was clearly displayed:

   - time – in large, legible font;
   - ringer setting;
   - battery level;
   - signal.

10. **APUs misplaced their mobile at home and forgot to charge it up**. Vodafone Simply had a dedicated charging cradle so the user would always know where it was at home and that it was always charged.

11. **APUs were reluctant to invest time in adding contacts to their mobiles: it was complex and they were likely to lose them.** Vodafone Simply was offered with an optional PC cable to back up and edit contact lists on a computer.

12. **APUs were overwhelmed by the array of accessories for mobile phones.** Vodafone Simply was offered with only the charging cradle and a hands-free kit.

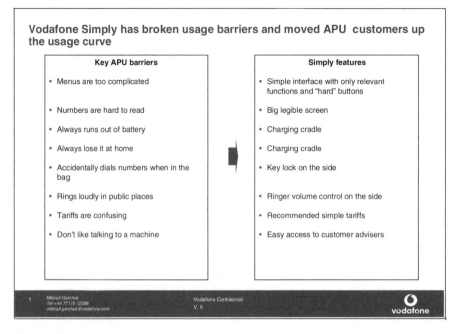

Figure 2.8

Ultimately, Vodafone Simply was designed to overcome APU barriers to mobile usage, to engage them in the mobile revolution and to stimulate their use (Figure 2.8).

Getting the marketing to work

The marketing communications for Vodafone Simply needed to get the message across as clearly as possible.

Initially, APUs were not particularly excited by the idea alone, or by a phone that looked somewhat different. What really made them sit up and take notice, however, was the user interface demonstration. This brought to life that Vodafone Simply really was a radically different concept in mobile phones. Launch communications were developed to dramatise the user experience and get across the radical and singular character of the proposition. The language and style used were implicitly straightforward and easy to understand.

Evaluating results

There were a number of measures of the success of Vodafone Simply, such as higher rates of new customer acquisitions in the 16 markets where it was launched and increased mobile usage. Other signs of success included:

- Enhanced mobile usage experience for APU purchasers. Vodafone Simply enhanced APU mobile experience in terms of satisfaction and increased accessibility by making their phone more readily available to them. Furthermore, it began to change the mindset of APU mobile users.
- Enhanced customer experience and satisfaction. Vodafone Simply purchasers were delighted with their purchase. 61% were very satisfied with Vodafone Simply, compared to just 51% of APUs who purchased a different mobile from Vodafone, and over 40% said it had exceeded their expectations (Figure 2.9).
- Vodafone Simply delivered high satisfaction through ease of use. Consumer satisfaction stemmed from ease of use and sheer simplicity, which

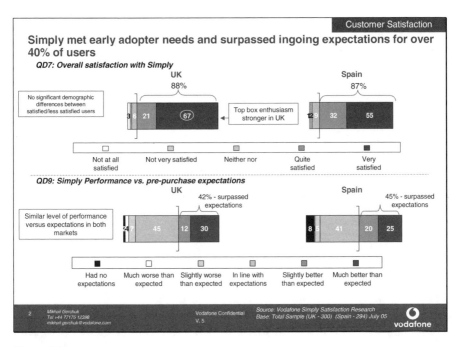

Figure 2.9

really delighted the user. Reasons for satisfaction were mainly given as "simple/easy to use" (56% UK; 77% Spain).

- Vodafone Simply succeeded in building APU confidence. A core aim of Vodafone Simply was to make APUs feel more confident about using their mobiles, which, in turn, would increase mobile usage. Vodafone Simply customers enthusiastically told the company that they felt much more confident about using a mobile and experienced fewer barriers or problems (72%/69% reported increased confidence in UK/Spain respectively). This also added to a greater satisfaction in using Vodafone Simply (vs. other handsets).

- Having Vodafone Simply led to APUs using their mobiles more. A third of Vodafone Simply customers found they were now more likely to have their phones charged and switched on, and therefore more likely to carry it with them. They were calling and texting more as a result.

There was also strong market endorsement and recognition. For example:

- Vodafone Simply was rated one of the "Ten best mobiles ever made" and one of the "ultimate iconic designs", in an article in the *Independent on Sunday* (October 2005) by Henrietta Thompson (author of *Phone Book*, a history of the mobile phone).

- The *Sunday Times* included Vodafone Simply VS1 in their top ten mobiles in the article "Evolution of the mobile moves to warp speed" (27/11/2005).

- Vodafone Simply was endorsed by daytime TV presenters Richard and Judy on their TV show.

Finally, on the day when Vodafone announced the launch, its shares were up 3.5 pence, helped by the launch of its Vodafone Simply service, according to *Forbes* magazine.

All images appearing in this case study are reproduced by permission of Vodafone.

3

Launching new brands

Introduction

Launching new brands is an exercise in both courage and risk. However, as these case studies show, different challenges call for different approaches.

For example, with the Toyota Corolla, where the company was launching what was essentially a new brand but with the baggage of the past, it took a lot of advertising money and steely determination. At Silentnight Beds, it demanded both an understanding of the consumer purchase cycle and creative thinking in a difficult, slow-moving and naturally uncreative category.

Strong consumer insight and persuasive communications combined to put BBC's Freeview on the map, while 3 decided to stop talking up the new generation of mobile technology and get back to the basics of price and delivery. Walkers did the unthinkable: it removed its parent brand as endorsement and used word-of-mouth to win over a new and elusive part of the market for snacks.

"Although these case studies illustrate different approaches to innovation, they do have a number of things in common. When it comes to cracking a difficult problem, the job of the innovator is to consider how to build the idea based on insight, in a way that enhances the brand and creates favourable economics – and to do this by considering all factors simultaneously.

It's not enough to focus on insight if you can't make money at it. Insights without fantastic, truly differentiated ideas to address them are an intellectual exercise. Truly great innovators have great judgement and fantastic flair. They know where to make the right trade offs to get a winning new product to market."

Syl Saller, Global Innovation Director, Diageo

Walkers' Nobby's Nuts: how a bag of peanuts got the nation talking

Snapshot: Walkers gained a firm foothold in a fiercely competitive market by developing a new stand-alone snack brand, Nobby's Nuts, and rewriting the rules of "peanut marketing".

Key insights

- Walkers found some clear market space and changed the rules by studying adjacent markets such as beer.
- The company didn't use the parent brand, with its association with crisps, in order to attract an audience which Walkers had traditionally found hard to reach.
- Word-of-mouth ensured that the brand was fast-tracked to nationwide fame, achieving the exceptional awareness and trial critical for a new product launch, especially without the parent brand endorsement.

Summary

Walkers is part of PepsiCo, a world leader in convenience foods and beverages, with 2005 revenues of more than $32 billion and more than 157 000 employees.

It is the leading grocery brand in the UK. Its portfolio of crisps and snacks has contributed to the company's impressive record of growth. However, in 2005, the company was facing a maturing and declining market, which meant that to grow the business, it had to find new and profitable gaps.

Research found such a gap: snacks that would appeal to hungry men in the 17–34 age bracket. The eventual creation of a pub snack brand, Nobby's Nuts, hit exactly the right note with an audience where Walkers had had little presence.

To get the message across in a high-profile way, the company rewrote the rules of "peanut marketing" – a challenge in a category that was both highly competitive and in the throes of commoditisation. Significantly, the brand was going to be launched without the endorsement of the parent brand.

The clever use of a limited budget to "get the nation talking" in a humorous way about the brand paid off in a big way, with awareness levels well above average. Even more importantly for the company, the brand single-handedly turned around the decline in the nuts category from −7% pre-launch to 22% afterwards. 20% of that was thanks to the new brand.

The opportunity: snacks for blokes

Walkers is the number-one grocery brand in the UK, with an enviable portfolio of crisps and snacks and a well-regarded story of rapid growth. The challenge the company faced in 2005 was the same massive challenge that it had been facing over the previous few years: how would it continue to grow the business in a mature market, with minimal cannabilisation to the existing portfolio? The big difference in 2005 was that market conditions were even tougher: it was no longer a steady market, but a saturated market experiencing its first significant decline.

Walkers conducted a quantitative segmentation study of the "macro" snacking market, and identified a part of the market and an audience that the portfolio traditionally ignored: "gap-filling" snacks among 17–34 year-old male consumers. This was not about snacking as a treat, or about snacks playing an emotional role (comfort, indulgence, etc). It was snacking with a clear, functional objective: to satisfy hunger. Walkers had little presence in this part of the market, so the segment offered huge potential for Walkers to grow its business with minimal cannibalisation.

The strategic rationale

Since Walkers dominated the salty snacking market, top-line growth had to come from gaining share in the broader macro-snacking market. While salty snacks satisfied the need to pick at something and keep the consumer going, they didn't satisfy real hunger. As a result, salty snacks performed well as a meal accompaniment but not as a missed meal. So this was a segment offering real growth.

Further qualitative research suggested that this audience found it difficult to find a convenient snack that could really satisfy hunger. Here was an opportunity to create a specifically "bloke-centric" snack that could really make its mark.

A tantalising target

The segmentation study identified the primary target audience as "care-free youth", who represented a significant 12% of the snack market:

- The group was predominantly pre-family (68%) and male (63%).
- The two occasions that came top of the scale were lunchtime (69%) and missed meal (71%). Together they accounted for over 25% of all macro-snacking occasions. Both occasions were characterised as impulse purchasing and eating out of home.
- This group was also a key audience for the Walkers business, since it was a group where the company had underperformed as youth switched out of the family brands they had grown up with, and began to make personal brand choices, usually for alternatives (e.g. McCoys) (Figure 3.1).

Qualitative research confirmed that this audience felt their strongest affinity towards brands that spoke directly to them. These, however, were rarely towards "family" brands. This presented Walkers with a big dilemma. The Walkers brand has an incredibly powerful equity. On a product level it is a

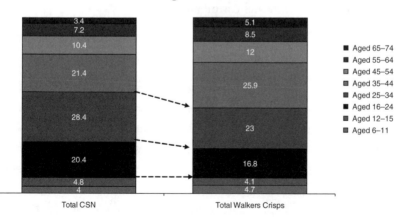

Figure 3.1

kitemark for five-star quality, freshness and flavour. On an emotional level, it represents British values, belonging, home, a family favourite.

But it was this ubiquitous appeal, and the very strength of its brand connection as the nation's favourite, that appeared to be turning off the younger adult audience. All indicators suggested that Walkers needed to look beyond the Walkers family to create a new brand that could to speak to them in their language and live in their world.

The solution: a pub snack brand

The company set about establishing a new brand that stood for the very things that mattered to this audience and satisfied their hunger in a no-nonsense way.

It started at a product development level with a clear blueprint for the new range: every product worthy of carrying this new brand had to be two things. First it had to be straightforward (not poncy, fluffy or fiddly), and secondly it had to be satisfying. The first two products to fit the bill were big crispy-coated peanuts and thick, strongly-flavoured ridged crisps. The crispy-coated peanuts represented the biggest hunger-busting innovation.

Rigorous qualitative and quantitative studies consistently proved that their launch was most likely to gain a lot of attention in a category that had seen little innovation or excitement for decades. So peanuts formed the start-point of the launch.

Once Walkers had developed the right products, it needed to find a new language with which to talk about them. One of the biggest insights for Walkers was the dissonance between the rules by which peanuts and snacks are traditionally marketed, and the marketing rules followed by brands that have a powerful connection with this target audience (John Smiths, Pot Noodles, Lynx, etc).

The new rules of peanut marketing

The target's language was the language of beer advertising, not the stale language of peanuts. To catapult the brand launch to nationwide fame, the company would need to rewrite the rules of peanut marketing.

This was about totally rethinking what a brand represents and how it behaves. Walkers was launching in a declining category, with a few long-established brands and little differentiation. Peanuts were a commodity, a market stuffed full of the same variants: dry-roasted, salted, honey-roasted, etc. So the company didn't set out to position the peanuts as crunchier than the competition, bigger than the competition or even that the peanuts were crispy-coated and available flavoured (which they were). Instead, the company decided this was a real opportunity to step outside the world of peanuts and create a pub brand.

The challenge: playing the fame game

The big challenge for the company and its agency, AMV BBDO, was how to build mass awareness and trial in a long-established and highly competitive category. And this had to be done without the strength of Walkers' branding: something that had never been attempted before.

Walkers studied other brands that did well within the pub environment (John Smiths, Foster's, etc.) and identified a trait they all shared. A phenomenon accompanied their marketing activity, one which would serve as the key benchmark for the company's own success: that, in every pub throughout the land, they were a topic of pub conversation.

Walkers sought fame for its new brand, and with a limited marketing budget, focused its attention on how to get the nation talking. The secret was in ensuring that everything about the brand, and every component of the campaign, had the "B factor": banterability.

Bring on the banter

Banterability (noun): 1. The ease with which a product or service can be talked about. 2. The likelihood that a product or service will be talked about. This activity is often experienced in school playgrounds, offices and public houses.

Banter, or pub-talk as it is sometimes called, is the most popular activity in all pubs. According to Kate Fox, author of *Passport to the Pub: The tourist's guide to pub etiquette*[1]:

[1] Fox, K. (1996) *Passport to the Pub: The touristis guide to pub etiquette*, BLRA.

> "Jokes, puns, teasing, wit, banter and backchat are all essential ingredients of pub-talk. In fact, you will notice that most pub-talk has an undercurrent of humour, never far below the surface. Pub humour can sometimes be bold and bawdy, but the stereotype of loud, beer-bellied males exchanging dirty jokes is inaccurate and unfair. Most pub humour is quite subtle – occasionally to the point of obscurity – and some participants have a command of irony that would impress Jane Austen."

So Walkers went on a quest to find that special marketing ingredient. It started with the name, a name that in itself would become a topic of pub conversation and which was the focus of the launch campaign.

Name that brand

A brand's name is perhaps the most important factor affecting perceptions of it. It can be incredibly powerful to have a brand name that not only refers to or describes the function or service of a product, but which lends it a tone, outlook and personality. Walkers sought a name that could conjure up just the right images to help position the product.

It toyed around with a range of names from Sailor Jack's to Rough Stuff, but settled with a name from further afield. In the wider international PepsiCo snack business there was a quirky brand from Australia that had just the magic that Walkers were looking for: Nobby's Nuts.

Pub research told the company that the idea of "Nobby's Nuts" was compelling. It came with inherent personality traits (northern, humorous, down-to-earth, local rather than chain pub), was highly memorable, would make a great bar-call and possessed the invaluable "B" factor (Figure 3.2).

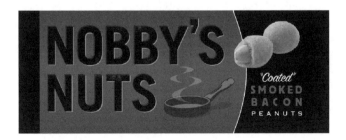

Figure 3.2

Figure 3.3

The packaging followed. Detail and, crucially, banter-stimulation, was incredibly important. Every element was designed to spark pub chat, from the phallic-shaped illustrations to the Nobby's Lessons on the pack: e.g. "how to double de-clutch", and "the origins of the pirate's eyepatch".

Walkers took the elements that were clearly working and created an entertaining TV commercial that would become one of the most talked-about ads of the year. It had all the necessary ingredients: it starred a pub jukebox favourite with pub icon status, it had a highly memorable and easily repeatable line – "Nibble Nobby's Nuts" – and was set in a pub. It quickly achieved cult status (Figure 3.3).

The company built on this by exploiting as much pub media as possible. Alongside beer mats and other pub elements, the campaign was accompanied by a launch event at football's Carling Cup final, and a pub was created for various sampling initiatives, with one involving the women's arm-wrestling team. All that was left was for the brand to hit the pub and wait for the regulars to start talking.

Soaring to the top

This was indeed a brand built on banterability. Nobby's Sweet Chili became the number one variant in the UK nut market, with Nobby's becoming

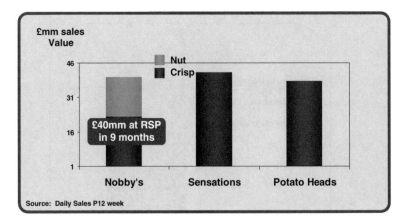

Figure 3.4

the UK's second largest nut brand, with a market share of 10%. Within nine months the brand was worth £40 million, which was the company's biggest launch since Sensations, the crisps range. In fact, the brand single-handedly turned around the decline in the nuts category in the impulse sector from −7% pre-launch to +22% post-launch in May 2004. 20% of that growth had been driven by Nobby's coated nuts (Figure 3.4).

Even better, Nobby's was taking a larger share of the 16–34 year-old market. Moreover, advertising tracking data demonstrated that the ads had been instrumental in driving sales.

- the ads reached top place in *Marketing* magazine's Adwatch, with spontaneous awareness of 73%;
- they fell into the top 3% of all ads in the UK, reaching 16 on the Millward Brown Awareness Index (Figure 3.5);
- among men, the ads hit a peak recognition of 78% (compared to the Millward Brown average of 59%);
- branding was incredibly strong, with levels of 90% among men (compared to the Millward Brown average of 48%) (Figure 3.6).

But perhaps most importantly for the company, the nuts became a subject of "banterability":

Awareness Index

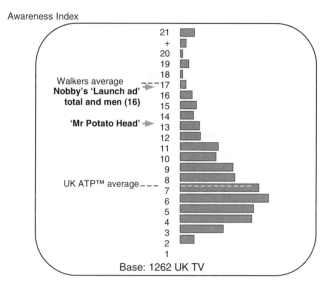

Figure 3.5

Branded impact

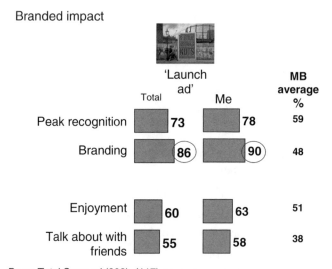

	'Launch ad' Total	Me	MB average %
Peak recognition	73	78	59
Branding	86	90	48
Enjoyment	60	63	51
Talk about with friends	55	58	38

Base: Total Seen ad (203), (117),· Not directly comparable due to methodology shift in

Figure 3.6

- talkability was high, with "talk about with friends" reaching 58%;
- 13 900 websites were listed as mentioning Nobby's Nuts according to the search engine Google in the UK;
- the phrase "Nobby's Nuts" was entered into the UK Google site over 80 000 times in 2005;
- the launch of the brand garnered extensive media coverage, generating £289 000 of free publicity.

The decision by the UK's favourite snack brand to launch a new product range without its powerful branding as endorsement was a huge risk, but one that was instrumental to the runaway success of Nobby's Nuts. It was not so much *in spite of* but *because of* going against every category convention that this phenomenon was achieved.

In completely rethinking what a snack brand represented and how it behaved, and in finding a new language to talk with, the company was able to build a powerful connection with a segment that it had struggled to reach before. Ultimately, it was Walkers' determination to make the brand the focus of pub banter that ensured that every component of the new brand, everything it stood for, everything it did and everything it said, found its way into public houses up and down the land, and helped it become the leading nut variant within nine months.

All images appearing in this case study are reproduced by permission of Walkers.

Toyota Corolla: making an unloved car desirable

Snapshot: Toyota transformed the prospects of the Corolla by mounting a big-budget campaign that broke all the conventions of traditional media planning.

Key insights

- A really good new product can reinvent a brand's equity.
- The rejuvenation of the Corolla – the biggest launch in Toyota UK's history – was achieved through a powerful combination of many factors: the car itself, the inclusive strategic process, the boldness of the huge investment and media strategy, the high-profile advertising and the consumer insights.
- Aiming at people's hearts rather than their heads transformed the car's prospects dramatically.

Summary

Toyota is Japan's leading vehicle manufacturer and one of the largest and most successful carmakers in the world.

In January 2002, Toyota launched the next generation Corolla in the UK. This was the company's most important launch ever. While the company had aggressive sales targets, it was missing out in some key market segments such as small/medium cars, which were dominated by the Ford Focus and VW Golf. The Corolla wasn't even in the top ten.

The challenge was intriguing. The Corolla was the world's best-selling car. A Corolla had won the World Rally Championship. It had topped J.D. Power's UK customer satisfaction survey for four years in a row. Yet, in image terms, it was nowhere. Marketing had to move the Corolla from supply-push to demand-pull by injecting desire and emotion into the brand.

The marketing and communications strategy was built around the concept of pride in ownership. An internal marketing programme was also undertaken to inspire staff, dealers and other stakeholders, while the advertising formed the heart of the external communications. Those ads emphasised the lengths to which people would go to be associated with the brand – a brand to be proud of. Bold media buying heightened the impact.

The resulting campaign achieved the company's aims: to sell more cars, more profitably, to a new audience in a much tougher segment of the market. Between March and October 2003, sales volumes grew 49% compared with the same period in 2001, or 7600 more cars.

The beginning: getting from supply-push to demand-pull

In January 2002, Toyota was set to launch the next generation Corolla. It is almost impossible to overstate the importance of this new model for Toyota worldwide. The corporation had set aggressive targets for growth. In the UK, sales had grown consistently over the last few years, largely through the success of niche models like the RAV4 and the Celica, but the company was missing out in the most competitive part of the market: the C segment, or small/medium cars. This was dominated by Ford's Focus in sales and VW's Golf in image. The Toyota Corolla wasn't even among the top ten cars. Its segment share was only 2.4%. For Toyota this was completely unacceptable.

The challenge facing the new Corolla was an intriguing one. In many ways, the Corolla had been a big success. It had been in production for a long time and was actually the world's best-selling car model (nearly 30 million had been sold worldwide since 1966; 440 000 in the UK). A Corolla had won the World Rally Championship. In the UK in the mid 1990s, it had topped the authoritative J.D. Power customer satisfaction survey for four years in a row.

And yet, in image terms, the Corolla was a failure. It contributed little or nothing to Toyota's overall appeal. Motoring journalists were routinely scathing about it. At the top end of the segment, the VW Golf and the Ford Focus were highly sought-after, aspirational and sold large volumes at a significant premium. At the other end of the market, the Nissan Almera and Citroën Xsara were bought principally on price and the number of extras thrown in. They weren't cars bought to show off to friends. The Corolla competed at this "commodity" end of the market.

Inevitably, this was reflected in the way the dealers sold them on the forecourts: more on value for money than on anything resembling "desire". At the sharp end, this meant that each car sold was pushed out with £750 in short-term tactical incentives.

The image deficit was also evident in the driver profile. C-segment cars were typically driven by mothers and fathers in their mid-forties (average age 46), while Golf and Focus drivers were younger still, with an average age of 43. The average age of a Corolla driver, on the other hand, was 57. Although Corolla drivers were intensely loyal and repeat purchase was high, there were few sales to those who did not already own a Toyota. What few there were tended to come from a small band of similar "value" models.

In launching the next generation Corolla, the challenge was to move from supply-push to demand-pull. This was an opportunity to be innovative and to create demand. The carmaker had to inject desire and substitute an emotional proposition for the current, purely rational one. Somehow the company had to "out-Golf" the Golf. That, in fact, became the rallying cry.

The launch strategy: from facts to feelings

The challenge was defined thus: "To make the Corolla the best loved car in its class. We want people who would never have dreamed of driving one to desire one with a passion." This was largely about presenting the Corolla as more "heart" than "head". From research, the company knew a lot about the strengths and weaknesses of the various models and the interplay of different motivators such as performance, safety, looks, practicality, economy and so on. But the company knew it had to go beyond the *facts* of why people chose C-segment cars. How it *felt* had to be addressed. In other words, how would such a desirable car make someone feel?

A new consumer segmentation offered a giant leap forward. To climb out of the commodity market and compete with the Golf, a new and more demanding audience would have to be addressed. These were people who owned cars not only to get from A to B but because they also attracted envious glances from the neighbours. They really cared about how it felt.

The company used quantitative and qualitative research and role-playing workshops. It identified a key group – called "Energists" – who would be the core target group. They needed a car that met functional needs but also expressive needs. They typically had nice, well-kept homes in nice, well-kept suburbs. They often looked a bit "perfect" with their tidy gardens, busy social lives, nice clothes and well-behaved children.

What's more, these people were role models among their peer groups. There were other groups who struggled with their untidy gardens, untidy clothes and unruly children, who looked at the Energists and wondered how they could be like that. Pride mattered to these people too, in an aspirational sense.

This led to the centrepiece of the communications strategy: the feeling the company was looking for was pride. This actually mirrored the emotion felt by existing Corolla drivers. Although they came from a different demographic group and would never shout about their enthusiasm, they were evangelical in their own quiet way.

A product good enough to change the brand

Crucially, people's reactions to the new car overwhelmingly endorsed the positioning: it really did inspire pride. The new car was the product of ED^2, the French design centre that had created the Yaris, and it was much more European in feel than previous Toyotas. It was a good-looking car, not necessarily breaking new ground but reflecting the best of modern C-segment styling. In addition, it had taken a leap forward in the perceived quality of its interior – the area where earlier generations of Japanese cars had often been criticised. And it was more fun to drive too.

The newness of the car even extended to a new system of grades and nomenclature. Out went the industry standard of S, GS, GLS, SR, etc. Instead, there was a fresh approach using T2, T3, T Spirit and T Sport.

The prospect of promoting this car at a premium to a more demanding group of buyers was looking not only credible, but positively attractive. It became clear that the new Corolla was good enough to change how people thought about Toyota. This was a rare opportunity and no time to be faint-hearted. The launch was to be the biggest in Toyota GB's history.

A review of the competitive position showed that, although well-liked, especially by its own customers, Toyota had a low profile compared with Ford, Vauxhall, Renault and VW. The company had to invest on a scale comparable with the biggest players to climb the rankings as worldwide management demanded.

Over £20 million was earmarked for communications, which was more than the company had ever spent on a single model in one year. The market was so competitive that this amount had to be invested just to compete with the leading brands. Even with a doubling of the total spend for 2002 to support the Corolla launch, Toyota still commanded less than an 8% share of voice.

The entire marketing mix was overhauled and the "pride" strategy was carried through into every medium and every communication vehicle. Toyota and Saatchi & Saatchi developed the positioning and initial ideas. These were used to brief all the other communications partners and agencies at the earliest possible point, so all activities had the same strategic starting point.

Getting everyone on board

The internal marketing programme designed to inspire staff, dealers and other stakeholders was crucially important. Over the years they had become almost as jaundiced towards the old Corolla as the British public had. All those who were to play a part in the launch were brought on board with the positioning at a very early stage, so their total "buy-in" was assured.

A series of interactive events was held in the six months before launch. In October, dealer managers were invited to a series of business forums to share the launch plans. Up to 2500 dealer staff were involved through a distance-learning programme and follow-up group sessions, emphasising the new selling approach that would be needed. Dealer principals attended a spectacular European launch event in Lisbon. The programme climaxed with a launch for dealers and 2500 Toyota staff. From here, dealers were able to drive away in a new Corolla. Meanwhile, a rolling programme of launch strategy presentations involved 3500 line workers at the manufacturing plant.

To convince the sceptical motoring journalists of the revitalised brand, the company gave 50 of the highest profile ones a Corolla of their choice for six months. In addition, large groups attended launch events in Paris and Malaga.

Cutting through the media clutter

The epicentre of the external communications was the advertising launch. Five TV commercials, accompanied by press and posters, showed the lengths people would go to in order to be associated with the Corolla – even if it turned out not to be theirs. The endline encapsulated the idea: "The new Corolla, a car to be proud of."

As well as five 30-second spots, there were five print executions, which appeared in the press and on posters (Figures 3.7–3.9 show three) and also ones aimed at the fleet audience.

The media approach had to stand out in a market where £2 million was spent every day trying to get consumers' attention. It also had to overturn the prejudice and apathy that existed towards the Corolla's old image. In addition, it had to address a new target audience which was quite atypical for a model of this kind.

Figure 3.7

Figure 3.8

New Corolla. A car to be proud of.

Figure 3.9

The strategy was designed to evolve over three phases:

- Two months before the launch, the company would first make people curious about the new Corolla.
- The month of January would be the time for the major impact, where the Corolla would rule the media landscape and the sheer weight of activity would see Corolla tower above other car advertisers.
- The strategy from February to the end of the year would be aimed at the Energist, with the communication becoming encircling rather than towering. The approach would be to talk to audiences in places where, normally, car advertising wouldn't be expected, even through channels that no-one had ever used before.

Making a huge splash

The main television campaign kicked off on New Year's Day, one of the highest quality and highest delivering viewing days of the year. In three days, 400 TVRs ran (one TVR – GRP in the US – is numerically equivalent to 1% of a target audience). An unrivalled 1500 ratings ran in the first three months of 2002. To make an impact unlike that ever achieved by any other car advertiser, the company bought complete advertising breaks and featured five different Corolla ads back to back. Over 10 million people saw these breaks across four different features on ITV, Sky One, Channel Four and Channel 5.

The biggest ever 96-sheet outdoor campaign was created, with huge banners draped across the biggest buildings in the UK. Special picture frames were built for the posters, while the company took 90% of the entire advertising on the rail network. There was also a heavyweight 48-sheet campaign in London underground stations.

The press advertising avoided the standard routes, with inside-cover, four-page gatefolds, pairs of half double-page spreads, colour strips on the front pages of newspapers, outside back covers of magazines and consecutive pages in reviews and supplements.

The radio airwaves were dominated by the Corolla for four weeks from January 2nd. The Internet was also used heavily, in addition to local radio, regional press and individual dealer advertising. Even the dealer activity was consistent. An online portal allowed dealers to customise a range of centrally-produced marketing materials. It also provided tools for them to plan and control their campaigns.

Capturing every moment

A range of activities of all sorts reiterated the "pride" positioning. For example, even Toyota's corporate Christmas card reflected the theme: a winter scene in which a Corolla owner has used Christmas lights to decorate the car rather than the house (Figure 3.10).

Figure 3.10

Another initiative was designed to harness and enhance the energy of the everyday lives of the Energists, with events specifically tailored to their leisure time activities, such as cinema showcases and the BBC Good Homes Show (with a facility in which visitors could design their own room "to be proud of " with touch-screen technology. There were also competitions with a number of health clubs to win a fitness instructor for a year to achieve "a body to be proud of".

Even before launch, an online profiling exercise with AOL and MSN began to build a database, which initially helped the company identify 100 000 Energist prospects using psychographic profiling. This was used for direct marketing and dealer-specific activity.

More direct mail featured a pack sent to existing Toyota owners. It contained a set of stickers which allowed them to stick the Corolla of their choice over their own car in photographs.

Remarkable results

The objective had been to sell more cars, more profitably, to a new audience in a tougher competitive arena. It worked.

First, the advertising made a huge impression, as Figure 3.11 shows. Secondly, the brand was firmly repositioned in people's minds (Figures 3.12–3.14).

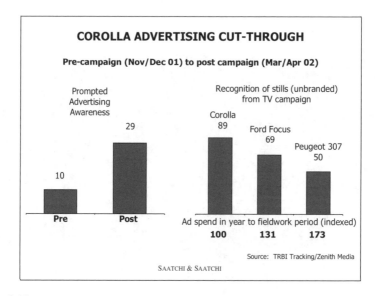

Figure 3.11

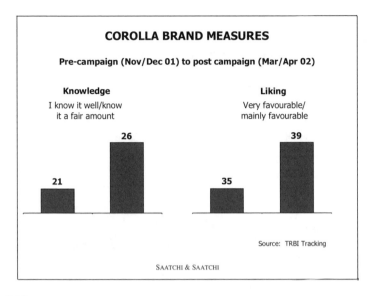

Figure 3.12

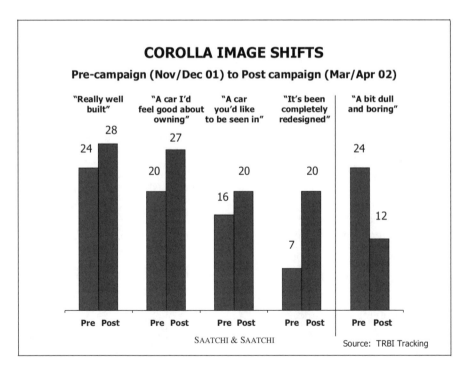

Figure 3.13

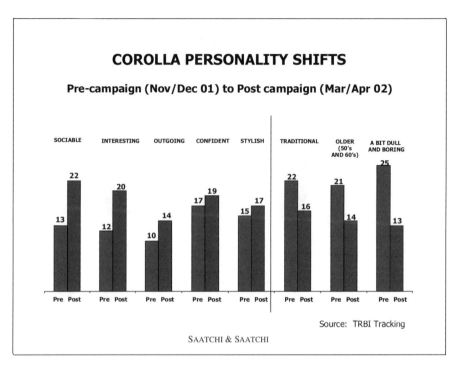

Figure 3.14

Finally, and most significantly, volume sales from March to October grew by 49%, or 7600 more cars. During the key September peak, sales were up by 88% (Figure 3.15).

In addition:

- Corolla leapt from 22nd to 5th in spontaneous purchase consideration;
- tactical incentives dropped from £750 per car to £400. Profitability improved;
- the proportion of high-end sales increased from 10% to 30%. Entry-level pricing increased from £8995 to £9995;
- average revenue per unit grew 22%;
- during the summer, on average, the Corolla sold for £700 more than the Golf;
- the number of buyers under 45 increased by 36% over 2001. In addition, more customers were won from aspirational models such as the Renault Megane and the VW Golf;

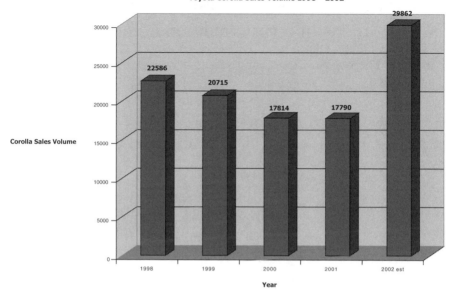

Figure 3.15

- brand tracking showed that the Corolla was now making a positive contribution to the image of the Toyota marque – something that would previously have seemed unthinkable.

The brand had thus been firmly repositioned, with increased ratings for sentiments such as "A car you'd want to be seen in" and "Stylish and good looking". The motoring journalists were more positive than ever before, with one TV car programme, *Top Gear*, calling it "Golf-worryingly good". Such a big investment had paid off in full.

All images appearing in this case study are reproduced by permission of Toyota.

Silentnight Beds' My First Bed: finding a profitable niche in a very traditional market

Snapshot: The company found and successfully exploited an exciting new gap for beds for children in what is a relatively slow-moving market.

Key insights

- The Silentnight strategy displays all the characteristics of great marketing: clever use of research and insight, innovative product development, internal marketing, informative and attractive marketing communications and a new approach to distribution.
- Creating a customised and cost-effective bed for children with over 2350 combinations appealed to children and parents alike.

Summary

Silentnight Beds is the UK's biggest bed manufacturer, with over 50 years of bed-making experience. In 2003, Silentnight Beds was the number-one bed brand in the UK, producing 8000 beds a week and commanding a 15% majority share of the divan market. The brand's product "characters", Hippo and Duck, were recognised by nearly 90% of all adults in the UK.

A significant increase in brand awareness had resulted from a four-year-long brand revitalisation campaign that included the brand's return to television with refreshed and animated Hippo and Duck characters. But there was still a growing realisation that to remain the leading player in the bed market, Silentnight Beds needed to take a far more innovative approach to development of the brand.

The solution, based on extensive market research, was a new range of beds aimed at children who needed their first bed. Using the iconic figures of Hippo and Duck, the range gave parents and children the ability to create their own, customised beds. It was backed by a media-led advertising and PR strategy, along with point-of-sale promotions.

The result was a gain of nearly 40% of the existing market within a mere ten months, along with growth of the market sector overall and distribution in key national retailers.

The beginning: exploring new market opportunities

The core strength of the company's business was mainly an older purchaser who bought into the brand attributes of comfort, support, homeliness and reassurance. However, since 1995, there had been a steady decline in the divan market, as younger consumers began to favour more fashion-oriented purchases, particularly bedsteads. Analysis suggested that major influences causing the shift in consumer demand were interior design TV programmes such as *Changing Rooms, Property Ladder* and *DIY SOS*, along with a range of different magazines.

The company begin to explore new sources of innovation. A specialist team drawn from many areas of the business, including marketing, quality assurance and continuous improvement, was selected to take part in an innovation project that encouraged them to explore market opportunities. The children's bed market was identified as one area with considerable promise, and one which seemed neglected by the Silentnight Beds core range, as there were no beds aimed specifically at children.

Census data showed that, on average, 700 000 babies are born each year. This statistic was used to estimate the "potential market". However, it was realised that much more research was necessary, particularly as there was an assumption that for most children, their first bed was a "hand-me-down".

Delving deeper with research

The company embarked on its first ever product research. It was conducted among mothers of children aged between one and eight years old. The respondents were selected to represent various family sizes, so they would be representative of the target market. Early stages of the research helped to establish that a new bed was the preferred option when a child grew out of its cot, dismissing the hand-me-down theory.

Reassuringly, 44% of mothers said that Silentnight would be their preferred manufacturer. The research helped the company to develop an understanding of customers and their requirements, so that product development could be driven by the priorities of parents. This included beds with storage, that were easy to clean, and that fit with the size of the child's room.

The two biggest lessons which emerged from the focus group were:

- Although those taking part in the research were presented with a selection of colour bed options, pink wasn't one of them. However, all parents of young girls wanted a pink option as the ultimate desire for their little girl.
- Given choice, parents and children favoured all of the suggested colours and accessories, which prompted the creation of the pick and mix "Create Your Bed's Personality" concept.

The quality and comfort of the product was considered to be good, and mothers loved the way that play and comfort had been combined with the use of plain, bright colours, the plastic storage boxes and the secret storage in the Play Pal accessories. The Play Pals and the feet were designed to be completely machine-washable, with the rest of the bed easily cleaned with a damp cloth. The separate plastic storage boxes were considered much more practical than traditional integral beech-effect drawers.

The final "My First Bed" product consisted of seven headboard and base options, six Play Pals, four feet options and two base types, which meant a potential 2352 combinations (Figure 3.16). Parents felt that Create Your Bed's Personality was a fantastic feature, provided that they would not have to pay a separate price for each component – there had to be one, all-in price.

Backing up the brand with expert advice

The company linked up with two authorities to ensure that "My First Bed" would satisfy every need of children at that age. The first was the charity BackCare, a leading authority providing independent advice on back care for all ages. Silentnight worked with their experts to make sure that its Miracoil Spring System would provide the ultimate support for a child. The organisation's advice was also included in the company's brochures.

Figure 3.16

Secondly, child psychologist Dr Dorothy Einon was consulted about childhood attitudes towards sleep, play and the effects of moving from a cot to a first bed. Dr Einon confirmed that My First Bed had many features that would help children settle into their first bed. The Play Pal accessories would provide emotional security for the child, as well as something to play with when they woke up. Many parents mentioned in research that they found the Hippo and Duck Play Pals to be almost "guardian-like", watching over the child as it fell asleep or woke up (Figures 3.17 and 3.18).

Figure 3.17

Figure 3.18

The marketing team at Clarks shoes was also a valuable source of information on the "My First . . ." buying process, as experts in selling high-quality, comfortable shoes with a personal fitting service. Silentnight felt that the opportunity to learn from the shoemaker's experience would benefit the My First Bed launch, and hoped for a link-up for future promotions.

Getting employees on board

A company-wide presentation given to all of the 25 managers in the business covered an overview of the market, the opportunity, research results and prototypes. The result of the meeting was very encouraging, with managers taking responsibility for their respective part of the order process and analysing necessary changes/improvements.

The company became increasingly aware that, should something go wrong, a child would experience a much greater degree of disappointment than an adult. A project codenamed "Emily's Bed" encouraged all employees to look more carefully at the consumer purchasing experience, simplifying internal order processing and production techniques to make the process more consumer-focused.

It seemed inconceivable that, as a business with a goal of achieving lean manufacturing techniques through simplification and standardisation, a product with so many variables could be brought into production. However, My First Bed had been designed to meet all current manufacturing techniques. Because the majority of the variable elements were late-change customisations, there was no need to alter production significantly. For example, the mattress was a standard single mattress, incorporating the company's Miracoil Spring System, tailored fillings and covered with one of the company's brand identities: the distinctive blue and white stripes. The two divan base variants were lower and constructed slightly differently than the standard product, but the basic construction techniques were the same.

The "Emily's Bed" project taught the company that delivery had to be fast and accurate. This could not be assured through the traditional retailer delivery system, where retailers store the product in a warehouse before delivery to the consumer, which could add as much as a week to the order process. Using Silentnight's Mail Order Delivery fleet, with its distinctive liveried wagons, meant that the product could be loaded immediately after production and delivered within 24 hours by a Silentnight driver.

Delivery of the product directly from the factory by trained drivers reduced product handling, and, hence, would minimise any damage. There would also be less chance of parts going missing. However, if that should happen, the drivers would have a full accessory kit. This also meant that the company could offer the fastest delivery lead-time in the furniture industry of a product, which would offer the consumer much more choice.

Building the brand identity

Effective marketing support was essential for My First Bed to succeed. The company needed to have consumers associate Silentnight with special beds for children, innovation, fun and a completely new level of choice, as well as still being associated with comfort and quality. The challenge was to communicate all of this to both retailers and consumers without diluting the message of causing confusion.

It was decided that to achieve this, the product should be given its own brand identity within the core Silentnight Beds brands. The new logo for the My First Bed sub-brand combined recognisable Silentnight elements, such as Hippo and Duck and an ellipse-shaped logo, with a new, brightly coloured pink and purple graded backdrop with stars. The name My First Bed obviously said instantly that this was a bed for young children (Figure 3.19).

Figure 3.19

The mix and match concept was a unique selling point, and a key element of the range. It would allow the child and parent to create their own, customised bed, expressing the child's personality in the finished product. The trademark "Create Your Bed's Personality" was created to articulate the choice of design available in the range.

Hitting the right target

As the brand leader, the company recognised that all of its marketing had to be responsible. The research and design process had successfully developed a product that would appeal to both parents and children. However, the company decided to concentrate on marketing My First Bed to parents.

For example, it was found in the earliest stage of research that parents had no information available to help them find a first bed for their child. So the marketing materials were made both informative and attractive. Much of what had been learned from Dr Einon and BackCare was reproduced on the website and in the My First Bed brochures. Brochure inserts were included in women's magazines, parenting magazines and national newspapers to target parents more effectively, while advertising was placed at times when it was known that both parents and children would be watching together – most effectively through national cinema advertisements.

Point-of-sale (POS) materials were created to help retailers display the product effectively and demonstrate the product features and benefits. Taking inspiration from the POS used by toy manufacturers and leading UK toy store Hamleys, the company's marketers designed the materials to appeal both to children and parents in a fun and exciting way. In addition, a website dedicated to My First Bed, www.myfirstbed.com, was set up to provide all the information parents needed, including the "Ask Dorothy" section, offering helpful hints and tips. The section "Create Your Bed's Personality" was created to help parents and children play together while designing the bed.

Other elements in the marketing package were:

- Accompanying the delivery of each bed with a blue and white striped envelope addressed to the child, which contained a Hippo and Duck room plaque and stickers.
- A form which allowed parents to enter the child into the My First Bed Club, which offered a welcome pack with gifts, a magazine and a website.

This was seen as a powerful way to begin an enduring relationship with the family over time.

- A heavyweight public relations campaign, including celebrity endorsement.

Achieving the right business results

The company achieved what it had set out to do: use innovation both to shore up the brand's strength and establish it in a new section of the market.

- The launch was very successful, gaining nearly 40% of the existing market within a mere ten months, while also growing the market sector.
- It strengthened relationships and floor model distribution with existing retail customers while gaining key targeted retailers as customers.
- It established a new brand extension, which helped gain awareness of 21% in eight months with a relatively small spend.
- The company won "Bed of the Year" at the Furniture Awards in 2003 for the first time in a decade, with the judges impressed by the way the bedroom became an extension of the child's personality.
- The project initiated the concept of the "Create Your Bed's Personality", which has been used with other products.
- It helped embed the idea of the company as innovative in consumers' minds.
- It boosted awareness of "consumer requirements" with the 800 employees of the company.

All images appearing in this case study are reproduced by permission of Silentnight Beds.

Freeview: changing the face of TV

Snapshot: The story of Freeview shows how an in-depth understanding of consumers is essential if a new brand is to thrive in a risky and competitive environment.

Key insights

- The big moment for the consortium led by the BBC came when research showed that people weren't rejecting digital TV as such, but the idea of having to pay for it. Consumer insight was put at the heart of the strategy.
- This led to a radical repositioning of the proposition to one which was simple and, more importantly, free. This would be an important step in the country's overall digital programme.

Summary

Freeview is the free digital terrestrial television (DTT) service owned and managed by a consortium of partners – the BBC, BSkyB, Channel 4, ITV and National Grid Wireless. It launched in October 2002 into a sceptical market, right after the high-profile collapse of its predecessor, ITV Digital.

However, Freeview has been a huge success. By 2004, it was in nearly three million UK households, or more than 10% of the country, and had overtaken cable to become the second largest digital platform in the country after satellite, making up 20% of the market. Digital set-top boxes for Freeview also became the fastest-selling consumer electronics product ever in the UK, selling 140 000 boxes in one week over Christmas 2003 alone.

Using a combination of TV, radio, outdoor, press and online, the brand positioned itself differently from the existing pay-TV services by offering a smaller range of channels and highlighting the non-subscription nature of the service. This positioning, much closer to existing analogue free-to-air television than to digital services, attracted a completely new market to digital TV.

Its success had far-reaching implications: it drove digital take-up above 50% for the first time and put government plans for switching off the analogue TV signal back on track.

The beginning: facing a digital dilemma

In early 2002, after four years of growth, the penetration of digital television through satellite and cable had stalled at 40%. Broadcasters such as the BBC were launching portfolios of digital channels to anticipate and stimulate the development of a fully digital TV nation, creating something for everybody.

The long-term strategy and success of these broadcasters' digital initiatives depended on getting those channels into every home. Unfortunately, research showed that only 11% of those who had not yet signed up to digital were interested in the exclusively pay-TV proposition then on offer from the commercial services. This meant that, unless there was a radical (and risky) change to the whole product offering, a whopping 15 million homes were not going to convert to digital.

In the meantime, ITV Digital collapsed in a blaze of publicity in April 2002. It was the UK's digital terrestrial television carrier, a joint venture between Carlton and Granada. The collapse, combined with all the questions about poor reception and unsatisfactory customer service, further fuelled the opinion of non-digital subscribers that they didn't need digital TV. Manufacturers and retailers of DTT equipment were losing confidence fast, and it began to look as though an entire digital platform, terrestrial, would be lost.

So, when the commercial television watchdog, the Independent Television Commission (ITC), advertised the now-available ITV Digital licences the following month, DTT stakeholders such as broadcasters and network operators had to make some quick and tough decisions.

Taking a radical approach

There was no obvious and conventional solution. The idea emerged only after a rigorous exploration of why people weren't buying into digital TV. In fact, they had no problem with digital television, but simply rejected the idea that they had to pay for what was already free on analogue. This fact suggested a radical repositioning of digital television through the launch of a new, simple and, most importantly, *free* proposition – an entirely new category in digital TV. Research suggested it could succeed with a limited number of channels if people thought the quality was high.

The consortium – National Grid Wireless, which owned a network of broadcast installations, satellite TV provider BSkyB and the BBC – produced a groundbreaking bid for the former ITV licences. It tipped the perceived industry wisdom on its head: digital TV, which had to be paid for by subscribers, now became free to everyone. In a shock win, the consortium had just three months to create and brand the service and launch it to consumers in time for the retail market's peak selling season – Christmas.

An integrated team of engineers, strategists, lawyers, marketers and communications professionals went to work, deciding to continue to keep consumer insight at the heart of the strategy. This led to a number of important outcomes:

- it fuelled the determination to improve the technical quality of the service, increasing the platform coverage from 66% to 75% of the country;
- the number of channels was reduced to 30 to also improve the technical quality since fewer channels meant better reception for viewers;
- the core brand attributes of "simple, honest, credible, free" underpinned the creative strategy and execution, setting the tone of voice across all communications;
- it drove the offer of a step-by-step information process via a new call centre, website, fulfilment and point-of-sale literature, including full details of whether consumers were in an area that could receive coverage and whether they might need a new aerial to receive the service.

The brand positioning moved digital terrestrial away from pay-TV operators and towards what people knew as "normal" TV. It provided a small but perfectly formed group of high-quality channels at no ongoing subscription cost. The marketing only needed to persuade people to pay a one-off cost for a small piece of hardware that allowed their TV to receive these channels.

Spreading the message

The communications challenge was made all the harder because many people had already rejected digital TV, being content with the existing five free analogue terrestrial channels. Again, consumer insight was invaluable in reminding the team that the message had to be very simple, and that clear space between existing digital offers and this new brand must be created. Don't overwhelm, don't confuse, and keep it simple.

The strategy encompassed a number of elements:

- The tone of voice was consistently straight-talking, positive and approachable.
- This was reflected in the brand name and logo. The name "Freeview" came out on top in research, while the logo consisted of a bold red graphic and approachable font to make sure it stood out in shops and was distinct from the more technically oriented brands (Figure 3.20).
- Positioning the brand closer to analogue TV than existing digital competitors. It had to be seen as a manageable increase in channel choice and high-quality programming.
- Emphasising the proposition that it was "a simple way to get digital TV".

The customer experience was also designed to be in tune with the brand values and overcome any confusion. A user-friendly postcode database was designed to give house-by-house information about Freeview coverage. The same approach applied to every consumer touch point, from the call centre, website and SMS postcode checking service to point-of-sale. Consistency was key to establishing the Freeview brand.

The brand values were also carried through into all consumer communications, including a consumer guide, public relations pack and in-store retail messages and creative work. A direct response element invited people to call

Figure 3.20

the newly established Freeview Call Centre or the BBC to receive a guide to going digital (including information about the other platforms). And the Freeview website had to be clear and simple too.

Finally, licences for the Freeview brand were restricted solely to retailers who could guarantee that they would check whether customers could receive the signal and give them accurate information about aerials before they sold a box. The onset of a BBC on-air campaign promoting digital television coincided with retailer promotions, including press advertisements, point-of-sale material and in-store promotions.

The launch

Freeview was launched on 31st October 2002, just 11 weeks after winning the licences. This was the fastest launch of any digital platform. Consumers were told about the new brand and what it offered through a combination of TV, radio, outdoor, press and online coverage.

In the first four weeks, a million people contacted Freeview for more information. That Christmas, over a quarter of a million set-top boxes were sold, meaning even the most sceptical commentators began to rethink.

To maintain momentum, Freeview continued its marketing campaign in Easter 2003, which tied in with the BBC's second phase of its digital TV portfolio campaign, which invited consumers to call for more information about cable, satellite and Freeview. In the meantime, sales were holding steady at an average of about 100 000 a month.

Conclusive results

Within only fifteen months after launch, Freeview became an outstanding success by any measure. It beat both Playstation2 and DVD players by selling two million units in that short time, even though coverage limitations meant that about a quarter of UK consumers couldn't receive it. And it changed people's minds: the 40% of households who had yet to take up digital TV said they were "interested in" or "actively considering" Freeview.

The government's plans for digital were back on track: just before Christmas 2003, digital penetration tipped over the critical 50% mark for the first time ever. People wanted Freeview, and the industry respected it. Over 650 000 set-top boxes were sold across November and December 2003.

Table 3.1 *Penetration of digital television (%)*

	2000	2001	2002	2003	2004	2005
France	14.7	15.9	17.7	18.3	20.3	25.0
Germany	6.4	7.4	9.3	10.4	11.8	13.6
Spain	14.4	18.7	16.5	14.4	13.3	18.3
UK	26.5	35.6	39.3	51.0	59.4	69.5
US	21.8	29.0	35.5	41.2	51.0	61.5

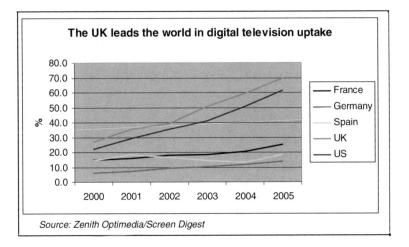

Source: Zenith Optimedia/Screen Digest

Figure 3.21

In a very short space of time, Freeview had become a powerful brand and market-changing service. And digital penetration continues to rise: by 2005, the UK was leading the world in digital penetration (Table 3.1 and Figure 3.21).

All images appearing in this case study are reproduced by permission of BBC Freeview.

3: branding a new network

Snapshot: Astute marketing saw this young brand take on the mass market and establish itself in record-breaking time.

Key insights

- 3 demonstrated the importance of focusing on consumer benefits, not just technical features, in the mobile phone market.
- The main turning point for the company thus came when it turned its marketing strategy on its head and relaunched the brand to focus on the customer rather than the 3G technology.
- The company aggressively repositioned itself in the centre of the market with a new mass-market offer and an aggressive comparative price campaign.

Summary

3 is the largest 3G network in Europe. Its core areas are communications, media and entertainment, and information services. With 11.5 million customers, it is part of Hutchison Whampoa, one of Hong Kong's largest companies.

In May 2000, the UK government awarded five licences to run third generation (3G) wireless services. A 3G network is able to deliver high-quality, media-rich content, including audio and video, to a mobile handset.

Hutchison (now 3) acquired the largest of these licences at the lowest cost, launching Europe's first 3G network in the UK in March 2003. Analysts and commentators were sceptical about the potential for the service, and the initial challenges indeed seemed to confirm the belief that not only would the technology have major teething problems, but, even worse, that consumers weren't interested in 3G mobile services.

By the next year, however, the management team decided on a new strategy that refocused the business around the consumer rather than the technology. This strategy targeted a core of mobile users whose needs could be met by the services enabled by the technology. 3 estimated this market to be about ten million across a range of ages and spending profiles.

An advertising campaign stressed the playful attitude towards technology of the 3 brand, as well as aggressively highlighting its value compared to other networks. Within a matter of months of this new marketing strategy, 3 had become the UK's fastest ever growing network. Despite entering a highly competitive and maturing marketplace, the company acquired over 2.5 million customers by the end of 2004, with average revenues per customer the envy of the mobile industry overall.

The advantage gained from launching ahead of the competition meant that 3 was well-positioned to meet its objectives of continuing growth, setting the agenda in terms of value and innovation and becoming the incumbent in the emerging 3G market.

2004: a new beginning

By the beginning of 2004, Europe's first 3G network had been in place for ten months. A new management team had since arrived, bringing together some of the key players who had successfully launched mobile operator Orange in the mid-1990s and made it one of the world's most recognisable brands. This included Bob Fuller, former Orange Chief Operating Officer, who became 3's Chief Executive, and Gareth Jones, previously Orange group Director of Sales and Distribution, who was appointed Chief Operating Officer. This new team could see that it was time to shake up what had become a very cosy mobile marketplace in the UK by putting renewed energy into building 3 into a compelling consumer brand.

The overriding objective was to refocus the brand around the customer rather than the technology. The key priorities initially were to get the basics right:

• develop a network delivering a good quality coverage for customers;
• create a range of high-quality, desirable and affordable handsets;

- build strong relationships with key mobile phone retailers and channel partners to secure distribution.

Once these basic operational issues were addressed, the management team could move on to the key marketing challenges:

- identify the most important customer segments to whom 3 could offer the most value;
- relaunch the brand to connect these segments with new propositions;
- create a marketing communications campaign that strongly differentiated 3 from its competitors;
- launch a mass market, pay-as-you-go proposition to appeal to the 50–60% of the market who wanted the flexibility of this type of service.

Gareth Jones took over responsibility for marketing and replaced the incumbent advertising agency with WCRS, which had worked with Hutchison for the launch of Orange in the UK.

Defining the target audience

As the company moved into 2004, the management decided to build the business around a core group of mobile customers whose needs could best be met by the new services the technology offered. Research showed that what could be called "the mobile generation", who numbered around 20 million, were comfortable with technology, wanted high mobile speed, were not afraid to download a ring-tone or use their mobiles to play games, and were most likely to switch handsets and networks in the next 12 months.

But while building the brand to appeal to this audience, care had to be taken not to alienate the other 20 million high-spending mobile subscribers. It was critical within this broader market that 3 be viewed as a credible alternative to the current providers in terms of value and the basic mobile offering (coverage, handsets and service quality).

The results spoke for themselves. 3 started 2004 with just 210 000 customers, and ended it with over 2.5 million, or over a 5% share of the UK mobile market, and an even greater share of the higher-spending consumer segments. The customer base had grown by a factor of 12 during the year.

Coming of age as a business

The company attributed its success to the steady availability of good-quality handsets, the investment in customer service, logistics and IT stability and the improvement and continued expansion of the network to the point where 3 had become the fastest-growing mobile network ever in the UK.

This growth was not achieved at the expense of value, however. In August 2004, parent company Hutchison Whampoa announced that 3 UK was generating average revenue per customer of over £43, or the highest in the UK, and well above the industry average of £24. In addition, non-voice revenues were over £6 per customer per month, again well above the industry average.

The brand itself had also developed strongly in 2004. It continued to build on its position as a fresh, creative and innovative company, gaining a reputation as a strong challenger brand and champion of great value for consumers. Both 3's contract and prepay propositions won 2004 industry awards.

Testament to this strengthening of the brand's position was the fact that the vast majority of new 3 customers went into a store knowing that they wanted to move to 3. The idea that customers would walk into a store and ask for a "3 video mobile" as opposed to a "Nokia + network tariff" was proof of the shifting brand dynamics in the market, with the network (brand) choice becoming ever more important. Interest was heightened with the launch of 14 new handsets during the year.

3's emerging brand position was taken a step further in the final quarter of 2004 with a distinct, vibrant, engaging and, most importantly, differentiated advertising campaign. It came on the back of an aggressive, comparative value campaign that had successfully launched the radical pay-as-you-go tariff, ThreePay, and formed part of 3's marketing strategy of building a brand to be admired by the target audience in the same vein as Nike, Apple, Diesel or Playstation. The campaign positioned the 3 brand around a playful attitude to technology, an attitude rooted in the Asian culture on which the creative strategy was based (Figures 3.22, 3.23 and 3.24).

Figure 3.22

Figure 3.23

Figure 3.24

By the end of 2004, 3 was available directly through the Internet and call centres, and through over 7000 retail outlets across the UK, including general and specialist retailers, plus the Superdrug concession of the parent company, Hutchison Whampoa.

All images appearing in this case study are reproduced by permission of 3.

4

Brand extension

Introduction

Brand extension can, more often than not, be a very bad idea, as countless failed attempts testify. The problem is that many of these extensions aren't rooted in consumer needs, but a desire by the company to grow volume. The results can be disappointing.

The two case studies are good examples of how to create both the functional and emotional bond necessary to make extensions work. However, they are both quite different. Tesco.com extended the brand into online shopping by keeping true to the brand promise of customer-centricity, convenience and consistency. Specsavers realised that extending the brand from eyes to ears was not only logical but would help a poorly served market.

"The 12th law of Al Ries from his *22 Immutable Laws of Marketing* is The Law of Line Extension. This states that there is irresistible pressure to extend the equity of the brand into adjacent markets, no matter what the cost or whether the brand values are competitive and relevant in the new market. That is why our categories often resemble over-cluttered graveyards of failed line extension attempts.

So it's refreshing to see these examples of well-executed ideas, where the promise of the brand extensions is delivered – outscoring competition on the quality of the product and service."

Roger Kirman, Head of Marketing Excellence, Unilever

Tesco.com: creating the sustainable online shopping experience

Snapshot: The story of how Tesco became the biggest online grocery retailer in the UK is a striking example of how the retailer maintains its market leadership.

Key insights

- Tesco developed its online channel with the realisation that unless the online shopping experience was consistent and seamless from computer to doorstep, customers would be lost.
- It also devised a carefully crafted communications strategy based on its extensive customer knowledge to encourage customers to become habitual users of the service.

Summary

Tesco is the UK's biggest supermarket group, and has an increasing international presence. Its group sales in the year to February 2006 were £41.8 billion.

Following a successful trial, Tesco.com's goal was to become the UK's number-one Internet shopping destination. By 2002, Tesco.com had emerged as the clear leader in the UK's grocery home delivery sector. With more than 65% of the market and 95% national coverage, it was taking more than 100 000 weekly orders and offered 20 000 grocery product lines.

Even more significantly, the operation had become profitable. First-half sales in 2002 grew 27% and profits increased to £1.9 million. In fact, profits had increased every quarter over the past two years, marking a turnaround from the early days of operating at a loss.

The company ascribed the success to the three Cs: customer, convenience, consistency. A customer-centric approach had been adopted, identifying that convenience was the key motivating factor. Consistency was brought to all points where the customer interacted with the brand. Website usability had also been improved, while regular customer communications were being aimed at individuals to encourage greater frequency of purchase.

Excited by e-commerce

Earning customer loyalty has been at the heart of Tesco values for years. Back in 1994, two key areas of development were identified. One of them was to launch Clubcard, the loyalty scheme as a thank-you for customer loyalty, through which, with the help of marketing consultancy Dunnhumby, the company was able to understand its customers better. The second was to develop a home-shopping business to meet the needs of those customers looking for convenience.

As retail marketing professionals, Tesco's management team was naturally excited by the opportunities presented by the Internet to expand the company's channels to market. With access to over two-thirds of UK homes and the technological capability (in theory at least) to deliver personalised offers matched to the individual needs of each customer, the Internet could offer the innovative retailer the chance to expand distribution at a stroke. However, in the real world, all too many companies had had to deal with the hype, over-expectation and technical dysfunctionality that had plagued the average e-business.

Since 2001, Tesco had emerged as the clear leader in the battle to become the UK's most successful grocery home delivery service. With over 65% of the market and 95% national coverage, it was now taking over 100 000 weekly orders and offering more than 20 000 grocery product lines. An ever-expanding range now included non-grocery products such as wine, CDs, books, videos, DVDs, electricals, flowers, finance, baby products and travel.

By 2002, however, Tesco.com could not only claim to be a successful business in terms of scale, growth and profitability, but it was literally defining the online shopping experience for the UK consumer.

Success was defined not just by size but by profitability: first-half sales in 2002 grew by 27% and profits increased to £1.9 million. As online shopping came of age, Tesco.com was clearly defining itself as the natural destination for online consumers in the UK.

The early days

Turning the clock back to the beginning of 2001, however, the situation was very different. Tesco.com was just one of a number of contenders for the e-commerce crown. Apart from most of the major supermarket brands (notably Sainsbury's, Waitrose and Asda), the line-up included electrical retailers such as Dixons and Comet as well as specialists in other competitive sectors such as HMV, Virgin Wine and Mothercare. Like Tesco, these were all brands poised for expansion into the new Internet channel following periods of testing at either regional or store level.

All were running at a similar level of unique visitors (200–300 000 per month). Tesco.com, however, was already beginning to pull away from the pack. It had exceeded the 500 000 unique visitor level for the first time towards the end of 2000 in an aggressive pursuit of its mission to become the UK's number-one Internet shopping destination.

2001/2 was thus to be a crucial period in the development of the UK e-commerce marketplace. While the online population was set to grow at a furious rate, regular online shopping was still very much in its infancy and had yet to catch up. Despite media hype and the undoubted potential of the channel to deliver to the needs of both business and consumer, the experience for many was (and indeed remained) shrouded in mistrust and mystery.

There was an obvious opportunity for a strong brand with a naturally prominent role in consumers' lives to seize the online shopping crown and grow the market. With so many high street retailers both ready and able to stake their online claim, Tesco.com needed to move fast if it was to dominate the sector and categorically establish a leadership position.

Invoking the 3 Cs: customer, convenience, consistency

From the earliest trials of Tesco.com in the late 1990s, the company had taken the customer-centric principles underpinning the Tesco brand and applied them to everything it did. Throughout the national launch in 1999 and the period of 2001/2, the company extensively researched customers' usage, attitudes to and satisfaction with Tesco.com and its competitors. As a result, it was able to continually improve the customer experience and meet customer needs more effectively. This meant introducing innovations in both site functionality and service delivery to ensure speed and ease of use, including:

- My Favourites: a short-cut which contained all items from previous shops, both online and in-store, and allowed customers to tailor their baskets without having to start from scratch each time.

- Previewing of delivery slots: Tesco quickly realised that convenience of delivery time was paramount. It made booking a convenient delivery time the first thing that online shoppers do to ensure available slots suited them before they shopped.
- More evening and weekend delivery slots to cope with the "out-of-hours" lifestyle of the typical dotcom shopper.
- Speed of download: pages designed to minimise download time, monitored by the company every day to ensure they met the stringent download performance targets.
- E-vouchers: offers and incentives to shop were delivered and redeemable electronically, maximising the value and convenience to the customer.

Customers were attracted to Tesco.com with the promise of convenience, but the company was well aware that one bad experience could destroy their faith in an instant. A positive experience of convenience throughout the customer journey thus demanded consistency of promise and service delivery at all points where the customer interacted with the brand.

So, from initial awareness and consideration of the service, from in-store or TV advertising, direct mail and digital communications, through to first site visit, registration and first shop, to delivery of goods in the home and subsequent use of the service, Tesco had to promise convenience and then make sure it was delivered to the satisfaction of the customer.

Consistent service delivery had been both a key to success and a leading point of difference between Tesco.com and other, less successful, online retailers. The company knew from its customer satisfaction surveys and research among lapsed customers that if they received inferior or poorly targeted offers, or had difficulty using the site, they could easily be lost to a competitor.

So the site had to be easy to access, simple to use and as user-friendly as possible to minimise the customer's time and frustrations online. That included being able to book a delivery slot that suited them and for those goods to be delivered to their home when the company said it would and for the order to be accurate, with minimal but acceptable substitutions.

Nothing short of a consistently positive experience from computer to doorstep would ensure success.

Understanding the online customer relationship

Another key focus for 2001/2 was to understand the relationship customers had with Tesco.com at each stage of their customer journey. The company wanted to nurture customers through their first online shopping experiences and beyond, ensuring that they became committed and valuable customers in the long term.

The knowledge of individual customers came from Tesco's Clubcard databases and included transactional, lifestage and attitudinal data. Additional data gathered from the website and individual response profiles was used to develop a segmentation model to identify customer profitability and potential.

A classic "recency, frequency value" (RFV) model measured customer commitment on six levels: dedicated, established, developing, cautionary, logged-on or logged-off. This was combined with a "basket cluster" classification system to identify groups of customers with similar profiles. It allowed the company to encourage positive customer shifts or react to negative ones using relevant offers and information, not just on groceries but across all the categories within Tesco.com (Figure 4.1).

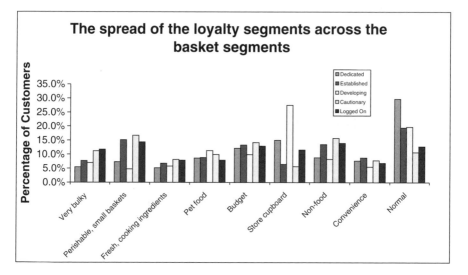

Figure 4.1

The company's aim was to move customers through these commitment profiles as they progressed along their customer journey. To this end, communications were targeted through online and offline media to individual customers to encourage increased frequency and basket value, guiding them through the various stages of their development from "cautious" to "dedicated".

Tesco knew from analysis that if it could get them through registration and first shop, they were still in danger of lapsing until they reached the magic "fourth shop". It was at this point that they were becoming habitual Tesco.com customers with the true potential to move up to the higher levels of commitment and value.

By planning exactly what messages needed to be communicated at each stage of the relationship, the company could be confident of talking to the right customers at the right time with the right offer, encouraging trial, repeat purchase, cross-sell, up-sell and retention. For example, offers could include money-off next shop in the form of £5 or £10 coupons, or else time-sensitive three-part offers giving up to £50 off over three shops within a certain period.

Maximising the effectiveness of communications

The company tested the communications programme extensively at every stage to identify the most effective and profitable way to move prospects along the customer journey with the help of its agency, EHS Brann (Figure 4.2).

1. **Acquisition**
   - A variety of trial incentive offers was used, including free delivery and money off first and subsequent shops. Recruitment results were intensely monitored throughout the process, allowing the company to understand fully and with immediate effect the optimum media, and to devise strategies to maximise the volume of new customers coming through.
   - Cold call lists were profiled against Clubcard data, allowing Tesco to identify potential dedicated customers before they registered. Both email and direct mail were used, while the company also tested a huge

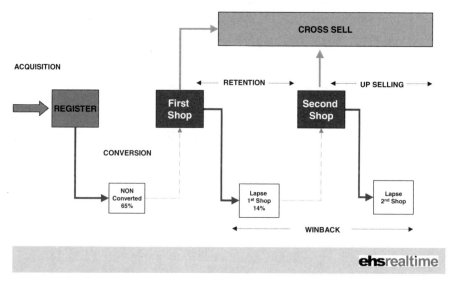

Figure 4.2

array of lists to establish the most cost-effective return on investment (ROI).

- Interestingly, word-of-mouth contributed approximately one-third of new customer registrations. Another third came through from in-store promotion, with advertising, web and direct marketing activity accounting for the rest.

2. Conversion

- Many customers registered but didn't shop immediately. These customers were called "registered not shopped", and they had a communication programme all of their own in order to nurture them over any barriers they might have to taking the plunge.
- Both email and mail were used to target them with relevant offers and information. The company could recognise first-time users with a personalised home page which effectively guided them through their first shop.

3. Retention

- The goal was to get customers to the fourth shop, where the company was more likely to keep them. There were many features on the website to encourage this, such as My Favourites, Express Shopper, recipes and tips, in addition to many thousands of pages of products, not just in grocery but across the whole warehouse, from wine to clothes to electrical goods to personal finance.

- For this reason, communications were staggered and focused on the most relevant hints and tips to get the most out of the site over a period of time as the customer got used to it. The company candidly told customers that while the first shop might take a while, the real time savings would come in future shops. They were sent a series of incentives to keep shopping with Tesco.com if they didn't fall into a preferred purchasing pattern at the early stages of the relationship.

4. **Loyalty, up-sell and cross-sell**
   - Tesco constantly tested monthly warehouse-specific emails and a weekly newsletter for the entire range of products to identify the key motivators for click-through and purchase by segment. Key tests included html versus text and content-rich versus offer-based emails, timing and targeting.

5. **Lapsed**
   - Both emails and mailings were used to reactivate customers who had been inactive for over 12 weeks. Even before 12 weeks, the company had set up a model to predict when customers might be likely to lapse. It contacted them during that period with an incentive to prevent them from falling into the lapsed category.

While word-of-mouth provided the biggest source of recruitment, cold acquisition activity now accounted for over one-third of the customer base. The subsequent loyalty communications programme involved approximately 100 individual pieces of communication annually, both on and offline in a variety of formats. All results were monitored closely and lessons learnt in rolling out activity to maximise effectiveness while minimising costs and wastage.

An unassailable position

By 2002, Tesco.com was far and away the biggest online grocery retailer in the UK, with over 65% market share. Any one of its retail competitors could have taken this enviable position. However, problems in site usability, delivery issues and logistical problems such as centralised distribution held them back. Many operated an unsustainable business model in an attempt to buy market share, which meant that even if they got the basics right, their operational costs (for example in delivering from a central warehouse location) prohibited profitability.

Tesco.com had greater success in developing a sustainable business model and overcoming the logistical and operational barriers to profitability. It operated from local stores and believed it now had the basics right in terms of consistency of site functionality and delivery. It meant it could now dominate the sector and maintain its unassailable lead. Only Amazon, the specialist book e-tailer, had more online customers than Tesco.com, and that company was in its sights. It consistently outperformed Amazon over the period in terms of growth and profitability.

The results for 2002 showed the extent of the company's achievement:

- profits increased every quarter, delivering £1.9 million in the first half of 2002 alone;
- turnover almost doubled to £400 million in 2002 from 2001 (Figure 4.3);

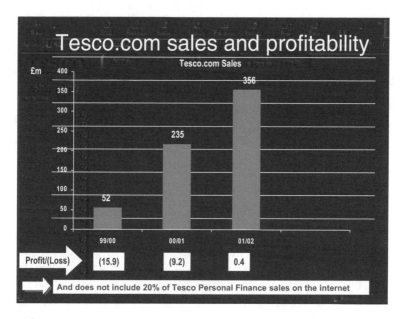

Figure 4.3

- 380 000 of the registered shoppers were identified as active customers;
- the sophisticated programme of relevant and targeted on- and offline recruitment activity was refined to the point where it could deliver a cost per customer of just £19 against a target of £20;
- regular customer communication produced directly attributable incremental revenue of £250–£500 000.

One additional aspect of this business success: Tesco.com increased overall Tesco spend per customer by 21%. Tesco.com customers tended to buy large shops for delivery, then top-up in-store, so that their combined spend was greater. This was just one more example of the value Tesco.com created for its owner.

All images appearing in this case study are reproduced by permission of Tesco.

Specsavers: extending the brand from eyes to ears

Snapshot: Specsavers moved adeptly to exploit the synergies between its well-established brand in eye care and the market for hearing devices.

Key insights

- Specsavers recognised the enormous potential for extending its trusted eye care brand into another, poorly served, part of the market: all aspects of hearing care.
- Consumers are much more sophisticated and flexible than they are often given credit for, in that they could appreciate the link between eyes and ears without the brand name having to be changed.
- Setting itself up in sharp contrast to the competition quickly propelled it into a top market position.

Summary

Specsavers Opticians is a UK-based chain of optical retailers with more than 800 stores in the UK, the Republic of Ireland, the Netherlands, Norway, Denmark and Sweden. Having successfully established itself in eye care, it began to appreciate the opportunities offered by extending its proven, trusted brand into another part of this market: hearing care.

This was a market that was not being well-served by existing suppliers, which included a mix of the National Health Service (NHS) and private sources. The company could see the synergy between eyes and ears, and began to develop a concept based on both value and customer focus.

Specsavers Hearcare was launched in 2004 with an aggressive and comprehensive promotional strategy. In just under two years, the company had become the fourth largest provider of digital hearing aids in the UK, and was on track to reach second place in 2006.

Eyeing up a new market

Specsavers was aware that nine million people in the UK (one in seven of the population) suffered from hearing loss. While hearing aids were free on the NHS, the service was poor, with little product choice and long waiting lists. The result was that 25% of people with hearing problems were already choosing to "go private", spending on average £1200 per hearing aid and creating a market valued at £200 million.

The company believed that people generally accepted that there was a synergy between eyes and ears and, as such, the brand attributes from the company's optical business would successfully extend to the provision of hearing services. Specsavers Hearcare was subsequently launched as an extension of the Specsavers Opticians brand to offer people with hearing problems a fast, affordable, professional retail service relating to all aspects of hearing care, from hearing tests to the sale, supply and aftercare of digital hearing aids.

Gaining insight

First, however, the company needed to find out more. During January–February 2004, it carried out consumer research, which revealed that people perceived most national hearing companies as outdated, hard-sell and untrustworthy, and that they charged extortionately high prices with little aftercare or customer service.

One-third of the people who initially ordered products from such companies reported that they subsequently cancelled or returned them, as they failed to live up to the pre-sales hype. The research also reinforced the company's belief that customers accepted Specsavers as a proven, trusted retail provider of healthcare services and would welcome its diversification into hearing services.

Standing apart from the competition

From the outset, the company designed the Specsavers Hearcare concept to be totally different from the competition, and to share the same value-based and inherently customer-focused approach that it had developed so successfully in optical retailing. In short, it was determined to revolutionise the UK private hearing sector.

Hearing centres were designed and added into the existing optical stores to offer easily accessible, modern retail services and displays, presenting prices and product features and benefits in a clear, transparent, up-front manner.

A free-trial programme was introduced that gave customers the opportunity to experience digital hearing aids free of charge before they chose whether or not to buy. The pricing structure was designed to undercut dramatically established industry pricing models, which it did: market research showed the company to be up to 70% cheaper than the national competitors on a like-for-like basis, which saved customers up to £3500 on some hearing aids.

The company also provided customers with free hearing tests and free, unlimited aftercare services. As a result, it enjoyed huge sales growth, with a returns and cancellation rate of less than 4%, compared to an industry standard of 25% or more. This reinforced the fact that the company was making sure that customers received excellent products and excellent prices without having an impact on the quality of the professional care and aftercare services provided.

Aggressive marketing

The advertising and promotional strategy was aggressive and comprehensive. The company first tested "two for one" as a limited promotional offer in April 2004, with an entry price of two hearing aids for just £595 (Figure 4.4). Based on the results, the promotion was rolled out during July 2004 and was then repeated, and the concept extended further, throughout 2005. By the end of 2005, it encompassed 95% of the product range.

At the same time, Specsavers significantly increased its advertising and customer communication programmes, from predominantly local press to include TV, national press, outdoor, radio advertising and online media. Marketing spend was the equivalent of around 10% of sales.

In terms of message, the main campaign led on the "two for one" offer in point-of-sale, local and national press and TV, although the company also ran national branding campaigns (using more quirky images, including dogs and penguins) to emphasise different attributes of its rounded offering (Figures 4.5 and 4.6). Customer response was via a freephone telephone number to its newly enlarged call centre in the British city of Nottingham.

The company also attacked its competitors head on with a major price comparison campaign in the national daily and weekend press, which highlighted the huge variations in the pricing of hearing aids across the industry. In fact, the advertising exposed the trading practices of some companies

2 digital hearing aids from only £595

If you haven't yet heard for yourself how good digital hearing aids are, you should try them. And while a hearing aid can never return perfect hearing, a digital hearing aid for each ear could give you a whole new perspective on life. That's why, at Specsavers Hearcare, you can now buy two digital hearing aids for the price of one - including 'in the ear' and ultra discrete 'CIC' models from Siemens, Starkey, Phonak and Sonic Innovations - from just £595.

Hearing tests from our registered hearing aid audiologist are free. As are hearing aid fitting, all aftercare and our 2-year No Quibble guarantee. You can even try a digital hearing aid free before you buy. Call us today for more details. Our two for one offer also applies to hearing aid batteries.

For your nearest store, or for more details about any of our hearing services, please call us free on 0808 143 1143 or visit www.specsavershearcare.co.uk

Figure 4.4

Figure 4.5

Figure 4.6

selling the same digital hearing aids at over £3000 per pair compared to the company's price of £995.

This message was reinforced with targeted lifestyle magazines (such as *Saga* and *Readers' Digest*), point-of-sale, local door-drops and through the website. Hearing messages were also incorporated into the optical direct mail programme. These reached some 15 000 new prospects a week, and integrated the "eyes and ears" messages on other point-of-sale and advertising materials.

A Specsavers Hearcare website, www.specsavershearcare.co.uk, was also launched to include full product, store and promotional details. It dramatically increased the company's Internet presence through sustained search engine marketing. There was almost ten times the volume of consumers hitting the website compared to the combined total of visitors to competitor sites.

In addition to new hearing centre openings (Figure 4.7), the company developed a "retail outreach" programme that enabled it to offer hearing services on a one-day per week "day centre" basis in smaller outlets which couldn't otherwise accommodate a dedicated hearing service. That meant the offer could be extended to over 80 locations.

Rocketing sales

Hearing sales for 2004 were £4 million. During 2005, following the expansion of the "two for one" offer and the price comparison campaign, sales rocketed to £12.5 million, making Specsavers the fourth largest provider of digital hearing aids within the UK, with 12% share by volume – and this was accomplished in just under two years (Figure 4.8).

The company predicted that within six months it would have overtaken the number-three brand in the market, and was projecting full-year sales of £30 million for 2006, which would see it in second place in the market.

In addition, hearing centres were repaying all set-up costs and generating incremental profits within six to nine months of opening. The company was continuing to open hearing and day centres at the rate of one per week to meet its target of 100 locations by the end of the financial year in February 2006. It was also targeting a further 100 locations (50 hearing centres + 50 day centres) for store openings for the period March 2006 – February 2007.

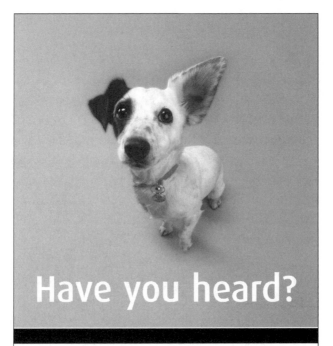

Have you heard?

There's a new Hearing Centre at Specsavers

Don't buy a new hearing aid until you've visited our new Hearing Centre at Specsavers in Redhill.

Now, Specsavers offers more than just glasses. We provide full hearing services in-store too, with hearing assessments, digital hearing aids and 'hearing helpers' for those of us who can't hear as clearly as we'd like to.

Hearing tests are free and, as you'd expect from Specsavers, we give outstanding value for money too. Our '2 for 1' offer now applies to digital hearing aids – you can buy 2 digital hearing aids for the price of 1, from just £595. Of course, we provide an expert, professional service too. Bob Maitland, RHAD FSHAA is our registered hearing aid dispenser, and he will provide you with impartial, friendly help and advice. And if you're not sure how digital technology can help you, we offer free hearing assessments and free digital hearing aid trials so you can hear the difference for yourself.

All you have to do is come and see us at Specsavers in Redhill. You'll find that better hearing has never been better value.

Specsavers Hearcare
1-2 Central Parade
London Road, Redhill
Telephone: 01737 772 990
www.specsavershearcare.co.uk

Specsavers Hearcare

Affordable - Digital - Hearing care

Figure 4.7

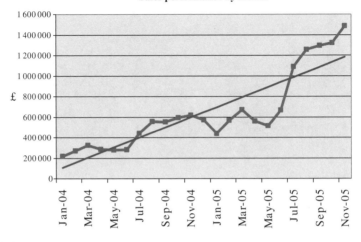

Figure 4.8

The company was thus well on course to become the UK market leader by the end of 2008, with an expected total store estate of over 250 units generating sales of over £60 million. In addition, it was planning to extend the brand into the Republic of Ireland and the Netherlands within the next 12 months.

5

Brand revitalisation

Introduction

Markets are tight. Innovation can be elusive. But businesses still have to find sustainable sources of growth. So it is hardly surprising that companies look within themselves to grow the top line and inject fresh energy into their established brands.

As the case studies in this chapter show, approaches to revitalisation may include market expansion, product modification or brand repositioning. They also provide interesting examples of how it can be done in different markets – and particularly in relatively slow-moving markets.

> "The striking thing I got from these case studies is that, although it is decades since brand management began, and we live in a radically different world on pretty well every level, the companies that are successful in revitalising their brands do it by doing 'the basics' well.
>
> Through comprehensive attitudinal and behavioural consumer understanding, they understand what the 'disease' is that is stopping the brand growing. They make clear *choices* in defining which consumer segment group they wish to target (the *who*), *choose* what they want to stand for among this target (the *what*) and they make still more *choices* about budget, product, packaging, media, geographical focus, etc. in order to cure 'the disease' identified at the start (the *how*).
>
> This is pretty well 1960s textbook stuff. One additional element that comes through is the importance of driving clear understanding of these choices

throughout an organisation and empowering the employees to be knowledge-able, passionate and empowered brand advocates.

So, recognising that this will sound like everyone's granddad: companies that successfully manage change and brand revitalisation do so by doing the basics right. They do so by making key choices, and then ensuring that they, and all of their organisation, understand, live and deliver these choices in everything they do.

On a final but happy note – as you read the cases you can be reassured that there is absolutely *no* conflict between simplicity, making choices and creativity."

Tim Seager, Marketing Director, Scottish & Newcastle UK

Green & Black's: taking a niche brand into the big league

Snapshot: Using limited marketing resources effectively has established Green & Black's as a leading player in the growing market for premium dark chocolate.

Key insights

- It is possible to translate a niche positioning with the right strategy into a mainstream proposition.
- The company's decision to build on its worthy, organic image by emphasising the luxurious nature of the chocolate transformed its fortunes.
- Clever timing and choice of marketing techniques, such as sampling, word of mouth and appropriate partnerships, gave the brand enough momentum to move into more mainstream promotional activities.

Summary

Green & Black's is a fast-growing, organic confectionery brand in the UK. Between 2002 and 2005, Green & Black's invoiced sales rose from £4.5 million to £29 million. This was a phenomenal growth of 544% in just four years, making Green & Black's the fastest growing confectionery brand in the UK. This success took place despite the UK's fondness for milkier chocolate. In fact, the intense dark chocolate produced by the company kicked off a revolution in the UK's tastebuds.

The company attributed this success to the brand positioning of intense, darker chocolate, which was embraced and communicated by all the brand's stakeholders. This was underpinned by applying this positioning consistently through a very select number of marketing disciplines in the earlier days to reach the right audience at the right time on limited resources.

This strategy has enabled the brand to compete successfully against much bigger, established players in the market, and it is one of the reasons why, by May 2006, it commanded a 7.4% share of the UK block chocolate market. In 2005, it was acquired for around £25 million by global confectionery group Cadbury Schweppes.

A brief history

Green & Black's was born in 1991, when Craig Sams, founder of Whole Earth, the pioneering organic food company, and his wife, environment columnist for *The Times* Josephine Fairley, made the world's first organic chocolate. It was a high-quality, bittersweet dark chocolate bar, packed with 70% cocoa solids.

By 1999, the company was ready to move to the next stage. A new set of investors took a stake in the business, led by William Kendall, formerly Chief Executive of the Covent Garden Soup company, a pioneer of fresh soup.

Over the next 18 months, a new management team was put in place, including Mark Palmer as Marketing Director, who had previously been Marketing Manager Burger King in the UK. This was a formidable combination of professional management and the brand's distinct personality.

Setting ambitious goals

With its bittersweet cocoa taste and organic credentials, Green & Black's chocolate had instant niche appeal, but never progressed beyond a 1% market share. It was viewed by supermarkets as a limited offering, with organic as its primary selling point. With the arrival of new management at the end of 2002, Green & Black's set out to:

- reposition the brand from worthy organic to luxury premium chocolate (leading on taste with organic as a supporting, rather than a primary, reason to purchase);
- operate in the premium sector, an emerging market with intensifying competition;
- create desire for dark chocolate in a milk chocolate-dominated market.

The market

The UK chocolate market is largely stagnant, with annual sales growth of just 0.5% in 2005. It has been dominated by long standing brands with big advertising and promotional budgets, such as Cadbury, Masterfoods and Nestlé, and there has been little room for volume or value growth for even the bigger players.

The market has also been dominated by milk chocolate as opposed to the intense dark chocolate that defines Green & Black's. In fact, dark chocolate accounts for less than 5% of UK chocolate sales.

Competition in the premium end of confectionery has also intensified in recent years, with Lindt, Guylian, Tesco's Finest and Sainsbury's Taste the Difference entering the arena at the same time as Green & Black's. In addition, brands such as Thorntons are supplying their products to supermarkets for the first time. As such, transforming Green & Black's – a low-profile brand with a small marketing budget – into a leading contender has been an extraordinary feat.

Getting people talking

Up until the end of 2002, Green & Black's had not carried out marketing activity of any real weight, but had built the brand by passionate word of mouth from a very loyal customer base. These consumers had in effect "discovered" the brand for themselves and were not only buying into the product taste, but were true believers in the brand story of organic and fair trade credentials.

The vision, therefore, was to take this small brand with its very loyal, passionate consumers and grow it. At this time the brand was known mainly for its organic credentials, but the trend towards eating more organic foods was in its infancy and many people still wrongly perceived that by choosing organic chocolate, they would sacrifice taste.

Based on an analysis of current buyers, two specific audience groups were identified: time poor, food rich (young affluent urbanites) and everyday luxury (home counties' mums). These were seen as offering the greatest potential for Green & Black's, because taste and quality were important for both groups. Positioning of any communications, therefore, focused on these two messages.

The long-term marketing strategy, developed in conjunction with its strategic communications agency Brave, was to reflect the experience of the Green & Black's early adopters, and the way in which consumers are introduced to brands by experiencing them in their social circle. The company

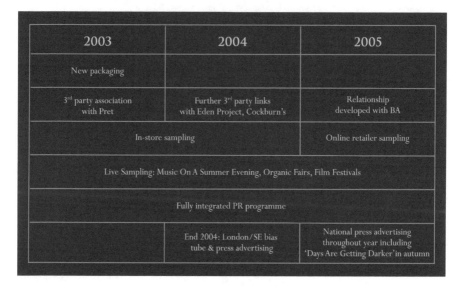

2003	2004	2005
New packaging		
3rd party association with Pret	Further 3rd party links with Eden Project, Cockburn's	Relationship developed with BA
In-store sampling		Online retailer sampling
Live Sampling: Music On A Summer Evening, Organic Fairs, Film Festivals		
Fully integrated PR programme		
	End 2004: London/SE bias tube & press advertising	National press advertising throughout year including 'Days Are Getting Darker' in autumn

Figure 5.1

set out to encourage and escalate this type of word-of-mouth behaviour that built the brand in the early days, resisting the temptation to "push" communications at them. The Green & Black's brand has an interesting story to tell consumers, and the company's key role is to retain interest and passionate advocacy from the early adopters while allowing new consumers to feel they are discovering the brand for themselves (Figure 5.1).

Attracting new consumers

One of the first applications of the marketing strategy came towards the end of 2002, when the company rolled out a new packaging design that placed the intense, darker chocolate positioning at the core. The dark brown background and coloured bands clearly communicated intense flavour first, while the gold typography acted as a cue to the brand's premium status. It was an image that created desire and encouraged consumers to pick up the product and try it (Figure 5.2).

Once the packaging reflected and complemented the quality of the chocolate more fully, the next task was to ensure the product was seen and tried by new consumers in the defined target audience groups. Sampling and

Figure 5.2

experiential activity were the primary marketing techniques in 2003 and into 2004.

The aim was not simply to sample, but to achieve a "Green & Black's moment" by reaching consumers and engaging with them in appropriate social situations. The primary focus was to maximise the attention given to consumer interaction with the brand and make consumers feel "selected".

The result was an ongoing brand experience programme that sampled 3.4 million target customers over three years. Sampling activity included the following:

- Offering complementary samples during sponsorship of English Heritage "Music on a summer evening" picnic concerts.
- Sampling in retailers such as Waitrose, Tesco and Sainsbury's, accompanied by branded customer information in keeping with other elements of the wider brand communication.
- Online sampling through retailers such as Tesco.com and Ocado (which is backed by Waitrose).

Extending the brand's reach

Brand partnerships were formed with a range of aspirational third parties, with bespoke activity tailored according to partner. For instance:

- A marketing partnership with the sandwich chain Pret a Manger included selling mini 40 g bars, the first ever co-branded product sold in its stores. In summer 2005, this relationship was extended to the sale of Green & Black's ice cream in jointly branded chilled cabinets.
- The Eden project is an international visitor attraction with a mission to "promote the understanding and responsible management of the vital relationship between plants, people and resources, leading to a sustainable future for all". The chocolate was sampled and sold to visitors by virtue of its organic and ethical attributes.
- Joint activity with Cockburn's Port to educate consumers on the complementary flavours of the brand's cherry bar and the port. This was supported by in-store sampling, point-of-sale support and press advertising (Figure 5.3).

Figure 5.3

Figure 5.4

- Bespoke 40 g bars are distributed to all of British Airways' first and club class customers (Figure 5.4).

PR has been a key element of the Green & Black's strategy, creating endorsement for the brand and increasing word-of-mouth communication. By seeding various elements of the Green & Black's story in various publications, from food to lifestyle titles, the brand has enjoyed unprecedented levels of editorial coverage. Evaluation of the 2005 campaign alone showed 746 pieces of coverage, of which 98% were favourable.

On the back of the pack redesign and the focus on getting people to discover the brand in 2003/4, sales started to climb, with an increasing number of customers tasting the brand through the trial activation programme and store-level marketing. In order to win greater awareness and reach, the brand then made its first foray into advertising in autumn 2004.

On a limited budget of £500 000, the company ran a combination of national press advertising and ads on the London underground. The underground ads reflected the London/Southeast bias for the brand (Figure 5.5). The quality press titles were selected because they would reach the key audiences identified by the company, and give the company the chance to attract them with the Green & Black's story.

Figure 5.5

The ad campaign self-confidently proclaimed the chocolate's "darkness", despite the fact that the majority of chocolate consumers expressed a preference for milk chocolate. It reflected the feelings of existing consumers towards the brand, as well as positioning it to new users as a darker, more intense chocolate (Figure 5.6).

Also, by introducing only one product/variant in each execution, and being very selective with the titles chosen, Green & Black's felt that consumers could still feel they were "discovering" the brand for themsleves. Different copy for the underground and the press increased the engagement and relevance of the advertising in the context in which it was seen.

The campaign succeeded in raising both national awareness and, more importantly, sales. In the 12-week period to the 1st of January 2005, year-on-year, the sales value increased by an eye-opening 72% – impressive results in a sector growing by just 0.5%.

Boosting the budget

On the back of such impressive sales figures, the marketing budget was increased to £2 million in 2005. The original strategy of trial activation, brand partnerships and PR remained, but the company continued to raise brand awareness with larger-scale press advertising campaigns.

The advertising campaigns continued to use consistent art direction and copy style, and to support an accelerated range extension strategy. New

Figure 5.6

products and tactical executions were introduced at key/relevant points in the calendar to capitalise on the key sales peaks in the year. In terms of the media schedule, the company was very aware of, and focused on, the relationship and dialogue developed with readers of a title over time. Executions and bespoke activity with any one title were built on what had been done previously.

The press was used in an increasingly creative way during the autumn of 2005. With agency partner Brave, an integrated media plan was developed with a core schedule of executions as well as innovative uses of space, with a heavyweight spike during the campaign to "celebrate" the end of British summer time on the 30th October: "the days are getting darker".

The campaign rebutted the negative perceptions of putting the clocks back by highlighting the extra opportunities to enjoy nights in and indulge in the brand's darker, more intense chocolate.

Significant success

Invoiced sales rose from £4.5 million at the end of 2002 to £29 million by 2005. It became the fastest growing confectionery brand in the UK, with an annual growth rate of 70% in a sluggish sector (Figure 5.7).

By May 2006, Green & Black's commanded a 7.4% share of the UK block chocolate market. Before the marketing initiatives carried out between 2003–2005, the share was under 1%. During this time, the brand's best seller, the 100 g Dark 70% chocolate bar, overtook the best seller of its closest rival, Lindt.

The breadth and appeal of the Green & Black's brand enabled it to evolve from its original base of health food stores through to some of the highest profile food retailers in the UK. The brand now had real diversity in distribu-

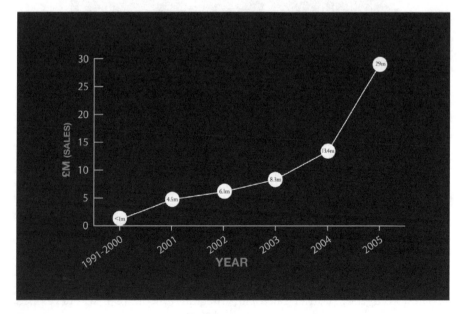

Figure 5.7

tion, from Oxfam and Tesco to Harrods and Selfridges. Moreover, between 2003 and 2005, the frequency of purchase increased from 2.7 to 3.4, and the average selling price rose from £1.19 to £1.54, which meant consumers were not only buying more but paying more.

Readers of the magazines *Good Housekeeping* and the *Observer Food Monthly* voted Green & Black's their "favourite indulgent treat" and "best organic product" for two years running.

This combination of the decision at the end of 2002 to focus on the darker, intense flavour of the chocolate rather than its organic heritage, engaging extensively with consumers and running an effective and carefully calibrated marketing communications programme, helped successfully transform the brand from a niche, worthy organic positioning into luxury premium chocolate.

J. Sainsbury: making Sainsbury's great again

Snapshot: Sainsbury's decision to rethink the way it attracted shoppers put the retailer back on track in the fight for market share.

Key insights

- Sainsbury's became aware that achieving complete loyalty from shoppers was unlikely to be successful. It recognised that increasing spend and frequency would be a powerful driver of brand success.
- It also realised that changes in shopping behaviour now called for a universal idea that connected with all shoppers, irrespective of demographics.
- This led to the development of marketing communications as a service to inspire shoppers with new ideas, rather than an advertising campaign as such.
- The aim was not to change image in the hope of influencing consumer behaviour, but to aim at changing behaviour and let the store experience change the brand's image.

Summary

J. Sainsbury plc is a leading UK food retailer with interests in financial services. It consists of Sainsbury's Supermarkets, Sainsbury's Local, Bells Stores, Jacksons Stores and JB Beaumont, Sainsbury's Online and Sainsbury's Bank. It employs 153 000 people. Its group turnover in 2005 was £16.6 billion.

The arrival of a new Chief Executive in October 2004 was the catalyst for the retailer, which had been losing market share over the previous few years, to start its sales and profit recovery. The first stage in this battle was to use pricing and distribution to win back lost customers to the stores by boosting the brand image.

But it wasn't enough. Sainsbury's became increasingly aware that not only were shopping habits changing dramatically, but that increasing sales called for more than an ad campaign. Rather than changing image, the company had to encourage new behaviour by actively persuading customers to put new items into their shopping baskets – to try something new. But this would also mean getting the message across to employees.

The new approach led to an uplift in sales of 5.2%, beyond any other contributing factors.

The road to recovery

In October 2004, new Chief Executive Justin King outlined plans for a sales-led profit recovery through sales growth of £2.5 billion. The project, called "Making Sainsbury's great again", began by fixing on-shelf availability and getting prices back in line with major competitors.

By 2005, great progress had been made in delivering improved availability. Investment in price was made in January 2005 and again in May/June 2005, and customers noticed. These changes had a big impact, but only brought the company in line with competitors, not ahead of them.

Marketing faced the challenge of delivering the next phase of growth. This required a fundamental change in the role of communication. The role of communication had been to make the retailer the choice for the main shopping journey. Ideas were tested in research to see if they would persuade people to "switch" to Sainsbury's. It was as though supermarket shopping was a bit like voting in elections. You were either a Labour voter or a Conservative voter, and each party attempted to change your attitudes to win your vote.

Thinking about Sainsbury's communication was thus dedicated to "winning the vote". This analogy had become so deeply ingrained that in 2003, a US polling organisation had been commissioned to conduct research in the UK for Sainsbury's. It had advised on Bill Clinton's successful presidential campaigns and now applied this thinking to UK supermarkets. A rigorous piece of analysis followed. But it was based on the wrong strategic thinking.

Flawed thinking

The first flaw in thinking was to try and change the way people shopped. The days when people chose one shop and shopped there once a week on a Saturday afternoon were long gone. Partly driven by the expansion to high street and small format stores, big supermarkets were everywhere, so everybody shopped in all of them at one time or other.

The political strategy was a noble attempt to turn the clock back, to change the reality of the market, to get more shoppers to do a main shop with just one supermarket. The first insight was to realise that the company's task was not to win more shoppers: it was to win more transactions from all shoppers and more pounds per transaction.

In 2005, retailers had to win the main shop, the top-up shop, the lunch-time sandwich and everything in between, every day of every week. Shopping behaviour demanded a universal idea. The company couldn't afford to focus on one high value group, like families or empty nesters. It needed a brand-driven communications idea universal enough to connect with any current or potential shopper, irrespective of demographics.

The second flaw in thinking was the lack of connection between the shopper attitudes the company wanted to change and shopper behaviour. While searching for a new approach, Sainsbury's looked at the attitude state-ments associated with first-choice supermarket. It had expected it to be all about the value equation, and that low prices and good quality would be associated with success. It was wrong.

The three statements linked with first choice store were "do everything they can to make shopping easier", "have really attractive stores" and "are always coming up with new ideas". The 2004 communication was dedicated to the retailer's high food standards to win the brand image battle. But key measures had been about delivery, not image. One measure stood out as neglected in Sainsbury's brand heartland: "are always coming up with new ideas" (Figure 5.8).

Changing behaviour

This called for trying something new. The company thus decided to reverse its thinking about the role of communication. Instead of trying to change *image* and then hoping for *behaviour* change, communication would be used to change *behaviour* and then let store experience change *image*.

But how could the company get everyone behind this behavioural change? The answer lay in further analysis of business goals. The £2.5 billion in growth seemed like a daunting target and was too big a number for any individual store colleague to see their direct role in achieving it. The size of Sainsbury's business offered a solution, however. With 14 million transactions a week and a few years to achieve the revenue goal, the company calculated

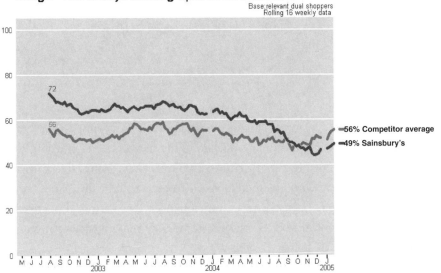

Source: Millward Brown/Sainsbury's

Figure 5.8

that it could reframe its task as simply earning one more thing in each basket or trolley.

The idea of one more thing had huge value. Suddenly the huge £2.5 billion target became user-friendly. Creative teams at the agency, Abbott Mead Vickers BBDO, said, "Now I understand what you want us to do". The idea of earning one more thing in each basket or trolley was to become common currency for store managers in the months ahead when discussing with their colleagues how to bring the idea to life in-store. Now everyone working with or for Sainsbury's knew that their job was to earn one more thing in every basket or trolley.

A brand idea rather than an ad campaign

Inspiration came by putting this observation with the image statement of "always coming up with new ideas". The company would achieve one more thing in the basket or trolley by giving people new ideas and by encouraging them to try something new, not just substituting something they usually bought. This demanded a brand idea, not an advertising campaign.

Sainsbury's
Try something new today

Figure 5.9

Advertising tells customers about a brand. Advertising runs to the brand owner's agenda, not its customer's agenda. This new brand idea would thus be different, transforming marketing communications from advertising to service. Customer research defined ideas customers would value. They would welcome ideas from Sainsbury's to enliven everyday eating. The retailer would inspire potential and existing customers by making marketing communication an ideas-delivery service.

There was already a slogan – "Making life taste better" – but it was just a passive advertising line. Now there would be a shift from a passive endline to a useful brand idea: "Try something new today" (Figure 5.9). This was not an idea that invited passive agreement. It was an idea that invited active engagement. It would change behaviour, not just attitudes, and was much more than advertising.

Inspiring employees

The first step was to bring the idea to life for store colleagues. The company tried something new to set the scene for them. The communication insight was that customers "sleep shop". This was inspired by an accompanied shop with a woman who conducted an unbroken conversation with her companion while subconsciously reaching to the shelves for all her usual items.

To dramatise sleep shopping, a man in a gorilla suit was released into a Sainsbury's store on a Saturday morning and the results were filmed. The gorilla wasn't jumping around or bellowing, but was an unusual enough presence in a store. The resulting film demonstrated that, despite this gorilla in their midst, customers didn't notice: they were too stuck in routine to look up. The colleagues got the message – sleep shopping was the enemy of try something new.

The company also wanted its colleagues to try new things themselves. For each wave of communication, samples were distributed to 125 000 colleagues (sausage and apples at launch, parsnips and maple syrup at Christmas). This would release store colleagues' potential to become brand advocates by inspiring them with the same ideas that were in the customer communication.

Inspiring managers

More was asked from Sainsbury's store managers. Try something new today was their call to action to try new things at work, come up with new ways of solving problems and adopt an open and constructive attitude to change. "Trying something new" was now enshrined as a leadership behaviour on their appraisal.

Inspiring customers

And finally, customers were showered with ideas. Between September and December in 2005, over 100 different ideas were given to customers. The existing media and point-of-sale strategy was adjusted to become an idea delivery system. In-store budgets were used to create idea cards delivered at the front of store, with hanging banners and barker cards (messages attached to the shelves) in the stores themselves.

The launch media spend was concentrated into a burst of ideas on TV, in print and on the website. Print, radio and leaflet spends dedicated to value and offer communications were now enhanced by adding ideas to them. Direct mail with vouchers and offers also distributed ideas to people's homes. And all this was achieved on a reduced media spend.

It was a simple deal – give customers useful ideas and they would reward Sainsbury's with more spend and/or more frequent visits (Figure 5.10).

Convincing results

When the campaign launched (in September 2005) it was the only significant change to Sainsbury's marketing and operations. Media spend actually reduced by 16% year-on-year over the period September–December (from £27.5 million in 2004 to £23 million in 2005), while competitive spend increased by 23%, reducing the company's share of spend from 30% to 21% (Figure 5.11).

Figure 5.10

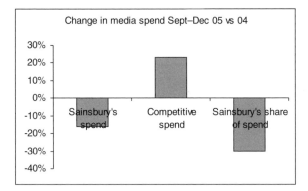

Figure 5.11

Prices and distribution were better than the year before. This change occurred in January 2005 and again in the summer. There were no major new sub-brands launched in store (the most recent had been the Basics range in January 2005) and promotional spend remained constant. No significant new direct mail activity or Nectar loyalty card promotions began.

New stores opened, but sales from these stores were excluded from the like-for-like sales figures. Sainsbury's TV brand spokesperson, the well-known British chef Jamie Oliver, became a national hero for his high profile TV programme, *Jamie's School Dinners*, but this was in March 2005. If this had benefited Sainsbury's at all, the effect would have been felt in the spring or summer of 2005, as Oliver was used consistently through this period. But the effects of the new idea were seen after September 2005.

The company's econometric model showed existing advertising and communications were already profitable, generating more sales than the amount invested in them. What this case study shows is the incremental effect of the new idea, not the effect of communications overall. Production costs were the same and media costs were lower, so the incremental cost of this idea vs. the previous idea was nil and every extra pound earned was the differential value of the idea.

Solid financial gains

Sainsbury's trading statements showed that fixing price and on-shelf availability kick-started its growth in the first half of calendar year 2005. Average

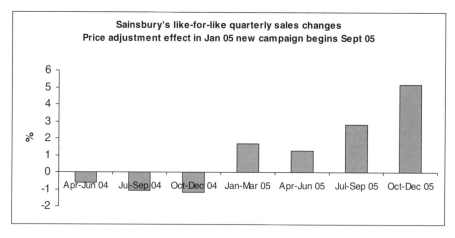

Figure 5.12

like-for-like growth during this period was 1.5%, following a like-for-like sales decline in 2004.

The new brand idea launched on September 19th, 2005. Sales responded almost immediately, but, for the sake of this analysis, assume that none of the additional growth in the July–September 2005 quarter could be attributed to it, and that this was the continual effect of store improvements.

The financial effect of the idea can be demonstrated in the additional growth in the October–December quarter (Figure 5.12). Without the idea, like-for-like growth could be assumed to be at an average of the previous three quarters (1.7%, 1.3%, 2.8%) or 1.9%. This was the ongoing growth effect of the considerable improvements in price and product availability. This would have produced like-for-like sales (excluding petrol) of £3.5 billion. The actual growth was 5.2%. Moreover, this was a conservative estimate, given that the idea drove sales for at least two weeks of the previous quarter.

The theory was that this behaviour change would lead to attitude change. This was indeed correct. Increasing frequency and depth of engagement of the store seemed to be exerting a catalytic effect, making more people realise the improvements in store delivery and accelerating growth rates as a result.

All images appearing in this case study are reproduced by permission of Sainsbury's Supermarkets Ltd.

Brains: the power of positive thinking

Snapshot: Regional brewer Brains revitalised its brand with a simple and unifying brand proposition that won over both external and internal audiences.

Key insights

- The adoption of "being positive" as the core brand value enabled the Brains brand to become symbolic of a progressive and positive new Wales. This was a position that no other beer and pub company brand could take.
- It demonstrates the value that can be gained through adopting a positioning that gives the brand an attitude and point of view on life that allows it to react quickly to marketing opportunities as they present themselves.
- This strategy has also been central to revitalising the company culture and driving organisational change.

Summary

S.A. Brain (or Brains) is an independent, family-owned brewer, pub operator and drinks wholesaler to the licensed trade. Brains is Wales's leading drinks and hospitality company. It is based in Cardiff and operates predominantly in southern and western Wales and adjoining counties of England.

However, by 2002, the company had become increasingly aware that its brand was perceived as old-fashioned and conservative. The company thus embarked on a far-reaching brand revitalisation programme that affected not just the brand itself, but every part of the organisation and its stakeholders.

The new Brains branding and "positive thinking" marketing campaign helped the company grow its turnover by 27% (from £96 million to £122 million) and profit before tax by 29% (from £7.2 million to £9.3 million) from 2003 to 2005. It also underpinned the internal cultural change programme required to deliver a revitalised "organisation brand".

Breathing new life into the brand

For the past few years, Brains has been undergoing a process of revitalising its brand from a typical regional brewer's brand (i.e. traditional, unadventurous, unaspirational) into a contemporary and dynamic brand. The Brains brand is being developed as a multi-faceted "organisation brand", with values that apply to all aspects of the company, including its beers, its pubs and its people (Figure 5.13).

The "being positive" brand positioning and "more positive thinking from Brains" strap line and advertising campaigns were launched in 2003. However, it was during 2004–5 that the company started to reap the rewards from its bold marketing strategy, with significant strides forward for the Brains brand and the overall business performance.

The Brains strategy built on its 120-year heritage by shifting consumer, trade and employee attitudes to the company and brand, so that in the future, the brand would be perceived to be forward looking (not conservative), innovative (leaders not followers), contemporary (not old-fashioned), Welsh (rather than simply Cardiff-centric), about great pubs (not average "boozers") and great people (not just great pints).

The brand revitalisation process was seen as a cornerstone of the Brains business plan:

• To grow sales of Brains' ale brands in a declining on-trade market and to expand geographically from the Brains heartland in southeast Wales into west, mid and north Wales, as well as into southwest England.

Figure 5.13

- To invest in the existing pub estate to improve its overall quality, diversity and retail standards, and also to expand the estate in numbers and geographical spread.
- To increase the motivation of Brains people through: effective training, development and team-building; improved employee communication and involvement in the business; and enhanced reward and recognition packages.

Gathering the evidence

At the start of the process, a comprehensive brand research programme was undertaken, including employee, trade and consumer research. In summary, this showed that the Brains brand had great heritage, but was no longer engaging effectively with its key target audiences. While there was genuine local affection for Brains, the brand and company were perceived to be:

- "old school";
- conventional;
- slow to change;
- followers not leaders;
- local to Cardiff (limited appeal in other parts of Wales).

Sales of Brains beers were in decline and the pubs were perceived as "traditional boozers" with low standards and a limited offer.

Crafting the message

An integrated marketing campaign based on the new brand positioning for Brains was developed. The core value was "being positive", and a consumer, trade and employee-facing tag line was created: "more positive thinking from Brains". The hero image for the campaign was the "always half full" image of a pint glass with the half pint of beer in its top half. This was used in outdoor, press and in-pub advertising as well as the end-frame of TV commercials (Figure 5.14).

The "being positive" thought tapped into the spirit of optimism in contemporary Wales (underpinned by developments such as The Millennium Stadium, The Millennium Centre, Cardiff and Swansea Bays) and the

Figure 5.14

Figure 5.15

ambition of the new board and senior management team. To the revitalised Brains brand, company and employees, the glass is "always half full".

Other elements included the development of a dynamic new identity, including new corporate logo, product liveries (hand pump clips, bar top "founts", cans and bottles) and striking new delivery vehicles (Figure 5.15).

The new livery was carried through to the point-of-sale through a substantial investment in branded glassware and point-of-sale materials. New signage was installed in all new pub developments and flagship free-trade stockists to signal the revitalisation of the Brains brand.

Developing new products

A programme of new product development was also undertaken, including the launch of Brains Smooth Extra Cold – the first "extra cold" product launched by a regional brewer – which was designed to appeal to lager drinkers, a younger male consumer and women. IPA, Brains's price-fighting beer, was rebranded from its secondary Buckleys brand to Brains, enabling the brewer to offer a Brains beer in every key market segment. It also allowed IPA to benefit from the over-arching Brains brand campaign.

To support the Brains sponsorship of Welsh rugby, a new draught and bottled beer called Bread of Heaven was launched. This was then reliveried as the Official Beer of their 2005 RBS 6 Nations Grand Slam, Wales's first for 27 years. A number of one-off or seasonal ales were also introduced, such as Welsh Pride (to celebrate the selection of ten Welsh players for the British Lions tour of New Zealand in summer 2005), WRU 125th Anniversary Ale and RBS 6 Nations Champions Ale.

Forging a rugby union

Brains's sponsorship of the Welsh rugby team, a four-year agreement that commenced on October 1, 2004, has been a major focus of its marketing campaigns ever since. The team took the Brains "positive thinking" positioning to heart by winning the Grand Slam in the 2005 RBS 6 Nations.

The support campaign, which began with the ultimate positive thinking announcement poster, "Brains – Official Sponsor of the 2007 World Champions" (Figure 5.16) and complementary TV commercial, was taken forward throughout the 2005 6 Nations, with a series of tactical and viral activities.

- The first of these was "Wooden Spoon", a cheeky image featuring the red rose logo of English rugby emblazoned on a wooden spoon, underpinned by the Brains strap line "more positive thinking from Brains". The

Figure 5.16

Figure 5.17

message was emailed by thousands of Welshmen to their English friends after England lost the first three matches of their 2005 6 Nations campaign.

- That was followed up by a change of branding on the Welsh shirts for the away match in Paris, made necessary by the ban on alcohol advertising in France. The name on the shirt was simply switched from "Brains" to "Brawn", generating massive interest and publicity. The Welsh team duly delivered a famous victory (Figure 5.17).

- There was a follow-up tactical advertising campaign featuring the slogan "Brains and Brawn: always a winning combination", which, following Wales's Grand Slam, was proudly amended to "now officially an unbeatable combination".

The sponsorship also meant that a Welsh beer was made available in The Millennium Stadium for the first time, an initiative that proved popular with Welsh rugby fans. Brains doubled its share of overall beer, lager, stout and cider sales in the stadium compared to the previous incumbent.

On match days, Cardiff city centre became Brains territory, with giant banners erected on the front of pubs, external bunting applied to all Brains stockists and replica Welsh shirts featuring Brains branding "de rigueur" for tens of thousands of Welsh rugby fans. Wales's 2005 Grand Slam provided unprecedented coverage for the Brains brand. This was supported by a number of initiatives, including the renaming of Brains's flagship Cardiff pub, the Yard Bar and Kitchen, as "The Grand Slam" and the launch of a range of celebratory merchandise.

For the 2005 Autumn Series, the campaign was once again moved on, with some of Wales's Grand Slam heroes featuring on a poster under the headline "Bred in Heaven", a positive take on both the players and the Welsh nation (Figure 5.18).

Figure 5.18

A comprehensive marketing mix

Advertising

Alongside the rugby-themed advertising, Brains created three other TV commercials. One featured two positive thinking hitchhikers who had the audacity to put up their entire address, including flat number and postcode, on their cardboard sign and were rewarded by being picked up in a limousine by two attractive women. Another was a specific campaign to support Brains Smooth Extra Cold under the theme "BRRRR! – Brrrrrrrrrrains Smooth Extra Cold". The BRRRR! thought was carried through into an outdoor campaign and a full point-of-sale package, including bunting, bar runners (the modern form of bar towels) and glassware (Figure 5.19).

Sales promotion

A series of sales promotions themed around the advertising and sponsorship was also developed: e.g. a text-in promotion to win the opportunity to kick for £50 000 at halftime in the Wales–Ireland match and a radio promotion on Red Dragon FM to win a trip in a limousine to watch a Welsh rugby international in the Brains Executive Box (tying together the TV brand campaign and rugby sponsorship).

Figure 5.19

Several other promotions were run on a rugby theme, including a free "Bred in Heaven" poster for every *South Wales Echo* reader; ticket and signed shirt competitions in regional and national press; and a series of activities geared to ensuring that a Brains pub or a Brains free trade stockist was *the* place to watch the big match for those without tickets.

Promotion Solutions, an online resource for pub managers, was also launched. This enabled managers to tailor promotions to meet the individual requirements of their pub's business according to its market template, e.g. Sunday lunch offers for "Destination Food"; "Watch it here" promotions for "Community Pubs" offering big-screen sport; wine promotions for "Quality Taverns".

PR

The "positive thinking" campaign and Welsh rugby sponsorship captured the imagination of the regional press in Wales, with Brains featuring prominently on four front page leads in the *Western Mail*, as well as receiving extended coverage for the various advertising and viral/tactical marketing campaigns in broadcast and print media.

The tongue-in-cheek "Wooden Spoon" and "Brawn" initiatives also received significant national coverage, including a full explanation of why the Welsh players were playing in "Brawn", not "Brains", shirts in Paris by the BBC TV live commentator in the first few minutes of the match. This was witnessed by millions of viewers in Wales and right across Britain.

Rugby aside, Brains consistently achieved excellent coverage in regional and national media for its advertising campaigns, new/refurbished pub openings and new product launches.

Constant listening and monitoring

- Qualitative consumer, trade and employee research was used as a foundation stone for the original brand positioning work and marketing campaigns. It was key to identifying the challenges and priorities for the brand revitalisation task.
- Quantitative consumer research was used at the launch of the new positioning to provide the context that made the campaign newsworthy, thereby achieving significant PR coverage. This provided a yardstick for

the mood of the Welsh nation, by measuring how many Welsh people see the glass as "half empty vs. half full". The initial and follow-up research generated considerable ongoing PR coverage, as it became clear that Wales was increasingly becoming a "half full" nation.

- The advertising creative approach was qualitatively researched among consumers to ensure that Brains was connecting with its core target audience and to help shape future creative solutions. The research showed that the Brains campaign had stature equivalent to any national or international beer brand.

- An ongoing independent brand-tracking study was undertaken across a representative sample of Welsh people to help understand how the new positioning and marketing campaigns were being received by consumers, as well as gauging how quickly the perceptions of the brand were moving towards the values identified on the desired brand map at the beginning of the process.

Internal marketing and culture

The "positive" brand positioning and marketing campaigns were in part created as a reflection of the increasingly upbeat spirit of the business identified in employee research carried out before the campaign, which had resulted from the appointment of a new Chief Executive and board team.

A comprehensive internal marketing programme has been underway since 2003. The key theme has been to promote positive thinking and behaviours throughout the company. This included presentations by the Chief Executive and senior marketers to all employees. Each member of staff was given a "one-pager" explaining the new brand positioning and company vision. Senior and middle management workshops were held to determine implementation strategy, while "half full" consultation sessions were carried out throughout the organisation to give employees the opportunity to air their views about the business – positive and negative.

The outcome of these sessions was then fed back to employees together with concrete actions, such as:

- new pay and grading structures and more comprehensive review processes;

- improved communications from the board downwards, including a quarterly cascade;
- abridged company report and accounts for all employees;
- greater visibility of directors on a day-to-day basis;
- improved inter-departmental communication and cooperation.

Progress was measured via regular employee feedback, mystery visits within the retail estate and informal discussion groups. Improved communication and consultation, including the setting up of an "Employee Communications Forum", led to a number of employee-friendly initiatives, such as a new and highly popular flexible benefits package. A testament to the developing "people brand" at Brains was the award of over 800 certificates to reward outstanding customer service in the retail team alone.

Hitting the right targets

The adoption of "being positive" as the core brand value and the inspiration behind the brand revitalisation campaign was in itself differentiating from other beer and pub company brands. The brand thought tapped into the ambition and optimism within the company and reflected the mood of contemporary Welsh people, enabling the Brains brand to become champions of a progressive and positive new Wales.

The "positive" new brand not only formed the inspiration behind engaging consumer marketing communications, but the backbone of the internal cultural change programme required to deliver a revitalised "organisation brand". The new brand positioning was used to drive behavioural change throughout the company, from internal departments and customer services to bar staff and draymen.

Finally, the sponsorship of the Welsh rugby team elevated Brains into a pre-eminent position in the minds of Welsh consumers and trade customers.

Rising sales

The new Brains branding and "positive thinking" marketing campaign helped the company grow its turnover by 27% (from £96 million to £122 million) and profit before tax by 29% (from £7.2 million to £9.3 million) from

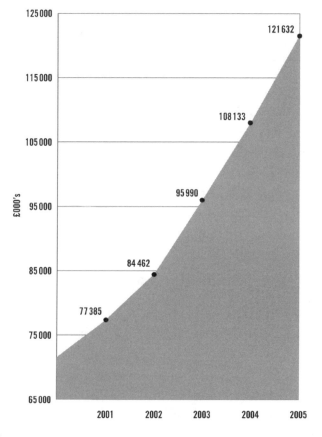

Figure 5.20

2003 to 2005. Managed house sales went up 4% year-on-year, a statistic which compared very favourably with other pub companies. Brains's draught beer brand sales were rising at 6%, in an on-trade ale market in Wales which was declining at 9% p.a., with over 1000 new distribution points achieved. Furthermore, Brains's take-home beers were growing at 14% year-on-year (Figures 5.20 and 5.21).

Increased awareness, trial and loyalty

In addition, quantitative consumer research showed that spontaneous brand awareness for Brains in south Wales was now higher than all other beer and lager brands. Brains S.A, the flagship ale, was enjoying higher levels of aware-

Profit On Ordinary Activities Before Tax
(before charging exceptional items & profit or loss
on disposal of fixed assets)

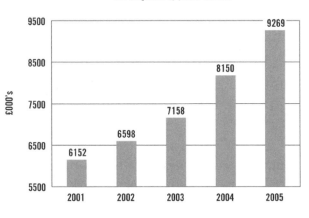

Figure 5.21

ness than all other real ale brands in south Wales, including Greene King IPA, Bass, Old Speckled Hen, Abbot, Marston's Pedigree and Fuller's London Pride.

Propensity to drink Brains beers also rose significantly over those two years, with beer drinkers who usually drank Brains more than doubling from 16% to 36%. Propensity to visit a Brains pub was up 23% over the same period.

Delivering the values

Focus groups held to explore reaction to Brains's positive new positioning and marketing campaigns revealed that it delivered on the desired brand values ("It gets Brains away from the flat cap, spit and sawdust image"); it was popular and humorous ("It's insightful and funny – it grabs your attention"); and it had stature ("It's slick and professional. It's what you would expect from a top flight beer brand").

It also worked internally. An employee satisfaction survey in 2005 showed overall scores were significantly up compared to the previous two years. For example: "Told when I'm doing a good job" was up 71%; "Receive regular communication of company strategy" was up 66%; "Training and development needs met" was up 40%; and "Morale" was up 23%.

Effective use of marketing resources

With a media budget of around £300 000 a year, by concentrating on its core trading area, Brains was able to match the spend of its key competitors in the region. In advertising terms, there was a concentration on a limited number of media options, primarily TV and outdoor, with campaigns being featured prominently in Brains's own pubs and other stockists of Brains beers. Other media, e.g. radio and press, were targeted through PR and sales promotions.

The Welsh Rugby Union sponsorship proved to be a key focus for marketing activity. Brains adopted a strategy whereby the sponsorship support budget more than matched the cost of the sponsorship itself, ensuring that the message got through to its customers.

All activity was underpinned by the core brand thought of "being positive" and true to the desired values set out in the original brand development work, thereby creating consistency of message and ensuring maximum impact. The strategy was extraordinarily well-received by local and regional press, which rewarded Brains with repeated coverage of its campaigns.

All images appearing in this case study are reproduced by permission of SA Brain.

Innocent: enjoying the fruits of living the brand

Snapshot: Ambitious growth targets and fierce competition meant that this young brand had to combine relentless innovation and clever marketing to build on its early success.

Key insights

- Three years after enjoying success as a well-received niche brand, Innocent was facing a market that was now attracting heavyweight players.
- It capitalised on its strong tone of voice, its relentless innovation and a quirky approach to marketing to keep the momentum going.
- There is no substitute for complete devotion and obsession if the brand is in a tightly defined niche.

Summary

Innocent Drinks had been on the market almost three years by January 2002, and had achieved an annual turnover target of £6.5 m and a 25% market share. Its brand had had a lot of success, helped by its strongly defined corporate culture. However, to reach future targets it needed to continue to grow by 50% a year. The firm realised it had to continue innovating, challenge preconceptions and strive for customer infatuation through a consistent message.

In response to consumer feedback on how the products could be improved, it launched six ranges of drinks with a total of 17 recipes. As a result, by 2004, Innocent was selling 450 000 bottles a week, with its take-home range alone generating £2.5 million in revenue since its launch in July 2004.

Much of the feedback came through a "banana phone": a consumer hotline through which Innocent received 10 000 calls and emails from customers. Queries were replied to within 24 hours and complaints answered with free product samples. As a consequence, the number of loyal Innocent customers grew to 6000.

Advertising, sampling and a series of PR stunts also helped the Innocent cause, increasing brand awareness from 25% to 37%. In 2004, it was the number one smoothie brand in the UK with a market share of 48%.

Creating the building blocks

When Innocent was started by three friends in 1997, they had a five-pronged business strategy that included building a strong brand. It was clear to them that for the company to succeed it would have to innovate and excel in five areas to achieve its goal: to become Europe's favourite little juice company with a turnover of £50 million by 2007 (Figure 5.22).

The five closely linked areas were:

- Wonderful drinks: consistently produce the best-tasting, all-natural drinks in segments through devotion to detail, innovation and research.
- Strong brand: build an engaging brand for a core target consumer which is marketed consistently, promotes trials and encourages loyalty.
- Robust supply: continually deliver what the company's customers want, when they want it, in the most efficient manner.
- Great team: invest in talented, ambitious people and their environment to help them do the best possible job and succeed personally.
- Solid customer relations: form strong, lasting relationships in target sectors with key customers.

By June 2002, the brand had been on the market for almost three years. The company had achieved its turnover target of £6.5 million in 2001 and captured a 25% market share. However, it had to grow the business 50% each year in order to meet its targets.

Figure 5.22

The smoothie market had started off with small, branded players. But, by this time, the major supermarkets had started to produce own-label smoothies, and competition to maintain market share was fierce. The market had doubled and was worth £25 million.

Finding the right way to grow

With a company that had grown as fast as Innocent, in a marketplace that was changing constantly, the company had to keep innovating and ensure that ruthless creativity kept up the momentum of the first three years. The company encapsulated this in the following way: "to keep marketing in an 'Innocent' way by always challenging the norm, striving for consumer infatuation and ensuring consistency in everything we do".

Having established a strong tone of voice from the beginning, it was imperative that it kept communicating to its four key audiences in a way that was compelling and relevant:

- Consumers: the "nice" people who bought the drinks.
- Customers: the people actually selling the drinks.
- Influencers: those who could help encourage others to try the drinks, such as journalists.
- Us: the team at Innocent who were each ambassadors for the brand.

The company hadn't always had lots of money to invest in marketing, so the solution was to create a mixture of big and small initiatives – all done in an "Innocent" way.

Relentless innovation

The company knew that its most important marketing weapon was the drinks inside the bottles. If they weren't what consumers wanted, the company would not have stayed the course. So the emphasis has constantly been on making the best possible tasting and most natural drinks with quality ingredients. Constant product innovation is thus at the heart of everything the company does.

At the start of 2002, there were five smoothie recipes and two thickie recipes. All adhered to the strong Innocent principles of crushed fruit, fresh juices and absolutely no preservatives, stabiliser or additives. By 2004, the range had been extended considerably (Figure 5.23 and Table 5.1). Each of these product launches involved a joint effort from the whole team.

A good example of the process of launching new products at Innocent is illustrated by the introduction of the one-litre take-home cartons in summer 2004, which generated £2.5 million in just over six months:

- running consumer trials and research to prove there really was a gap in the market for this offering;
- testing new packaging formats;
- designing the new packaging;
- gearing up the rest of the business, from products to operations to finance to sales, to cope with the impact of the launch.

 **innocent**   our drinks

Meet the whole family...

Fresh Fruit Smoothies
100% Fruit
No preservatives or concentrates
No artificial colours, flavours
No added water

Super Smoothies
100% Fruit
Ingredients chosen for their nutritious –VitC/
Detox properties

Thickies
100% low fat pro-biotic yogurt and
fruit/spices
One guest (rotating) recipe

Juicy Waters
100% Spring water and Fruit
No preservatives or concentrates

Really lovely juices
Freshly squeezed juices

Fresh Fruit Smoothies Take Home
Same exact ingredients as in our little bottles
Convenient pack with longer shelf life

Figure 5.23

Table 5.1 *Innocent range expansion to 2004*

Range	Consumer need	2002	2003	2004
Really lovely juices	Something as natural but a bit thinner than a smoothie	Range launched with three recipes		
Seasonal smoothies	Variety offering tastes of the season	Four recipes launched	Four new recipes	Five recipes (two for the summer)
Juicy waters	A truly thirst-quenching soft drink for adults		Range launched with three recipes	One new recipe added
Thickies	Healthy indulgence		Two new recipes added	Guest thickie launched for extra variety
Super smoothies	Drinks with natural functionality		Vit. C and Detox recipes launched	Fruit and Veg. added
One-litre take-home cartons	Bigger pack format, great for keeping in the fridge			Range launched with four recipes

Going bananas over consumers

In 2003, Innocent had set up a sophisticated database to help it care for its consumers even better, by keeping track of what they were saying. Between September and December of that year, the company had over 1000 forms of consumer contact. 2004 saw this rise to over 6000 (one customer loved the company so much she even made a quilt for it).

By 2004 it was responding to 10000 forms of customer contact by phone and email. It encourages people to ring its consumer hotline, the "banana phone", even if they just want to have a chat because they are bored. All letters and emails to the "hello" box are answered within 24 hours. The company also invites people to pop in and visit Fruit Towers, which they do. Anyone who has a bad Innocent experience gets sent a case of "sorry smoothies" to arrive the next day. This is all well in line with the company's philosophy that little things don't cost much at all, but make an enormous difference and definitely add richness to everyone's Innocent experience.

Putting the message out there

The company ran a quirky advertising campaign in 2003, which led to £100 000 worth of new listings and grew brand awareness from 25% to 37% (Figure 5.24). By 2004, Innocent was more highly regarded than its competitor PJ across a range of major criteria such as "good quality", "good value for money" and "I would recommend".

Events have also played a prominent role. For instance, in 2003, the company chose to reach its consumers in a totally innovative way with the launch of its first Fruitstock music festival (Figure 5.25). It had several objectives:

- To say a big thank-you to all the outlets. They were all invited to come along and spend some time in the Very Nice People area, equipped with deckchairs, free drinks and food.
- To have a nice fourth birthday party for everyone at Innocent and all its customers and suppliers.
- To have a major free event that the company could invite all its regular consumers to as a way to thanking them for buying its drinks.
- To get the Innocent brand out into a major park in London (Regent's Park), in the press and on ads to reach new consumers.

Figure 5.24

Figure 5.25

The first year saw over 40 000 people popping along to Regent's Park, and in 2004, the company's festival attracted 80 000.

Building up the brand

There have been a number of other activities aimed at boosting the brand.

- **Stay Healthy Be Lazy.** People enjoyed the company's tone to such an extent that it wrote a little book with tips on how to be healthier. This also gave the company a chance to reach out to a new audience not necessarily associated with the brand: book shops.
- **Little Innocent forests.** This was an urban tree-planting programme across the UK and Ireland that began in 2003. The objective was primarily environmental, but it was also a great way to help get the "natural" message to the local community in line with the company's ethos.
- **Sampling.** Getting drinks into people's hands has been critical to the company's continued success. It has invested a lot of time training its Innocent "angels" to ensure that they (as well as the vans) communicate clear messages about who the company is. 2002 saw the first ever Dancing

Grass Van summer roadshow. By 2004, over 2.5 million consumers had been sampled so far.

- **Promotions.** The company wanted a promotion that would look great at point-of-sale, engage consumers, drive sales and hopefully raise money for charity. This led to the project called "super gran", where lots of nice grannies and consumers from around the UK knitted little hats for the drinks (Figure 5.26). For each drink with a hat sold, 50p went to the charities Age Concern and ExtraCare, directly helping those who knitted the hats in the first place. In 2004, the company attracted 24 000 hats and raised £12 000 for charity.

The company has continued to invest in the category to grow awareness and help generate sales. In 2003, it introduced grassy chillers for special outlets, while, between 2001–2004, it sent out over 7000 Christmas gifts,

Figure 5.26

ranging from little trees to knickers to coins. It also entertained over 3000 retailers in the Very Nice Person (VNP) area at Fruitstock.

Journalists have been key targets as well. In 2003, the company had set up an in-house measuring system to allow it to log and record press coverage. It has also enticed the media over the years with events such as elderflower picking in the summer, while they have regularly been invited to Fruitstock and have received Christmas presents. The company estimates that in 2004, for instance, press coverage alone was worth £1.4 million.

Internal innocents

The three founders set the company up with basic principles of being absolutely passionate and hard-working, but also having fun along the way. They were well aware that motivated and excited employees are amazing ambassadors for a brand. So there are company Monday morning meetings each week, and quarterly meetings to discuss long-term goals to ensure that everyone knows what everyone else is up to, and how they can personally affect and drive the brand's future success. In addition, each employee receives his/her own bowl and free cereal, fruit, tea and coffee, while everyone goes away skiing together once a year.

There have been a number of other ways in which the company has boosted employee morale:

- The distribution of excess stock to the homeless.
- In July 2004, the company established a separate registered foundation, the Innocent foundation. It works to give grants to charities and non-governmental organisations which operate in areas where the company buys its fruit or sells the drinks. The remit of all these groups has been to bring nature and communities closer together. The foundation is run by a team of volunteers, and each year is given part of the company's profits.

Hitting the targets

By 2004, Innocent was the number one smoothie brand in the UK, with a turnover of £16.7 million. Other signs of its success included:

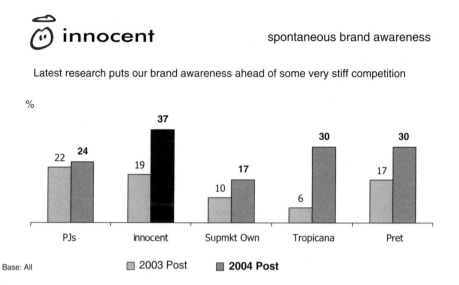

Figure 5.27

- market share grew from 20% to 48%;
- it was rated the third fastest-growing company in the UK, according to the *Sunday Times* Fast Track 2004;
- brand awareness had grown to 37% (Figure 5.27);
- the company was selling over 450 000 bottles each week;
- over 120 000 people had attended a Fruitstock festival;
- up to 2.5 million consumers had been sampled;
- it had dealt with 10 000 forms of consumer contact.

All images appearing in this case study are reproduced by permission of Innocent Drinks.

The Independent: brand invigoration through defying conventions

Snapshot: *The Independent* turned the market for broadsheet newspapers on its head by devising a new category of compact.

Key insights

- *The Independent* had to do something dramatic to bolster its once-dynamic position in a declining market.
- While keeping the content, and hence the brand values, the same, it used the change in size to draw in new readers.
- It flew in the face of accepted newspaper wisdom that a serious newspaper couldn't be a tabloid, and used research, careful market testing and "controlled migration" to get its new size accepted by both its current and new readers.
- It pioneered a trend followed by other key competitors.

Summary

The Independent is one of the UK's national newspapers. When it was launched on the 7th of October, 1986, it was the UK's first new national quality daily newspaper for 131 years.

In 2004, the company defied preconceived ideas by launching a compact version. It was contradicting the received wisdom that quality journalism had to be supplied in a broadsheet format. To do so took a great deal of courage, since the company was overturning many years of accepted wisdom. However, as the smallest brand in a declining market, such drastic action was essential.

The company used a powerful combination of research, market testing and clever marketing to make the launch so successful that a year later, the newspaper had achieved a 15% increase in circulation, taking it to a daily average of 260 000. The bold and innovative strategy was adhered to, despite the fact that the overall broadsheet daily newspaper market had declined 10% between 2000 and 2004.

A new-reader drive was undertaken, while the newspaper sought to maintain loyalty among its existing audience. TV, outdoor and radio ads were supported by regular visits to retailers by the sales force to discuss supply figures and point-of-sale needs. The two sizes existed side-by-side, so the company could gauge the state of reader acceptance.

Being a pioneer paid off: a year later, the increase in circulation for the new compact had proved the wisdom of the decision and reaffirmed the title as a market leader for innovation. The results were rising sales and readership. Over time, most of the other UK national broadsheets followed suit.

Facing a daunting challenge

The original launch of The Independent – its very name symbolised its distinctive stance – in 1986 demonstrated that it was prepared to be mould-breaking by being different and innovative. However, by the beginning of 2000, times were becoming challenging in terms of attracting quality newspaper readership. Between 2000 and 2004, there was a 10% decline in the number of regular quality daily newspaper readers.

As lifestyles evolved and developed, the traditional habits of newspaper readers were changing. Not only was there a growing and fragmented supply of news media from cable/satellite TV channels, the Internet and radio, but traditional newspaper-reading habits were changing.

The Independent was in the most invidious position as the smallest brand in a declining market. Research showed that it had simply fallen off the consideration list of many people. So perceptions needed to be changed, and something of the early dynamism regained.

The notion of a quality newspaper in a tabloid format was a logical one. Indeed, most of the long-established tabloids were once in a broadsheet format. Yet the received wisdom was that there would be considerable opposition to this change. Somehow, a broadsheet format was perceived to be an intrinsic element of a title's quality credentials. Accusations of "dumbing-down" would be levelled at any newspaper that dared to step out of this orthodoxy. But, if any paper had the ability to do it, it was The Independent.

Mocked-up copies of a tabloid Independent were examined in extensive qualitative research, both group discussions and in-depth interviews. Reactions were overwhelmingly positive. Such a radical move was perceived to be a part of The Independent's pioneering heritage. And any doubts about the dissonance between quality journalism and a tabloid format were effectively removed by generating an entirely new name for this format: a quality "compact" newspaper.

Taking the plunge

The compact *Independent* was launched in the London area in September 2003, traditionally the paper's heartland. Its objectives were to:

- increase the presence of the title in the market;
- increase loyalty among occasional readers;
- reassure that all aspects other than the format remained unchanged;
- generate trial through being the first in the market to launch;
- establish a new format for newspapers: the quality compact.

The compact launch was sold alongside the broadsheet version. It was important to see whether it was actively selected by readers rather than simply an enforced choice in the absence of the broadsheet. If the relaunch was seen to be arbitrary or rushed, there was clearly a risk of readers rejecting the new style. Unless the relaunch was properly managed, it might have proved disastrous. Considerable benefits could be attained through encouraging a sense of discovery of the new paper that would lead to positive word-of-mouth. Early adopters of the new format would act as ambassadors, strengthening their bond with the paper and encouraging others to do the same.

Once successfully established in its London heartland, the compact format could be rolled out nationally in a process referred to as "controlled migration".

A comprehensive approach to marketing

Marketing activity for the London launch focused on distribution. *The Independent* needed to be certain that the retail trade would give its support, especially when it meant allowing the paper more shelf space in an already cluttered retail environment. The entire sales force was relocated to London and the merchandising force was quadrupled. Over 3000 retailers were visited pre-launch to discuss supply figures and point-of-sale requirements.

Above-the-line support developed by agency Walsh Trott Chick Smith (now Chick Smith Trott) took the form of a TV campaign, 6-sheet posters, the sides of buses and a radio campaign (Figures 5.28 and 5.29). As the lead medium, the 30″ TV commercial showed how innovation has always

Figure 5.28

Figure 5.29

provided smaller versions of products which improved on the original. Concentrated bursts of media activity were supported by a huge merchandising programme of posters, display units and a deal with leading UK retailer WH Smith for a strong presence in key stores at main railway stations.

Price promotions, for so long the staple activity of the newspaper market, were decisively rejected. *The Independent* was a premium product and it was essential not to impugn the value or endanger the integrity of the product. There was no trial discounting at any stage.

In London the compact outsold the broadsheet from the start, and sales increased by 35% in this area. This turned an ABC decline of 3% into year-on-year growth of over 6% in just one month.

Extending the reach

So compelling were reactions from the media industry and sales results from consumers that the launch was rolled out first to the Granada and Meridian areas, and then nationally. Geodemographic mapping systems were used to highlight the areas where sales uplifts could be maximised. The London launch activity was duplicated in each region, with concentrated advertising support and focused distribution support. Extensive trade advertising was undertaken to ensure the retail trade was fully aware of the launch.

Sales patterns were analysed, both by postcode and down to individual retailer, so that distribution could react to sales patterns on a daily basis. To cover sales potential and ensure maximum awareness and availability, launch compact supplies were 50% higher than broadsheet supplies. Compact "hot spots" could be targeted for merchandiser calls and promotional activity.

Once the compact *Independent* was available nationally, the decision was taken to withdraw the broadsheet version and concentrate resources on the compact. The broadsheet withdrawal took place region by region over a period of three months, from March 2004 to May 2004. Each region was supported by a concentrated TV and poster advertising campaign focusing on small objects that stand for style and innovation.

The deal with WH Smith for heavy promotional support (including in-store TV, dump bins and window posters) in key stores at main railway stations and airports continued, and the sales force was again deployed to provide heavyweight support to retailers during the period of transition.

Changing the face of British journalism

A year on from the launch, *The Independent* continued to enjoy the sales success of the launch period, and proved that the quality compact newspaper

The Independent sales (Mon-Sat)

6 Monthly Headline Sales ABCs since Jan 2000

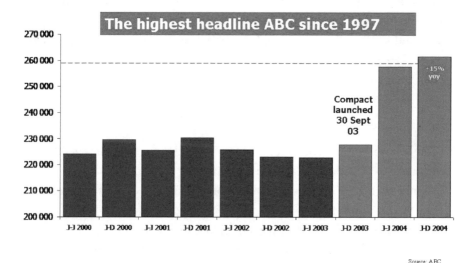

Figure 5.30

was here to stay (Figure 5.30). Street interviews were conducted with *Independent* readers immediately after the launch in October 2003 and nearly a year later in September 2004. Comparison between the two sets of results showed that there had been a sustained change in readers' loyalty towards the paper. By September, regular readership had doubled. In October 2003, 22% of readers said that they read *The Independent* every day or most days. By September 2004, that proportion had increased to 45%.

Asked their opinion of the paper, 32% of readers said "excellent" in October 2003. A year later, 46% said "excellent" and 34% said they were reading it more frequently.

For so long, it had been accepted wisdom that no title had the courage to launch a format like this. Like all major innovations, however, it now seemed like the obvious thing to do. *The Times* (see the following case study) and the *Guardian* have since followed suit. However, it was *The Independent* which created the first new category in the newspaper market for years. It changed the face of British journalism.

All images appearing in this case study are reproduced by permission of CST Advertising and The Independent.

The Times: reinventing a national institution

Snapshot: *The Times* made fundamental changes to a long-established brand to attract a younger readership in the face of potentially fierce consumer opposition.

Key insights

- *The Times* shows how an established brand can use a format change to flag a repositioning.
- While making *The Times* smaller was a huge risk, it allowed the company to signal to the market the change in brand values.
- It created a carefully orchestrated marketing campaign in a bid to prevent alienation of current readers while attracting new ones.

Summary

In May 2004, *The Independent* went fully compact. Six months later, *The Times* followed suit. Why? Both had to make the change as they sought to cut operating costs and boost circulation levels. But that is where the similarity ends.

For *The Independent*, changing format was less risky. As the UK's youngest broadsheet, launched in 1986, it had always had a challenging, avant-garde agenda and little historical "baggage". Besides, the circulation base was so low that it had little to lose.

For *The Times*, however, which had been a broadsheet since 1788, changing format was a huge risk that could potentially damage the heart of one of the world's oldest and most established broadsheets. The doubters were out in force, arguing that this would be a gamble too far.

These predictions turned out to be wildly inaccurate following the launch in November 2004. By 2005, *The Times* was a much-revived brand with a growing circulation to match. This is largely attributable to the marketing programme developed to bed in the compact Times, from initial launch in November 2003 to 100% compact conversion twelve months later.

Why *The Times* had to change

After a patchy decade in the 1990s, the broadsheet market took a nosedive between 1999 and 2003, losing around 18% of its average daily sale. Some of this was self-inflicted. Big promotions had become the default marketing *modus operandi* during this period. These rarely enhanced brand reputation, especially when the brand was a broadsheet newspaper (Figure 5.31).

However, the main drivers of decline in the sector were the changes happening in consumers' lives, and these were having a telling effect. They included:

- an ageing population;
- lack of time;
- media fragmentation;
- increasing pressure on disposable income, with cover-price charges having to compete for disposable income against mobile phone services, Internet costs and pay-TV subscriptions.

There were three factors in particular which had an exponential impact on sales during this period:

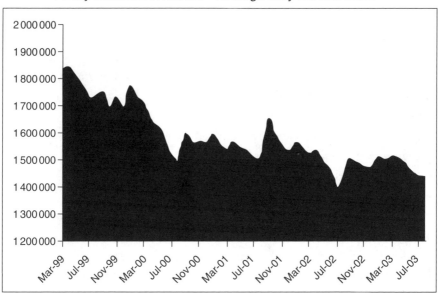

Daily broadsheet market – Average daily full-rate sales

Source: TNL Circulation

Figure 5.31

- Consumer needs had changed in terms of news delivery. Ever since the arrival of the digital age, consumers had come to expect a high level of immediacy from the goods and services they used. Consequently, 24-hour TV, the Internet and mobile phone companies had entered the realm of serious news delivery, where once broadsheet newspapers dominated.
- The free press was highly successful. At the time, there were around 7.8 million commuter "freesheets" circulating daily across Europe, with the Metro group leading the charge. London had become the most competitive marketplace, with Express Newspapers predicted to enter the market and Associated Newspapers recently launching the *Evening Standard Lite*.
- The British political landscape was homogenising under New Labour. Election turnouts were at an all time low as generation after generation were finding reality TV more engrossing than real politics. The blurring of old traditional political boundaries and the growth of "centrist" politics meant that broadsheets had to seek out new sources of differentiation.

While every broadsheet's circulation suffered over this period, *The Times* suffered the most. Its rate of circulation decline outpaced the category, losing around 26% of its average daily sale (compared to the market drop overall of 18%).

Just as worryingly, *The Times* was also losing brand strength. Young & Rubicam's Brand Asset Valuator (BAV) showed that *The Times* brand closely tracked the broadsheet category at large – not a good thing when broadsheets were lagging behind other news and information brands in terms of key attributes like energy and emotional connection.

As it was for *The Independent* before it, something radical was called for. But, for *The Times*, the risks were far greater, as one commentator made clear:

> "What it (*The Times*) has failed to understand is that *The Independent* readers are, by their very nature, 'eclectic individuals', and so are receptive to radical change. *Times* readers like predictability, status quo, a sense of timeless order and the badge of a broadsheet. They don't like change."

Murray Chick, Brand Strategy, Dec/Jan 2004

Preparing for change: what to lose and what to retain

Despite the scale of the task and the obvious risks, the marketing and editorial teams at *The Times* were determined to make the most of the move to the compact format. While the primary focus was to manage the risk of losing core, traditional readers by reassuring and retaining them, this was also a chance to exploit the "freedom" of no longer being a broadsheet, and begin to attract new readers from across the newspaper spectrum – and readers who rejected the notion of broadsheets more than they did any one broadsheet brand.

For this to happen, it was important that *The Times* was able to:

* retain the values that regular *Times* readers held dear;
* acquire the ones that non-*Times* readers would find attractive;
* abandon the ones that simply anchored the brand in the past for everyone.

Quantitative research showed big differences between readers and non-readers. Regular readers had fundamental concerns about it no longer being a broadsheet and the consequent "lowering of standards" in content and editorial terms. Non-readers of *The Times*, on the other hand, welcomed the increased accessibility and ease of the compact but still had reservations over the newspaper's traditional broadsheet "stuffiness".

Finding the middle way

This seemingly intractable conundrum – where one group wanted the opposite to the other – had to be resolved. The company and its agency, Rainey Kelly Campbell Roalfe/Y&R (now RKCR/Y&R), had to find a communications approach that made the new, compact *Times* appealing to both groups, despite their different needs. Comprehensive qualitative and quantitative research, including the BAV, was thus undertaken. Three core values were identified that defined *The Times*'s brand and that, crucially, were likely to have broad appeal for readers and non-readers alike: trust, quality and leadership.

Further BAV analysis showed, however, that these values had become at best passive and at worst infected with an overall sense of tired decline. *The Times* needed to find a way of injecting these values with new meaning.

The solution lay in bringing the renewed energy, fun and innovation of the compact to *The Times* brand overall. By making it more than a change of format, the compact represented the opportunity to grow short-term sales actively (as *The Independent* had) but also to boost the health and scope of the brand over the longer term. The newspaper might lose a few of its older and more traditional readers, but this would be more than outweighed by the influx of the commercially coveted ABC1 25–44s, and the successful retention of the paper's upmarket business audiences, who were ABs aged 30–50.

What is more, the company believed, such reinvigoration would further differentiate *The Times* from its arch-rival, *The Telegraph*, which had remained heavily associated with being arrogant, upper class, restrained and unapproachable. Changing to a compact format would thus involve a reinvigoration of the brand, where the format size would be part of a bigger brand story, not the story itself.

The integrated marketing programme

The Times compact was introduced in three phases:

- as an alternative to the broadsheet in London (in November 2003);
- as an alternative to the broadsheet nationally (in June 2004);
- in 100% compact format in November 2004.

Getting the message across

Communications were developed to announce and support each phase of the move. The first two phases targeted new (and light) *Times* readers primarily with a confident and upbeat campaign that announced the new format. In terms of tone, these ads were very different from those of the past. There was a new sense of wit and humanity, where previously the advertising was more concerned with "what was important". TV, outdoor and radio were the core media, with PR doing much of the basic announcement work.

The TV commercial used commuting as its context to dramatise the thought that, unlike people who still find themselves having to apologise for the ungainliness of their broadsheets on public transport, compact *Times*

Endline: 'The new Compact Times. Read it – you won't be sorry'

Figure 5.32

readers were an altogether smarter breed, liberated from having to say "sorry" every day because of the convenience of the new size. The endline was: *The new compact Times. Read it – you won't be sorry*" (Figure 5.32).

By targeting commuters, not only did the company find a smart way to talk both to traditional and prospective readers about a need they both shared, but it also enhanced distribution and retail thinking at the paper. For example, it led to unique partnerships with Starbucks and WH Smith.

Outdoor 48-sheets extended the message with the succinctness that the medium demanded, but still managed to incorporate the wit and savvy approach of the TV ad: "*It's not big but it is clever*".

As the move to the 100% conversion got nearer, more activity was introduced to communicate *The Times*'s new dynamism and modernity, and also to reassure that this was a positive move by a paper that was fully aware of what it meant to its readers. A broad range of subject matter and celebrities were selected for their ability to reflect the new, inclusive but still high-quality agenda of the new-look paper: from traditional *Times* territory, like business and finance, to newer topics, such as health and entertainment.

There were a number of other elements:

- outdoor, press, radio and point of sale were used to extend the campaign;
- a one-off sampling booklet was distributed at key train stations evoking the heritage of the newspaper and, crucially, positioning the compact within this context.

Building reader relationships

In April 2004, a reader helpline and website were set up to manage requests from readers who still wished to read the broadsheet *Times* and had noticed the increased presence of the compact. When the decision was taken to convert to the 100% compact, based on previously registered preference for the broadsheet format, the company knew the approximate number of readers that it needed to manage carefully through to transition.

A multi-stage, "contact and response" strategy was put into place to support and reassure these people. Everyone who had contacted the paper to register their preference for the broadsheet edition received either a personal call or letter from, or on behalf of, the editor. These explained the reasons for the change and sought to reassure them of the paper's continued commitment to quality journalism. A letter was also printed on page two of the last broadsheet edition of the paper on 30th October 2004, highlighting a free helpline. *The Times* had anticipated calls from 15% of its broadsheet readers. In fact, only 3.9% called the helpline, while 1.8% contacted the paper by letter or email. Such low volumes clearly suggested the success of the campaign had so far reassured worried readers.

As well as answering 95% of calls within 20 seconds, *The Times* followed up all calls, letters and emails within 48 hours of receiving them. Each received a further letter from the editor, vouchers for the compact edition and a free gift.

Finally, all readers for whom *The Times* had contact details received a further personal call after their vouchers expired, to understand how effective all these efforts had been in convincing readers to stay. Amazingly, 98% had.

Getting a good business result

Contrary to the dire predictions, the sales performance of *The Times* turned around following the launch of the compact – with exponential year-on-year circulation growth (Figure 5.33). In addition, *The Times*'s share of the quality

Times year on year full rate sales

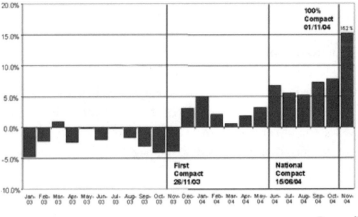

Source: TNL Circulation

Figure 5.33

Market share & quarterly averages: The Times (Jan '03–Dec '04)

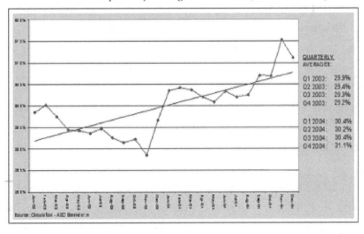

Source: TNL Circulation

Figure 5.34

newspaper market strengthened over the launch period (Figure 5.34). *The Telegraph*, on the other hand, fared much worse. And, for the first time ever, sales of *The Times* overtook those of *The Telegraph* at full-rate sales in the month it went 100% compact.

All images appearing in this case study are reproduced by permission of *The Times*.

6

Sustaining the brand promise

Introduction

Sustaining brands over time is one of the toughest, but also one of the most important, areas of marketing. It is sad but true that marketing triumphs can come to an end all too soon, with today's success becoming tomorrow's disaster. One indication is to consider how many beer brands have seen their fortunes slump throughout the period that Stella Artois has thrived. The same goes for a number of the competitors Tesco and Lynx have faced.

What unites these three case studies is that, although the marketing communications may have changed through the years, there has been a remarkably consistent proposition underpinning whatever they do. This is all too rare, whatever the sector.

> "To me, these three cases simply reinforce the old truths about brands. That is: be very clear about what you promise, make sure that what you promise is meeting some fundamental needs, and keep delivering on that promise. Then, at a brand communications level, you have to stay up-to-date with changes such as fads and fashions and new media.
>
> A sharp distinction has to be made between the brand and what it stands for and the communications. For instance, Lynx has done an absolutely brilliant job with a notoriously difficult target market which keeps moving. What it has gone for is a very simple need: young males are basically interested in sex.

The brand has hit on something that is not going to go out of fashion. It is a good example of being clear about the underlying benefits and then also being in tune with how to communicate those benefits and to evolve the brand over time.

Stella's adherence to a premium price as an indicator of quality has also been extremely consistent through the years. Its positioning is that product superiority is worth paying more for. Throughout the years it has had a sophisticated tone of voice which says that people who drink this are rich and clever.

And the communications have been creative and distinctive, such as those campaigns which were based on the evocative Jean de Florette film. Unlike Lynx, it hasn't had to keep on top of such a faddish market. But it has had to cope with adapting the communications from the 1980s to the 1990s, which it did very subtly.

Finally, customer focus has been Tesco's defining characteristic. It decided to go against the conventional wisdom (for which there is actually no evidence) that says a company shouldn't get stuck in the middle. It aims for both quality and value, which are deep consumer benefits. Tesco consciously said it was going to be the best supermarket for almost everyone, with different channels, different price ranges and non-food offerings, while also being operationally excellent and, of course, incredibly close to customers.

We mustn't allow fashionability and the fact that new trends are always emerging to blind us to the fact that sustained shareholder value creation is usually based on focusing on some fairly simple, deep, long-term human needs and meeting them obsessively."

Patrick Barwise, Professor of Management and Marketing at
London Business School and co-author of *Simply Better*,
winner of the American Marketing Association's 2005 prize
for best recent marketing book

Stella Artois: reassuringly consistent

Snapshot: A consistent focus on the quality of the product and a refusal to compromise its positioning over time has kept Stella Artois top of its market.

Key insights

- The temptation to change tack when growth faltered in 1990 was strong. By sticking to its "Reassuringly expensive" theme, Stella thrived despite a vigorously competitive market.
- It did so by developing a subtle alteration in its creative approach which challenged rather than pandered to consumers.

Summary

InBev is a global brewer, with leading positions in the Americas, Europe and Asia, and is ranked number one or number two in over 20 key beer markets around the world. InBev was formed in 2004 when Interbrew and Companhia de Bebidas das Américas (AmBev) combined to create what is now the world's largest brewer by volume. Its portfolio includes brands such as Stella Artois, Bass and Beck's.

In an economy-conscious world where many products and services are marketed on price, Stella Artois has long stood apart as a brand that was not afraid to promote itself as "Reassuringly expensive".

This undeviating approach had proved highly successful from the brand's launch in 1976 until the beginning of the 1990s, when Stella Artois began to lose market share and volume in the face of a number of entrants in the premium lager sector.

With consumer attitudes having moved beyond price, the "Reassuringly expensive" slogan seemed inappropriate, and the obvious solution to the decline was either to relaunch or reposition the brand. However, Stella Artois refused to abandon consistency and its core product focus. Instead, the vital strategic breakthrough came in a subtle shift in the message that the brand communicated, opting for a non-explicit emphasis on price and quality. This revision essentially relied on the consumer working out for themselves the quality offered by Stella Artois.

With this positioning underpinning every piece of strategic thinking and marketing brief for the brand since 1990, Stella Artois fought back from decline and was re-established as the biggest premium lager brand in the UK. Between 1996 and 2003, Stella Artois saw volume growth of 217% compared with premium lager category growth of 66% over the same period. This rise made it the third-biggest lager brand and the biggest premium lager brand in the UK, selling 3495 million barrels in 2003.

Building the brand 1976–1990

In 1976, Stella Artois was marketed in the UK by Whitbread. It was advertised only in the quality press, targeting a niche product at a niche, upmarket audience. Focusing squarely on the product, it didn't attempt to mirror consumers' lives, but said simply that Stella Artois was expensive because it was produced with the finest ingredients and the longest brewing process. In 1982, *Reassuringly expensive* became the brand's end-line, and the campaign directly challenged consumers to afford the precious brew – perfect for the brash, materialistic spirit of the Thatcherite 1980s (Figure 6.1).

Figure 6.1

Unfaltering repetition of this *Reassuringly expensive* mantra, and unswerving focus on the product, transformed Stella Artois from a nice-tasting, expensive pint into the *Reassuringly expensive* lager.

Between 1976 and 1989 sales grew rapidly, increasing by over 500% to 500 000 barrels a year. Then growth faltered. Stella Artois had demonstrated how lucrative the premium lager sector was, and new brands were being launched at a frightening rate, peaking in 1990 at three a month. The stock market crash of 1988 and prime minister Margaret Thatcher's resignation in 1990 finally destroyed the "greed is good" philosophy that had supported the brand's positioning so well. Stella Artois began to lose share, and volume, dropping 20 000 barrels in a single year. Stella Artois marketing faced its biggest challenge to date.

1990: time to start again?

As growth reached a plateau in 1990, the marketing objectives were simple, but not straightforward:

- reassert the strength and distinctiveness of the Stella Artois brand;
- return Stella Artois to volume growth;
- protect Stella Artois's position as market leader.

It was the consumer who needed to be won over, so a standard marketing solution was tempting. The temptation was to renounce the brand's heritage and follow the lead of other lagers, repositioning in accordance with consumers' lives and preoccupations. This would mean rejecting the now-incongruous and possibly off-putting *Reassuringly expensive* positioning, which had worked by challenging rather than courting the consumer.

But reinvigoration was vital, and *Reassuringly expensive* seemed to stand in its way. Anyway, the *Reassuringly expensive* positioning was 15 years old. Surely it was high time for a repositioning?

Standing firm

Had consistency and product focus been rejected, along with the *Reassuringly expensive* positioning, the story of Stella Artois might have been very different. A vital strategic breakthrough came in a subtle shift in the message the brand communicated – through each element of its marketing mix – that took account of the changing times while remaining true to Stella Artois's heritage. The message changed from:

Stella Artois is expensive . . . because it is good quality
to
Stella Artois is worth paying more for (. . . so it must be good quality)

This crucial difference meant that marketing would no longer talk explicitly about what made Stella Artois good quality, allowing consumers to work that out for themselves. This revised message was encapsulated in the brand proposition: *Stella Artois is a lager of supreme quality and worth.*

This simple phrase would underpin every piece of strategic thinking and every marketing brief for Stella Artois from 1990 onwards.

The value of consistency

Lager

Stella Artois was set apart from other lagers from the outset, refusing to compromise by conforming to consumer tastes and market rates. While other lagers had reformulated, or diversified into light/ice/low-alcohol varieties, the Stella Artois product remained consistent.

Packaging

The packaging had, of course, evolved over time. But the mandate for the design brief had not changed: all packaging must be of supreme quality and worth. Rather than courting consumers by modernising, Stella Artois packaging became ever more exclusive. Embossing on the can was introduced in 2001, increasing its "quality–expensive" image relative to other cans from 2% to 23%. The outer box was redesigned in 2003 along the model of champagne packaging; largely white, it stood distinct from other lager packs (Figure 6.2).

Glassware

The Stella Artois pint glass was introduced in 2001 to reinforce Stella Artois's image in the real world by ensuring that the lager of supreme quality

Figure 6.2

Figure 6.3

and worth is served appropriately. It became the 9th most stolen item from pubs. Within 12 months of launch, 66% of UK households possessed at least one glass.

The design brief employed the supreme quality and worth mantra, mandating a quality glass worthy of being filled with a lager of supreme quality and worth. Hence the logo was embossed rather than printed to avoid degradation with use, while its shape and weight were determined by concern for optimum delivery of the beer itself. Consequently it couldn't be stacked, upsetting the trade, but demonstrating Stella Artois's unswerving prioritisation of its product (Figure 6.3).

In 2002, a "free glass with six bottles" promotion sold 900 000 glasses. In 2003, a not-insignificant outlay of £10 was required to secure a glass. This time, 1.4 million glasses were despatched, improving key brand image measures among users: "worth paying more for" moved from 72% to 83% post use and "high quality" from 82% to 90%.

Draught barrel

After five years' development, the Stella Artois Draught Barrel was launched in 2003, using high-specification technology to ensure that the lager was served in optimum condition in the home, consistent with the brand's supreme quality and worth positioning. The draught barrel sold 4.5 million pints through the off-trade in its first year of launch, at a 37% premium to the average off-trade Stella Artois price point, and brought in new buyers, with over 40% of purchasers new to the beer category.

Proper placement

By 2003, Stella Artois was the most widely distributed lager in the on-trade. It had grown ahead of competitors and was now in 52% of all pubs, driven by strong growth in draught (Figure 6.4). Behind this distribution growth was

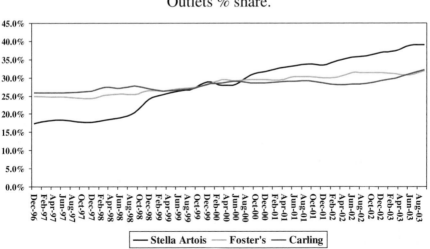

Outlets % share.

Source : CGA Qtr 3 September 2003.

Figure 6.4

the On-Trade Quality Programme, an initiative designed to ensure Stella Artois would always be served in a manner commensurate with a lager of supreme quality and worth. The programme, which by 2003 was in 70% of outlets, trained staff to ensure Stella Artois would always be served in a clean, branded glass, at the right temperature and with the correct head. These outlets commanded a 10p premium per pint, and saw a 6% greater return on sales (ROS) than pubs without the programme.

An object of uncontrollable desire

Advertising played an important role in reinvigorating the brand in 1990, giving it a revised, coherent and effective identity for new premium lager drinkers, without alienating existing drinkers.

The campaign that began then, and continued into 2003, was as radical as it was successful. The differences between Stella Artois commercials and the lager norm were obvious: Stella Artois ads were not famous for beautiful women. Nor did they make use of flash cars and cool bars. The dialogue was in French, which limited the scope for gags lads could play back in the pub on a Friday night. It was a very different kind of lager advertising.

Fundamentally, the product was elevated above the drinker, placed on a pedestal and revered beyond all logic – to the point where drinkers would do anything to get their hands on it. Amid the foreign jabbering and the subtle narrative, the supreme quality and worth of the product was the one certainty of the drama. The consumer felt proud and flattered to understand the narrative, despite the film's opacity and its perceived appeal to someone more sophisticated.

The campaign, playing on the imagery of the famous French film *Jean de Florette*, began in 1991 with *Jacques*. A French flower-grower first exchanges a bunch of carnations for a sandwich, and then his entire day's haul for a Stella Artois. The transaction and worth-equation were straightforward (Figure 6.5).

Twelve years on, the consumer now knew what role Stella Artois would play in each ad (the object of uncontrollable desire), enabling grander, subtler tales to be spun around this constant. In the execution *Devil's Island*, for instance, an inmate on a prison ship fortuitously comes into possession of a bottle of Stella Artois and attacks a guard so he will be put into solitary confinement to drink his beer in peace. The worth-equation here was less

Figure 6.5

concrete – it occurred over an indefinite timescale, with nothing of monetary value changing hands. Absurdly, light and liberty are sacrificed for a bottle of beer.

Yet the consumer delighted in the advertising's increasingly fanciful assertions of worth, each successive execution proving more effective than the last at building desire for Stella Artois. The benefits of a consistent, long-running campaign were evidenced in steady spontaneous awareness growth. The contrast with Budweiser, which aired eight different campaigns over the same period, was marked. This correlated with sustained salience levels from 1999 to 2003 in the face of competitor fluctuation in response to new campaigns.

The advertising was also the most involving in the category, with Stella Artois scoring 67% (vs. Carling 65%, Budweiser 55%, Foster's 53%, Grolsch 48%, Heineken 46% and Kronenburg 1664 39%). Qualitative research attributed this to the peculiar nature of the creative: *"The advertising is admirably different from the frenetic weirdness of the competition. It has great stand-out against its rivals, which all tend to plough the same furrow"*.

Consumers were conscious that the overall quality message (intrinsically linked with "desire") was constant: *"None of the other beers could do quality so convincingly because Stella has been saying it for as long as I can remember, and anyway it's true."*

Econometric modelling in 2000 proved that every £1 spent on advertising generated a direct uplift of 30 000 barrels, or £12.60 of additional revenue, for Interbrew UK, and a further £3 through increased distribution.

Choosing the right media

Demonstrating strategic consistency once again, Stella Artois advertising only ever appeared in media deemed appropriate for a lager of supreme quality and worth.

The 1980s *Reassuringly expensive* print campaign was almost exclusively confined to the pages of the *Sunday Times* Magazine. This was the only suitable magazine for colour double-page spreads, and the Stella Artois brand would settle for nothing less than this most extravagant of sizes.

When volume targets necessitated the move to TV to reach a wider audience, a similar demand for quality prevailed: Stella Artois commercials were a minimum of 60″ long, with extended 70″, 90″ or 100″ versions running in the most upmarket programming. This discipline enabled the creative strategy to work effectively on a modest spend, relative to the competition.

Quantity of ratings was sacrificed to quality of impact: media buying centred on film, a more premium viewing environment and synergistic with a filmic campaign. Only certain films were deemed worthy; often mass-audience blockbusters were ignored in favour of late night avant-garde showings on Channel 4, which attracted a smaller audience, but provided a more appropriate medium. Despite its huge reach, Stella Artois ads never appeared in football. A large proportion of the media budget was spent in the cinema, the environment where the quality of the commercials worked best.

Selective sponsorships

Unlike the many and varied partnerships built, then dismissed, by other brands, in 25 years Stella Artois has run only two sponsorships.

The first is films on Channel 4, which Stella Artois has sponsored since 1997. This made it one of the longest-running TV sponsorships, and it was, in a "beer 'n' sport" world, unique. Consistent with the Stella Artois brand, the cultish films shown on Channel 4 were somewhat highbrow, niche and consequently deeply aspirational. The sponsorship identifications were similar in tone and feel to the advertising, thus benefiting from and adding to the brand affinity it generated.

Consumers appreciated and respected these five and ten second films, which reinforced and elevated their relationship with the brand:

> "A lot of thought has gone into it, I just know it's Stella".
> "It's all about quality".
> "They've got their own way of sponsoring that's unique".

The same relationship exists with the Stella Artois Tennis Championships. This event, held in the run up to Wimbledon at the Queen's Club every year since 1978, epitomises the "supreme quality and worth" of tennis. An invitation-only event, it regularly draws the top male players in the world, a capacity crowd with disproportionate numbers of film stars, and extensive coverage on BBC1 and BBC2. Association with such an exclusive event has helped Stella Artois maintain the paradox of the brand: perceived exclusivity despite virtual ubiquity.

Keeping promotions aligned with brand values

Appropriately for a *Reassuringly expensive* brand, Stella Artois has run relatively few, and only value-added, promotions itself (Table 6.1). This was evidenced by the glasses promotion, which was advertised in a very different way to most retail promotions – barely mentioning the deal in 2002, and then not mentioning it at all in 2003 so as to retain exclusivity. However, as a sure-fire footfall driver, retailers loved to promote Stella Artois.

However, frequency of promotion in no way impaired effectiveness. Modelling showed Stella Artois promotions generated a four-weekly penetration gain of 2.8%, 1.6% points greater than gains generated by the second most successful brand, Carling.

Table 6.1 *Numbers of promotions in multiples 1999–2001*

	Stella Artois	Budweiser	K1664	Carling	Foster's
1999	107	99	79	57	65
2000	200	121	91	121	79
2001	195	102	105	105	79
Total	502	322	275	283	223

The reverence in which Stella Artois was held (high brand preference and high position in brand repertoire) meant that when it was on promotion, its promotions were seen as better value than its competitors. For instance, only when Carling was promoted with "buy one-get one free", which is generally recognised as the best deal by consumers, would they prefer it over Stella Artois, on which they might only save 25%, or get 3 for 2.

Consistent communication of the supreme quality and worth positioning across all other elements of the marketing mix protected Stella Artois's brand image from potential damage by these promotions. Overturning received marketing wisdom, econometric modelling proved that promoting Stella Artois in the off-trade not only generated short-term sales uplifts but also increased long-term penetration without eroding brand image. It allowed people who desired Stella Artois but couldn't afford it at the normal price point to buy, thus making an abstract brand relationship more concrete.

Making its mark

Within a market where beer penetration had declined from 31% in June 2001 to 28.9% in June 2003, Stella Artois was the only lager brand to have grown penetration, to become the most widely drunk brand in the UK (Table 6.2).

Other results were equally impressive. Between 1996 and 2003, Stella Artois enjoyed volume growth of 217%, compared to premium lager category growth of 66% over the same period. This gave the brand an 8.9% share of the total beer market, over three times more than its 1996 share of 2.2% (compared to a share increase of less than double for the 1st and 2nd placed brands, Carling and Foster's).

Table 6.2 *Lager penetration changes 2001–2003*

	Y/E June 2001	Y/E June 2003
Stella Artois	18.00%	21.80%
Foster's	18.30%	16.70%
Carling	16.40%	15.40%
Budweiser	9.60%	7.90%
K1664	5.00%	5.40%

Figure 6.6

This wasn't just a case of a smaller brand growing more quickly than larger brands. Over the same period, Stella Artois had almost doubled its share of the premium lager market from 20% in 1996 to 38% in 2003, stealing share from its nearest premium competitor, Budweiser, whose share dropped from 12% in 1996 to 7% in 2003. In addition:

- In the on-trade, Stella Artois move from fifth to fourth largest lager brand between 1996 and 2003, increasing its lead over premium lagers (Figure 6.6).
- In the off-trade, Stella Artois was now the largest lager brand, with a volume share of 15.5%, a clear 5% points ahead of the closest competitor Carling.
- Stella Artois became a top four grocery brand behind Coca-Cola, Walkers and Müller, having moved up from 34th in six years.
- In value terms, Stella Artois's growth was still more remarkable, growing from £849 million in 1998 to £1.4 billion in July 2003.
- This value growth was driven by the off-trade, where Stella Artois was the biggest beer brand, with a 17.2% value share of the total market, and still growing.

All images appearing in this case study are reproduced by permission of In Bev UK.

Lynx: the power of seduction

Snapshot: Lynx has managed to thrive over the years, despite the fickleness of its target audience, through a dedication to reinvention and evolving creative strategy.

Key insights

- Lynx has lasted because it is rooted in a core human need – young men think about sex a lot.
- Its simple and consistent proposition has been constantly reinvented to follow changes in fashion and culture over the years.
- By adding the concept of fragrance to deodorant, it has given young men "permission" to use it.
- The brand has been built on regular reinventions of the formula and evolution of the creative strategy to keep reconnecting with its consumers.

Summary

Unilever is an international manufacturer of leading brands in food, home care and personal care. Its 2005 revenues were almost €40 billion.

One of the company's business goals in 1984 was to create a deodorant brand which could penetrate the male youth market. There were two key challenges:

- young men weren't interested in deodorant;
- youth brands had a history of being short-term fads. How could the company build a long-term business?

The company's insight was that deodorant had a motivating and unchanging benefit for young men, but it was different from the normal "adult" one. Lynx was developed to deliver the promise of fragrance and seduction. This brought the appeal of the fragrance product marketplace to young men, who previously would have waited until they were old enough to use after shave products.

The two challenges were answered in two ways:

- A new type of product and marketing mix, which merged deodorant with fragrance behaviour. The product was fragrance, communicated with a fragrance benefit, but in a deodorant can, merchandised and priced as a premium deodorant.
- Long-term performance was built through constant innovation and reinvention of the fragrance parts of the marketing mix. Marketing resources were focused against fragrance rather than the deodorant aspects of the mix, because this is where the highest added value was. This was instrumental in enabling the product to be reinvented regularly, to match major shifts in youth culture.

By 2002, seventeen variants had been launched, each with its own identity and launch advertising. Each year, a fragrance was introduced and an old one delisted.

The brand by now was worth 6100% of its launch year values, in a category that had grown 267%. It had a 37% share of the male deodorant market, and penetration of the core target of 15–19 year-olds of more than 80%. It was, without doubt, Unilever's leading male personal care brand.

The beginning: facing the impossible

In the early 1980s, Unilever was determined to grow its deodorant business by targeting young men. This posed two key marketing challenges.

1. Young men weren't interested in deodorant for several reasons:
   - the category was defined by functional promises;
   - but young men were focused on their social and emotional needs: with becoming a man and with attracting women;
   - promises of staying dry were boring.
2. How could the company build a long-term business in a volatile environment? Unilever had long been a company that demanded long-term performance. However, youth adopted and discarded brands as fast as bands shot in and out of the charts. It seemed an impossible task.

Gaining insights

The company started with developing a deep understanding of the market. It found that deodorant had an incredibly motivating benefit for youth, but one which was quite different from a normal "adult" one. For young men, the end benefit was not odour control. It was about smelling good, so that they were attractive to women. The brand proposition was thus summed up as the need to seduce: Lynx grooms young men to seduce.

This insight underpinned two strategies (Figure 6.7) to answer the two challenges. Both of these overturned the conventions of the time:

- The first was to create a new type of product and marketing mix so that Lynx would appeal to young men.
- The second was to develop a dynamic model of promotion and product innovation, which enabled Lynx to survive in a fast-moving, fashion-led environment.

The solution was a new hybrid product category – deodorant body spray – which married the appeal of fragrance to the accessibility of deodorant. The rationale was clear: young men believed that fragrance attracted women, as with Brut and Denim. However, using fragrance was a sign of dubious sexuality. They needed "permission to use" – or a functional alibi.

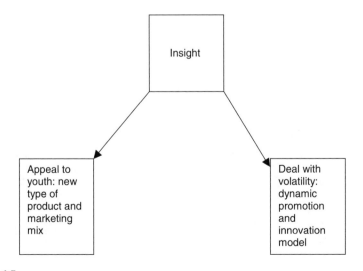

Figure 6.7

Adult men used shaving as their alibi – hence "after shave". But 11–16 year-olds didn't shave. Their only alibi was deodorant. So, Unilever combined them into deodorant body spray: a fragrance applied like a deodorant. The marketing mix could then work on a spectrum of both deodorant and fragrance, without reference to the older man's practice of shaving. Lynx had a formula that gave appeal and permission to buy.

The defining characteristics of the brand would be along a spectrum from fragrance behaviour to deodorant behaviour. The fragrance element would create the greatest emotional connection and value for consumers.

- The "fragrance" would be outsourced to the same consultants and fragrance manufacturers used by top luxury brands such as Dior.
- The communications would focus on the emotional benefit of seduction.

The deodorant end of the spectrum would give consumers permission to use and offer functional deodorant reassurance.

- The pricing would be that of a premium deodorant, to suggest superior brand value and to capitalise on it.
- The packaging would be that of a deodorant, by having an aerosol spray can, but would establish difference by using a better-looking, short, stubby, black can, instead of the normal, tall, thin, light-coloured one (Figure 6.8).

This formula would give both appeal and permission to buy.

Figure 6.8

Building a dynamic model

The key theme was that Lynx signalled seductiveness as defined by youth culture. Youth culture changes continually, but, by 2002, Unilever had been able to maintain the credibility and currency of Lynx for 17 years. It did this by understanding what not to change, what to change and how.

The company appreciated that while young men appeared to be fickle, this was only at the superficial level of style and expression. Their underlying need was stable, which meant that the brand could stick to the proposition of seduction over the long term as long as its style and expression was constantly reinvented. That meant restimulating consumers with new expressions of the product and executional formula at least once a year.

Moreover, innovation had to be focused on the areas of highest added value to the consumer: the fragrance rather than the deodorant element of the mix. Thus, the brand's defining characteristics were:

- Lynx was not one product but a "house" with a range;
- every year, a new fragrance would be launched and an old one delisted;
- each fragrance would have its own packaging icon and associated imagery that would re-express Lynx in new and culturally relevant ways. The brand would thus be constantly evolving via a series of annual product steps.

Regular reinvention

Advertising continued to create desire for the brand by adding the promise of seduction. However, it changed over time to keep the emotional side of the brand in tune with evolving youth culture. The brand started with one "theme" ad a year, focused on the promise of seduction, and one to launch and position a new variant. By 1998, the company realised that youth culture had got to the point where two ads a year wouldn't keep pace with it. So, 10-second TV ads and tactical press ads provided refreshers.

One of the most important decisions, and one which required a great deal of bravery, was to reinvent what was a proven formula regularly, even at the moment when the variant seemed to be at the height of its popularity. But the success of Lynx depended on never being left behind. After all, during the life of the brand, youth culture had been characterised by "New Romantics", "Ravers", "Grunge", "Crusties" and more. Continuous research, cultural

Table 6.3 *Lynx new fragrance variants from launch to 2002*

	New variant name	Strategy
1985	Launch: Spice, Amber, Musk	Ingredients signal fragrance credentials
1987	Oriental	"Real locations" build richer imagery through
1989	Marine	links to travel aspiration
1990	Java	
1991	Alaska	
1992	Nevada	
1993	Tempest	"Mythic locations" develop fewer literal
1994	Mirage	references as real travel becomes
1995	Africa	more accessible
1996	Atlantis	
1997	Inca	
1998	Apollo	"High concept" borrows luxury fragrance
1999	Voodoo	language as these products become
2000	Phoenix	more accessible
2001	Gravity	
2002	Dimension	

and semiotic analysis (of media, films, music, experts, etc.) kept the company in touch with those trends. When those trends demanded, the brand team reinvented the executional formula.

A new variant was launched every other year until 1989, and then annually thereafter. Each had a concept which was used to develop its name and the dedicated launch advertising (Table 6.3).

Adapting the advertising

During this period there were three eras of advertising.

1985–1995: Alpha male, heroes
(ads such as "Ocean Liner", "Waterfall", "Hotel")

This was a time when wealth, luxury, strength and status were admired. Bruce Springsteen was "the Boss". Sylvester "Sly" Stallone played Rambo and Rocky. "Iron" Mike Tyson was the youngest-ever heavyweight champion of the world at 20. Gordon Gecko wore his braces and declared "greed is good".

A scruffy ex-popstar united the forces of charity, youth idealism and big business to create Live Aid. Men fought epic battles. "We could be heroes".

Women were beginning to enter male roles, but had not confronted popular consciousness. Madonna, one of the few survivors from those times, was a "material girl", but still looking for a man to spend on her. The advertising reflected this with aspirational heroes, wealthy men in suits, ocean liners going to exotic locations, romantic strangers.

As the 1980s turned into the 1990s, popular heroes became more thoughtful. The Berlin Wall came down. Nelson Mandela was freed. But still, a man was a man. The Lynx world became a rugged, sweaty place. All it took was one spray and you were Harrison Ford as Indiana Jones. There was a very slight nod to the New Man (sensitive glasses in the "Waterfall" ad). But it was never more than a nod.

This mirrored the less sophisticated grooming and seduction attitudes of the time. There was little advice for the regular teenager, so Lynx could operate as a simple guarantee of seduction.

1994–1999: Ironic fantasy ("House Party", "Tribal Women", "Revenge")

By the early 1990s, male culture was becoming less heroic. While in 1991 pundits declared the advent of the "caring" decade and sought out the "new man", Johnny Fartpants, Buster Gonad and the Pathetic Sharks propelled sales of Viz magazine to 1.13 million – approximately double that of women's monthly magazines.

By 1994, Lynx was at a watershed. Loaded magazine was launched. The "new lad" had arrived. And while it was goodbye to the new man, it was nearly goodbye to Lynx as well. In qualitative research, consumers were ready to write it off as "the Brut of the nineties". Or, as one young man said, "As cool as Roger Moore in a safari suit".

Much of this was driven by advertising that was perceived as "OK" but not first division. There was a cultural shift going on, and Lynx hadn't acknowledged it. So the new advertising had to tear up the rule book. New lad was knowing, sassy and irreverent. The right tone had to be found; one that acknowledged "mate to mate" that Lynx wasn't the panacea, but with tongue firmly in cheek they had permission to enjoy the fantasy – and live in hope. So it was out with the Chippendales and their sultry babes on tour. It was in with your coolest mate.

Bartle Bogle Hegarty (BBH) took over the account in May 1995, and the executions moved from fantasy guys in real situations to real guys in fantasy situations. Pre-testing of the first new execution, "House Party", indicated that the company was on to a winner. Millward Brown tracking norms showed that it had over three times the impact of any previous Lynx theme advertising.

The retail trade was enthusiastic:

> *"Lynx has performed one of the hardest tasks known to advertising. They've acknowledged that the macho commercials they were using weren't fooling anyone, not even their spotty, sweaty secreting (sic) target market. Consequently they've done a 180 degree turn and put their tongues fairly and squarely in their cheeks."*

> *The Grocer*, March 1996.

Subsequent advertising addressed this take on seduction in new ways. For example, in "Dream Dates", Jennifer Aniston waits patiently in bed (1997) while in 1998's "Tribal Women", legions of tribal women wave their fur bikinis.

But even this annual theme ad wasn't fast enough for youth culture. So a range of combined media/creative solutions that could run faster was developed such as the White House during the Monica Lewinsky affair, with an empty Lynx in the rubbish bin (Figure 6.9).

Figure 6.9

2000–2002: Commentary on the seduction process
("Ideal Woman", "Rituals")

By the end of the 1990s, the new lad was beginning to look a little worn-out. The circulation of lads' magazines had been falling since 1998. The public face of relationships was more mature. Girl power had become Posh 'n' Becks, Madonna had married a Brit and had kids. Online chat rooms and texting had made communication less scary. Heroes were multi-talented, multimedia chameleons such as Robbie Williams.

It wasn't enough to drink beer and smoke tabs any more. "Tribal Women" had defined a high watermark for the brand's relationship with the lads' movement. But it was beginning to have a glorious past rather than a glorious future. "Ideal Woman" engaged in a subtle debate with women, sharing Henry Higgins's wish that "a woman be more like a man".

With consumers becoming more sophisticated, the brand's positioning could be seen to share jokes about the process of seduction, rather than focusing on the score at the end.

Other factors affecting performance

Advertising and new variants had thus been the two key drivers of Lynx's long-term success. Their contribution could be broadly split: advertising contributed more to penetration gains, while new variants accounted more for retention of existing users. Word-of-mouth was also important in this market, promoting "changing room currency".

Areas such as packaging, pricing and merchandising were kept relatively stable, with "invisible" evolution of pack design in order to create an iconic presence and reassure about its deodorant "permission to use" credentials.

Pricing strategy was critical to exploit the brand value created. The brand launched at a 50% premium, with subsequent brand success allowing the company to increase that. Meanwhile, the competitive environment had been intensifying. At launch, the format and packaging of Lynx was highly distinctive, creating a new category. Nor had it altered radically over time, since the deliberate intention was to create an icon.

However, it was under attack from "me toos", both from retailer own brands and other brands. Despite this, the brand continued to prosper, suggesting that the strategic emphasis of the mix on fragrance and communication was the right one. In addition, Lynx grew mainly through increased penetration, not weight of usage, and within a static category.

Impressive results over time

Growth had thus come from establishing a unique marketing mix, innovation and reinvention which focused on the area where the greatest consumer value was added: fragrance. Its emotional approach had built a valuable brand.

By 2002, the brand was worth 6100% of its launch year values, in a category that had grown 267% (Figure 6.10). It had a 37% share of the male deodorant market, and penetration of the core target of 15–19 year-olds of more than 80% (Figure 6.11). In addition, 25–34 year-old men endorsed the brand's key style values of fun, sexy and young (Figure 6.12).

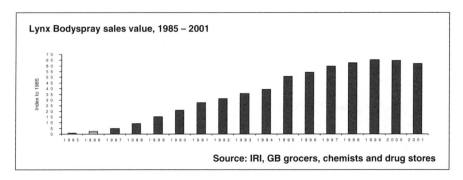

Figure 6.10

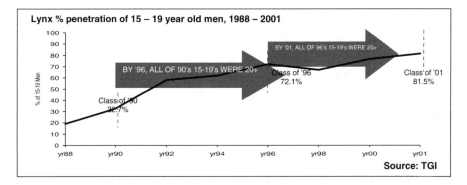

Figure 6.11

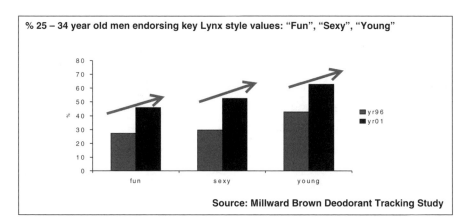

Figure 6.12

For 17 years Lynx had been deft enough to keep one step ahead by being reinvented repeatedly. And this has continued. Further product launches have included:

- Pulse   2003
- Touch   2004
- Unlimited   2006
- Click   2006

All images appearing in this case study are reproduced by permission of Unilever.

Tesco: from a company with a marketing department to a marketing company

Snapshot: Tesco has become a world-class retailer by building up a deep knowledge of customers, and having a sustained commitment to giving them what they want, when they want it.

Key insights

- Tesco's seminal moment came in the mid-1990s when it decided to focus its entire business around customers through an ongoing dialogue.
- Its attention to detail over the years, based on this customer knowledge, has affected every part of the business.
- Tesco doesn't "do" marketing. Marketing is in the corporate DNA.

Summary

Tesco is the UK's biggest supermarket group, and has an increasing international presence. Its group sales in the year to February 2006 were £41.8 billion, and profits were £2.2 billion.

Tesco has, without doubt, been the retail success story of the past decade, and its success owes a great deal to its decision in 1995 to ditch its "pile it high, sell it cheap" philosophy in favour of a strategy that put consumers at the heart of its business.

In the early 1990s, the supermarket was caught between rivals Sainsbury's and Asda – between quality and value. It has since outperformed the market consistently and expanded into telecoms, financial services, non-food and international markets. And it has done it all under the "Every little helps" banner.

Introduced in 1995, the initiative means that everything is measured against whether it is helpful to customers and whether it makes shopping easier. This major change in organisational behaviour was built on the ethos that Tesco could deliver on the customer's desire not to have to choose between price and quality. The use of Tesco's customer insight unit in implementing the strategy has been particularly impressive, with business decisions informed by an ongoing dialogue with the consumer at local and national levels.

This continual conversation has enabled the brand not only to extend its range of services, but also to increase choice in its core products, such as its own-label *Value* and *Finest* ranges. This has allowed the chain to make good on its desire to become all things to all people. As with any marketing-led initiative, the crucial aspect has been the activity's effect on the company's bottom line.

Ten years ago, Tesco was Britain's third-biggest grocery retailer. By 2004, it was the third most successful grocer in the world. The supermarket had substantially outstripped its rivals in the UK to achieve an undisputed market dominance.

Defying convention

In 1995, Tesco was stuck in the middle of a market which was defined by two dominant competitors. Sainsbury's had a clear quality food positioning, and Asda occupied the discount end of the market. Tesco's defining moment from market follower to leader can be traced back to its decision to put customers at the centre of the decision-making process. This changed Tesco from a company with a marketing department, to a marketing company.

Two fundamental decisions emerged which have been pivotal to Tesco's growth ever since:

1. Tesco decided to stop following the competition and start following the customers. The company talked to its customers to find out what mattered most to them and what made one shopping experience better than another. With hindsight it seems obvious – a good shopping experience meant being able to get around the store easily, find what they wanted, at a good price, and then get out again as easily as possible. This initial dialogue with customers was the start of Clubcard, developed and managed for the last ten years with the help of the marketing consultancy Dunnhumby, and which is still pivotal to Tesco's ongoing understanding of its customers today.

2. Tesco realised that it could be all things to all people. In conventional positioning terms, "the middle ground" is not generally a good place to

be. Based on what customers told them, however, this is where Tesco decided to stay. Customers didn't want to make the choice between price and quality. They wanted it all and, importantly, no-one else was giving it to them.

Translating ideas into behaviour

Tesco's vision was not about the company it wanted to be, but rather about what it wanted to do: "Create value for customers to earn their lifetime loyalty". This has become the driving principle for everyone in the company.

Everything Tesco has since done, at any point in the customers' experience of the brand, has been to make them want to come back. Implicit within it have been two ideas to ensure the relevance and longevity of this vision for the company in any part of the business:

• an ambition to deliver what customers want continuously;
• a defined organisational behaviour in order to make sure that the company remains true to its core purpose and values, irrespective of category.

This core purpose has remained part of the Tesco DNA since its inception in the mid-1990s. The expression of Tesco's good intentions was supplied by the guiding principle that "no-one tries harder for customers" and the phrase "Every little helps". As a creative thought, "Every little helps" has spoken to staff and customers alike down the years, across everything from the advertising to the carrier bags. This outward expression of Tesco's values has continued to be the measurement for every new idea: Is that helpful to our customers? Will it make their shopping easier? (Figure 6.13).

Figure 6.13

Creating value for customers

The 1% inspiration to get to this clear purpose has been followed up by 99% perspiration in getting it right ever since. There have been many successes and a few mistakes along the way, but its endeavour towards customers has kept the company on track. In every part of its business, Tesco has tried to make things simpler and easier for both its customers and its staff (Figure 6.14).

Fundamental to this is an ongoing dialogue with customers. Tesco's insight unit encompasses a broad range of research disciplines and is the guardian of all customer knowledge. This ranges from day-to-day buying behaviour to research into new formats, store openings or bigger macro trends. Importantly, this bank of knowledge informs every key business decision.

Tesco Personal Finance (TPF)

Customers told Tesco that they found the financial market complicated and bewildering. They felt that Tesco would make it simpler, easier to understand and better value. The company launched its personal finance offering in 1997 to set about giving them an alternative. By 2004, TPF had surpassed the milestone of one million motor insurance policies, making it the fastest-growing motor insurance provider ever. Instant travel insurance allows Clubcard holders to buy their holiday insurance conveniently at the checkout.

Figure 6.14

Nor does the dialogue with customers stop when a new initiative has been launched. For example, regular customer question times (CQTs) with customers and staff across individual stores are held on a continuous basis. CQTs allow customers to express their views on stores, products and Tesco as a company. There is no fixed agenda: real views emerge which can be acted on. This local feedback generates local changes. In Skegness, for example, covered motorised scooter parks were installed outside the store to cater for the elderly population.

In the ten years up to the end of 2004, the company had held 1100 sessions, talking to 55 150 customers and 12 153 staff.

In addition, in 2002, Tesco introduced TWIST, or Tesco Week in Store Together. Directors and managers (from the Chief Executive down) are encouraged to spend one week a year on the shop floor. This gives the people who are making the decisions the chance to listen to the views of staff and customers, and to see how to deliver initiatives simply and successfully.

Details make the difference

Tesco' s successful communication of its endeavour for customers through "Every little helps" has been well documented. But it is the way in which it has been woven into the real nuts and bolts of the business that has set the company apart.

What the company has long appreciated is that it is the detail that makes a difference, and that there is not much room for error. After all, Tesco is only ever as good as a customer's last shopping experience. That is why trying harder for customers has been built into the bricks and mortar. Customers told Tesco that they needed plenty of space at the entrance to find their trolleys, fasten the kids in, etc. In response to that, Tesco devised a policy to reduce clutter around those areas. The stores have been designed with wider aisles and a uniform layout so that customers can get around easily.

Beyond the shopping experience, Tesco has delivered its inclusive offering through the choice of pricing, products and store formats.

Price transparency

Customers told Tesco that they wanted peace of mind when it comes getting good value for money. It has been one of the main reasons why customers have been choosing Tesco, and have kept coming back. To ensure that this is always the case, Tesco checks 10 000 prices against competitors every week. In an attempt to reassure customers further, Tesco gives customers the opportunity to interrogate them at Tesco.com/price checker (Figures 6.15 and 6.16).

From Value to Finest and beyond

In 1995, Tesco introduced two branded lines to span the whole range from basic to premium within its own product range. Ten years later, *Value* was even cheaper than it was at launch, with 70% of customers buying from the

Figure 6.15

Figure 6.16

Value range and over 37% buying from both *Value* and *Finest*. This proved that it was right to listen to customers rather than marketing convention, and to create a range that catered for everybody (Figure 6.17).

Evolution of the product range

Tesco's range has expanded in response to customers' increasingly diverse demands, and in line with the consciousness around health and food origin. By the end of 2004, the retailer led the market in organic and Fairtrade alternatives. By that time, the organic range contained over 1245 lines, with most superstores stocking at least 600 lines. This made Tesco the UK's largest

Figure 6.17

organic retailer. In the same period, it stocked 90 Fairtrade lines, which saw sales double over the year, contributing to a market share of 32%.

Tesco also introduced the *Free-From* range to cater for the growing number of people who suffer from a food allergy or intolerance. By the end of 2004, it was the market leader with over 40% market share, stocking over 120 *Free-From* branded items, including 40 own-brand products. Ranges have also been adapted at a local level to cater for local tastes. Wherever practical, products are sourced from within each national market. By the beginning of 2005, Scottish stores were selling around 1000 Scottish products from 183 Scottish companies, and in Wales, stores were carrying around 800 Welsh lines.

Evolution of the ways to shop

One size no longer fits all. Customers' shopping habits have changed and Tesco has developed new formats to cater for every need and occasion. Extra is the ultimate "one-stop shop" with everything under one roof, and Tesco. com has successfully built up online shopping (see the Tesco.com case study in Chapter 4). In 2004, Tesco was handling around 120 000 orders online every week in the UK.

Tesco Express has been another case in point. Customers told Tesco that they wanted the company's range, fresh produce and good value but in more convenient locations. In response to this, the retailer developed the Express format, with a well-thought through range and a focus on freshness. Customers' positive reactions and excellent business results have proven that Express has met these demands. Most Express stores have an in-store bakery and a wide range of fresh produce, from fruit and vegetables to herbs, fresh meat and fish.

Acknowledging the value of customers

Detailed customer information captured through Clubcard has meant that the company has been able to develop targeted promotions to reward customers' loyalty (Figure 6.18). Importantly, it also means that, wherever possible, the company has avoided sending meat vouchers to vegetarians or nappy vouchers to bachelors. With each Clubcard statement, between 250 and 300 different types of vouchers are sent out. Some give money off things they already buy, while others encourage customers to try new products.

By the end of 2004, there were 11 million active Clubcard holders. The data gathered relates to real shopping behaviour, captured every time customers shop. Regular surveys among Clubcard holders supplement the behaviour data with attitudinal data, which informs many areas of the business. During 2004, there was a 20% usage beyond the store environment, which has meant that the company can see the real effects of customer behaviour in adopting the brand, whether it be in finance, telecoms or online.

Living the brand values

What has set the company apart in marketing terms is that it doesn't talk about its "brand" but its business. Tesco's customer focus has made it a

Figure 6.18

marketing company to the core, aiming to cater for all customers and let them make their own choices: what they want to buy, how much they want to spend, when, where and how they want to shop. The decision-making process of the business has constantly revolved around the customer – and the results speak for themselves (Figure 6.19).

The attention to detail at an operational level has also ensured that every customer's experience is as good as it can be. Testament to this is the fact that "Every little helps" has been the constant outward expression throughout the years. Its continuing relevance is tied to the core purpose of Tesco itself. It has represented many things, from customer service in 1995, to every aspect of price, quality, range and service in 2004 and beyond.

As a business, Tesco has behaved consistently through its stores, product range, pricing, innovation and communication. There has been no need to

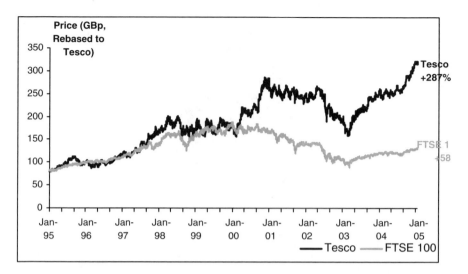

Figure 6.19

add any superficial marketing spin. In fact, as the business has become increasingly complex, communicating the small things that Tesco does for customers becomes even more essential.

Many people have asked over the years just how long Tesco can keep talking about "Every little helps". The answer from the company is quite simple: as long as it keeps trying harder for its customers.

All images appearing in this case study are reproduced by permission of Tesco.

7

Marketing communications: getting the message across

Introduction

It is often argued that marketing should be about far more than a communications campaign. And it is true that communication is only part of the story; the product, or the customer service, has to deliver too. But the case studies included in this chapter remind us that an outstanding communications campaign can establish/transform a brand to an extent that few other marketing levers can. Additionally, the good news is that developing such communications appears to be a matter of the right execution based on the right insight – which should give hope to us all.

For Waitrose, marketing communications transformed its image and put it on a platform where it could easily justify its premium positioning. Unilever broke the mould of advertising beauty products by using "real" women rather than anorexic models. The Number made something as boring as directory enquiries fun. TNT also threw out the usual approach to advertising delivery services by emphasising emotion rather than function.

> "All these cases demonstrate good strategic thinking and sound common sense which have been executed really well. One should probably ask why this perfect combination is managed so rarely when so much expertise is used. However, these cases have managed to produce the 'hat-trick' and their business results have paid out.

For example, I can't think of Waitrose without my taste buds starting to water, and its reassuring me on price can justify my desire or twinge of guilt. Simply perfect. And Dove – hooray on behalf of all women (even those working for Procter & Gamble) – shows how brilliantly refreshing this approach was, giving a crystal clear, firm reason to buy.

The Number 118 118 (and I was working for BT at the time) was a brilliant and formidable competitor. Not only did the company develop a superb creative strategy, from the symmetry of the number itself through to its approach to all market channels, but the media strategy to go early and get awareness ahead of the pack was brave and should never be forgotten.

TNT is a wonderful demonstration of customer insight brought to life and made into a benefit. The case is an inspiration to us all, in that it is still possible to 'get into the mind of the customer' and fundamentally change a business and deliver top line growth because of it.

Finally, Make Poverty History defined the early summer of 2005. It is the ultimate case history in using word-of-mouth to mobilise an opinion change, resulting in doubling of aid to developing nations. Furthermore, it engaged the hearts and minds of nations across the world. It's a brilliant example of a question which isn't 'can we do x?' but 'what will it take to do x?'. The rest, as they say, is history.

In summary, what we learn from these five cases is:

- think what is needed to be achieved;
- think as broadly as you can about what it takes to make something happen;
- get in the customer's head;
- apply common sense;
- apply creativity and freedom in the thinking;
- execute well in every dimension.
- don't stop competing."

Amanda Mackenzie, Director of Brand Marketing, British Gas

Dove firming cream: authenticity is the best policy

Snapshot: Unilever hit upon the clever and innovative idea of using "real" women in its integrated marketing communications for Dove body firming cream and achieved a stunning breakthrough for the brand.

Key insights

- The company realised the power of aligning the brand with the authentic voice of the consumer to challenge existing industry norms.
- Dove realised it could capture the high ground and differentiate itself with a more honest approach to women's bodies. This was a radical departure.
- Its non-traditional media planning, particularly using the power of integrated PR in recruiting "real" women, was a winning approach and effectively formed the basis of its TV ad campaign.

Summary

Unilever is an international manufacturer of leading brands in food, home care and personal care. Its 2005 revenues were almost €40 billion.

Unilever had been successfully extending its leading global personal care brand Dove into new segments of the market, such as bodycare. When the company decided, in 2004, to enter the highly competitive market for body firming creams with three products, however, it knew it had a big battle on its hands. The two leading competitors were already well-entrenched, having extended their strength in firming face creams into this growing sector.

On researching the success of these competitors, Dove discovered an undercurrent of dissatisfaction with the beauty industry. Advertising was increasingly bombarding women with artificially constructed images of unattainable beauty, and it was evident that many women felt a disconnection between the familiar ad messages and their own, real world.

This consumer truth formed the basis of an integrated marketing campaign which centred on the idea of "real women, real curves". Dove had previously used "real women" in its launch advertising in 2000, but had not used the idea to portray the aspirational image the brand now needed.

The creative idea not only met the marketing challenge, but it was enhanced by Dove's clever mix of intelligent media planning and innovative use of PR and in-store marketing, which were used to support the advertising campaign. The launch exceeded its business objectives, growing purchase intention and market share above and beyond the original goals.

The business issue

Globally, Dove is the number one brand for Unilever Home and Personal Care, with a presence in over 100 countries (Figure 7.1). Since its first introduction in 1990 as a cleansing bar, the Dove promise of ¼ moisturising cream had formed the basis for a rapid strategy for line extensions into shower, deodorant, bodycare and haircare markets.

By 2004, the UK market was now managing a portfolio of over 60 skus, with a retail value of over £120 million. The Dove heritage of moisturisation clearly offered a strong functional platform from which to enter new categories and establish line extensions successfully.

In line with this, Dove launched into bodycare in 2000 with its Intensive Body Moisturiser. This was introduced with the marketing campaign of bringing the consumer "the other ¾ moisturising cream".

In 2004, Dove proposed to further its presence in bodycare by entering the highly competitive firming segment with a range of three firming products. This was a clear stepchange for Dove line extensions. The firming segment of bodycare required product credentials and claims above and

Figure 7.1

beyond moisturisation. Moreover, the market was dominated by Nivea and L'Oréal, which could claim strong skincare credentials from their presence within the facial care market, where the concept of firming had originated.

The company thus wanted to launch the Dove Firming range with communications which would challenge the dominance of the beauty power brands.

Getting real

The UK Dove team worked closely with the global brand team to develop a new brand positioning which would not only provide a platform for Dove's launch into firming, but would also leverage the trusted functional heritage in order to deliver a longer-term, more engaging, emotional positioning for the rest of the brand.

While researching the success of the beauty power brands, Dove discovered an undercurrent of dissatisfaction with the beauty industry. Advertising was increasingly bombarding women with artificially constructed images of unattainable beauty, such as flawless skin, tiny bodies and wrinkle-free faces. For some women, this represented the holy grail. However, it was evident that more women were feeling a lack of connection between familiar advertising messages and their own real world of beauty.

This was proven by a research study undertaken by the UK team into body image. Dove could see the potential for a brand which could champion a more honest representation of beauty, and believed that this could not only be aspirational, but ultimately more credible to the consumer.

Already a trusted brand, Dove could take on the role of championing real beauty for real women by using real women with real curves in its advertising as the true test of a firming product. This would have far more credibility with the increasingly cynical consumer. Dove Firming would communicate the simple truth that "firming the skin of a size 8 supermodel was no challenge".

Recognising that the new positioning was based on a consumer truth and therefore differentiated from the industry norm, the UK team was committed to maximising the potential of the campaign with a high impact, standard-setting execution. This resulted in a fully integrated marketing communications campaign based on the campaign idea of "real women, real curves".

Finding the right image

A recruitment campaign was started in newspapers to find the women for the advertising. It invited them to take part in the shoot, informing them that they would be selected based on their spirit and attitude to life, not on their looks. The six women chosen were happy, fun-loving women who were confident in their bodies, despite round hips and curvy thighs. They also represented the most popular dress sizes in the UK: 12 and 14 (Figure 7.2).

To add another dimension of talkability to the campaign, the advertising agency Ogilvy & Mather commissioned Rankin, a world class photographer, to take the shots. But, in keeping with the vision of "real beauty", there would be no airbrushing and no retouching. The brand's credibility based on using real women could not be undermined by resorting to "beauty tricks".

Dove had previously used real women in its launch advertising with "testimonial" TV ads. This had resulted in a great functional story, but had not delivered the aspirational image the brand now required. The communication challenge now was to make "real women" aspirational for the consumer, and to make other women "want to be like them". This challenge was met through a combination of superior media planning and an integrated PR and consumer activation campaign.

Figure 7.2

Making a splash

Historically, TV had always been the lead medium in bodycare launches. By challenging the standard media plan, the company recognised that it would deliver a campaign with more impact than other bodycare communications by disrupting the norm. Ten years earlier, Wonderbra had generated a huge amount of publicity with a stereotypical portrayal of beauty with its "Hello Boys" strapline. The Dove team recognised the inherent opportunity to juxtapose this with Dove's point of view on beauty. Posters, rather than TV, were therefore the lead medium in above-the-line communication.

A poster campaign with high impact was created to deliver maximum exposure of multiple images of the Dove "real women", to give up to 100 viewings in the first two weeks alone:

- 48-sheets showed a group of size 12–14 real women together;
- buses crammed the high street with the women – this use of bus sides was a bodycare-first category;
- escalator panels on the London underground showed further images of the women in changing poses.

Magazines further showcased the images to support the posters and give the campaign longevity. TV followed the posters a week later, showing the actual casting and photo shoot to emphasise the fact that it was real women in the campaign, and to describe how the posters were made.

Engaging consumers beyond the visuals

The role of PR was to stimulate debate and get the media to pick this up as a consumer story, which would really engage with the target consumers beyond just "seeing it" to "talking about it" and even "taking part in it".

The Times newspaper was the first to run the story in its Saturday magazine. This gave Dove the full front cover and six pages of editorial coverage, including images from the advertising. This was a substantial win for the launch: a first for personal care advertising to dominate the front page of a major newspaper broadsheet magazine. This elevated the campaign beyond the product message and started a national debate about

Dove's new beauty philosophy. It was followed up by every national UK newspaper.

To further the momentum, research findings on body images were released on the day the poster advertising was due to break. The research was used to illustrate why Dove had chosen to break beauty advertising convention by using "real women", and to assure the media that this was a long-term vision of the brand. This made it newsworthy rather than just a one-off publicity stunt. That gave the brand overwhelmingly positive coverage in every newspaper the week of the launch.

The company also released a "behind the scenes" film of the advertising shoot itself to TV broadcasters. It featured on BBC news and GMTV as editorial items.

In addition, to create a second burst of support for the campaign and to engage with consumers even more, the team developed a consumer-led campaign. It consisted of a competition called "Firm Friends", which invited more real women to "bare all" in a follow-up ad. The team negotiated an exclusive editorial piece in the *Sun* newspaper to launch the competition, and also used an advertorial in *Red* magazine to provide further opportunities. A website, www.firmfriends.co.uk, was established to allow friends to enter the competition and to view other entrants, as well as to request product samples and information.

Nine regional winners were chosen from the competition in June 2004 in order to ensure more regional coverage, while the national winners' stories appeared in the *Sun* and subsequently in other major newspapers. This was unprecedented for what was essentially a consumer competition.

The in-store materials, meanwhile, were designed to reflect the above-the-line images to stimulate recognition at point of purchase and amplify the visual effect of the campaign. To do this, free-standing units which included pictures from the ads were placed in key retailers to increase recognition and communicate the launch offers.

Beating targets

Clearly, the campaign had created substantial publicity for the brand and the products. However, the acid test for project success would be to determine if this had translated into successful results for the business against the objectives set before the campaign. A typical product in the hand and body market had to achieve at least a 0.5% value share in order to justify a position on retailers' shelves. It was imperative to exceed this benchmark.

The first business objective of reaching a combined market share of 2% of the hand and body sector with Firming Lotion and Gel by the end of 2004 was surpassed, with the actual figure of 2.3%, including a peak of 6%. The market share of Firming Body Wash in the shower wash segment by the end of 2004 was 0.9%, with a peak of 3.2%, compared to the original target of 0.7%.

Marketing objectives were also met, with purchase penetration in the hand and body sector reaching 1.1% for Body Lotion and 0.6% for Gel-Cream against a combined target of 1.4%. Purchase penetration of Body Wash reached 1% against a target of 0.5%.

Stringent communications targets were also met:

- Dove Firming achieved exceptional awareness of the product range during the launch period, as shown by substantial increases in prompted awareness, with communication awareness moving from 19% to 50% and aided awareness from 60% to 74%.
- Body Wash enjoyed substantial gains in communication awareness, moving from 28% to a high of 50%.
- The TV ads for both the Dove Firming and Body Wash achieved significantly differentiated scores on a Millward Brown tool which measured the level of engagement of a piece of communication.
- Post-viewing measures showed that Dove Firming advertising, compared to previous Dove advertising, was much more memorable because of higher enjoyment and involvement.

One final ingredient was that, along with the launch of Dove Firming, competitors were also marketing their firming products to make the most of the spring seasonal peak, when consumers get their bodies ready for summer. Retail sales data showed that, thanks to a campaign that cut through competitor communication, Dove outperformed the two market leaders during

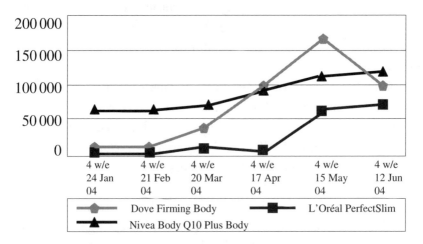

IRI data showing Retail Unit Sales of the 3 highest selling firming ranges.
This data has excluded Firming Body Wash, to compare only bodycare products on a like-for-like basis

Figure 7.3

this crucial period (Figure 7.3). It went on to form the basis of the "real beauty" campaign for the brand as a whole.

All images appearing in this case study are reproduced by permission of Unilever.

Waitrose: supermarket advertising that broke the mould

Snapshot: Waitrose developed a distinctive advertising campaign with a relatively small budget that gave it an enduring position in the market by evoking its special brand qualities.

Key insights

- In 1997, Waitrose became increasingly aware that, as a niche player, it was time to embrace marketing to make prospective and current customers realise just what quality and value it could offer.
- Its evocative and beautiful advertising campaigns improved sales by persuading more shoppers of its price/quality offer.
- Its imaginative creative and media choices allowed it to out-gun its rivals, despite its much smaller budget.

Summary

Waitrose is the supermarket arm of the John Lewis Partnership, one of the UK's leading retailers. Sales for the year-end 2005 were up 13% at £3.3 billion, driven by like-for-like sales of 4%.

In 1997, however, the sales growth of Waitrose was steady, but below the rate of category growth. The evidence suggested that a radical approach was needed. Other supermarkets benefited from economies of scale, with more and bigger stores, and more profit per store. And they enjoyed hefty marketing budgets. But the company had one special ingredient: its passionate and motivated employees. The problem was one of visibility: Waitrose needed to get its story across more effectively, but without shouting.

Customers perceived Waitrose as a quality food supplier. However, this meant many people incorrectly thought it was expensive, so did not feel justified in shopping there regularly. It had more promiscuous shoppers than its rivals. This had to be changed, although it would have to be done over time. The solution would involve persuading these people to put more in their baskets, more often.

But the communication of Waitrose's everyday food expertise needed to be balanced with a price message. That way, people could feel justified in shopping there as they could see the quality they were getting was at a fair price. This, after all, is the real meaning of the word "value" – a definition often forgotten given the frequency with which it's used to mean simply low price.

The communication of this message began with press ads for individual products whose unique or superior quality was described with a short "nugget of information" and an evocative image, all balanced with a simple price statement, demonstrating that Waitrose offered true value. These product quality statements evolved to emphasise that the chain knew its suppliers and remained loyal to them. Then, with competitors striving to change their images, the company decided to use TV advertising for the first time in 2001.

Incremental sales attributed to the advertising more than paid for the first TV campaign. The overall effect of this marketing activity improved and shifted perceptions of Waitrose, which, in turn, contributed to a gradual change in shopping habits and a subsequent increase in sales.

How it all began: the quiet revolution

In 1997, the sales growth of Waitrose was steady, but below the rate of category growth. All the evidence suggested that a radical approach was needed. Other supermarkets benefited from economies of scale: Tesco and Sainsbury's didn't just have more stores, but they had larger stores with higher profitability *per* store. Their marketing budgets matched their magnitude. All these components together contributed to greater visibility and awareness. Despite Waitrose's limited growth, however, the passion and commitment of its employees were unrelenting. The Waitrose story was not being properly told to potential customers.

The company could be described as a small fish in a big pond. In a loud retail environment, how could it communicate effectively with customers? Not only did it face a challenge from its weighty competitors, but also from its own culture. As part of the John Lewis Partnership, the tenet that "We don't do advertising" very much affected Waitrose.

Until, that is, in 1997, when the retailer decided to appoint a Marketing Director. Mark Price became Marketing Director in February 1998. Advertising agency Banks Hoggins O'Shea FCB was then briefed to create a national advertising campaign, from which point the role for marketing (and a marketing department) really began to evolve. Marketing Waitrose did not mean shouting, as this would be at odds with the subtle nature of the brand. Nevertheless, this supermarket needed a communications solution which would enable existing resources to work as powerfully and efficiently as possible.

A brand apart

It was the brand values of quality, honesty, care and commitment that differentiated Waitrose and contributed to consumers' perceptions of the brand, leading customers to see the retailer as a class apart from the rest. These perceptions also affected the way that people shopped there. Analysis found that the retailer was more of a "top-up shop" for many shoppers. Indeed, it had more secondary shoppers than other major supermarkets and had a higher proportion of promiscuous shoppers (i.e. regular shoppers who were also regular major shoppers at one or more rivals). This meant that for most of its customers, Waitrose was not a "main shop" destination.

Qualitative research highlighted these perceptions:

"There is a snob value".
"A more classy shopper".
"A bit more select".

It also found that the Waitrose brand culture stood apart from its competitors in four ways:

- **Quality**. Despite being in the retail arena, the company's primary consideration was in providing quality, not in fighting its rivals.
- **Honesty**. Waitrose aimed to persuade through an honest presentation of information, without hard-sell tactics.
- **Care**. Waitrose staff are partners whose philosophy is to inform customers, using their expertise. Customers are ultimately left to make their own decisions (this is consistent with the original John Lewis retail philosophy).
- **Commitment**. While other supermarkets moved swiftly into non-food areas, Waitrose chose to continue concentrating on its core area of excellence – fresh food retailing.

Because people perceived Waitrose as a quality food supplier, and saw it as a destination shop for special food, they had a part-time attitude to shopping there. In addition, research showed that people mistakenly derived "expensive" from "quality". Because many customers were going to Waitrose to buy those special items, they had become blinded to the prices or offers on everyday items. Therefore, the perception was that because it wasn't a "regular" supermarket, consumers didn't feel they could do their regular shopping there.

Waitrose was indeed different from its competitors. However, marketing could help consumers connect to this difference, to realise the benefits and to see that the supermarket should be as much a part of their shopping habits as other mainstream supermarkets. But the company had to be realistic. It could not expect "basket shoppers" to become "trolley shoppers" overnight through the effect of marketing communications. Nevertheless, a clever marketing campaign could encourage secondary shoppers to put a couple of extra items into their baskets.

In fact, if Waitrose could increase the frequency of visits and the size of baskets by 10% among secondary shoppers and promiscuous regular shoppers, the result would be an extra 7.9% in turnover per year. All it had to do was convince these shoppers to add an extra half dozen pack of eggs or an extra block of cheddar cheese to their baskets to make a big difference to the bottom line.

Again, qualitative research showed that when shoppers were actually shown prices of "regular" items, they were surprised: *"We've been brainwashed into thinking Waitrose is expensive, but it's not the case looking at these prices."*

When people thus saw Waitrose without blinkers, they realised it was just a supermarket that offered a normal range of food and drink. The retailer needed to grab the attention of secondary shoppers so they felt justified in putting a few extra items into their shopping baskets.

The first stage: creating a consistent and compelling image

At the same time, blasting a price message was "just not Waitrose". The challenge was to confront its price and range perceptions in a manner consistent with its reputation for quality. Quality and price needed to be balanced, like an equation. This brought about the value proposition that the company could genuinely offer: Waitrose is committed to bringing its customers the finest quality fresh foods at prices which make them outstanding value in the true sense of the word.

The other large supermarkets could easily fragment their marketing communications, because the sizes of their budgets ensured high exposure and almost instant familiarity with the varying messages. Waitrose was consistently spending at levels of less than 10% of its competitors, so a distinctive and consistent advertising voice was vital.

In 1998, a national campaign began in the press. The creative execution was a departure from traditional retail advertising, and supermarket and food advertising in particular. The creative idea was not to show the specific product in a colour double-page spread execution, but instead to show an evocative image that captured the provenance behind a Waitrose product, accompanied by a caption which simply and honestly gave the name and, importantly, the price of the product. Additionally, there was a single half line of copy with a simple "nugget of information" about the product's quality.

The juxtaposition of a beautiful visual product story with a price message was the surprise element that made the campaign distinctive. Once this identity for the brand had launched in the press, it began to pervade through to all points of customer contact. The communications budget was used efficiently by making communications consistent with the brand strategy and visual identity, thereby helping the brand to become more easily recognisable to consumers, such as the ads for sunflower spread and fresh cod fillets in Figures 7.4 and 7.5.

This "food commitment" and "price commitment" was enforced at varying levels, such as in-store promotions and with microsites for the products featured in the brand advertising on waitrose.com, to satisfy the target audience's desire to be educated about food.

Because Waitrose's commitment to food was being brought to life in marketing communications, it was important that this positioning was reiterated within the company as well. Through working closely with the company buyers, the elements that comprised this core commitment were identified and an "everyday food expertise" spectrum was developed by the marketing department.

The next stage: building on trust

The company tracked the perceptions of the brand through continuous research to see how perceptions of the brand had developed since the

Figure 7.4

Figure 7.5

campaign launched in June 1998. By 2001, food scares were regular occurrences and the outbreak of foot and mouth disease in the UK only served to reinforce the public's belief that supermarket standards were falling in the battle for low prices. Consumer trust in supermarkets declined significantly. The boom in demand for organic produce was further evidence of a growing consumer concern over the source and traceability of the food in the food chain.

Waitrose, however, appeared to be the exception to the rule. Its brand tracking study showed that, since June 1998, the perception that supermarkets "ensure food meets the highest standards possible" had declined for all other major supermarkets, except Waitrose. In fact, for the first two months of the foot and mouth outbreak, this perception actually improved for the retailer.

That is why, from October 2000, the brand advertising campaign began to focus on supplier relationships to convey one of the key dimensions of food expertise (Figure 7.6 shows an ad for English farmhouse lamb). From October 2000, the perception that Waitrose was a store that "tends to stay loyal to its suppliers over time" improved significantly. This impression improved faster for secondary shoppers who typically had less contact with the retailer, which suggested they were responding to external marketing communications.

Figure 7.6

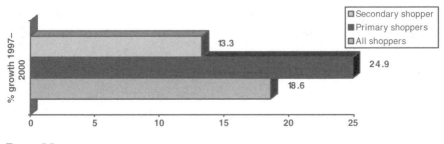

Figure 7.7

In recent years, the company had had to battle with the trend that shoppers were becoming more promiscuous in where they chose to shop as more choice was opened up to them. For example, smaller retailers, such as Marks & Spencer and Somerfield, had seen their proportion of secondary shoppers increasing.

However, since 1997, the proportion of Waitrose's primary shoppers had increased from 45.6% to 48.0% in 2000. This demonstrated that customers were beginning to become more loyal to the brand. In addition, the rate of growth of primary shoppers had been twice as fast as secondary shoppers from 1997 to 2000 (Figure 7.7). Furthermore, both primary and secondary shoppers who were aware of the ads claimed that they visited the store more often and spent more (Figure 7.8).

Year-on-year growth for Waitrose had been 2.60% for the trading year 1997/98, which was less than the 3.05% industry rate. Almost three years since the advertising campaign began, however, the year-on-year growth rate for Waitrose was 3.28%, double the industry rate of 1.57% (for the 2000/01 trading year.

Creating a stronger image

While it was clear that Waitrose's marketing and advertising was having a visible impact on sales and shopper behaviour, research showed that spend was not as efficient as it could have been. Expenditure hadn't entered the "zone of efficiency", where a minimum ad spend would yield £7 million (+/–£2 million) in gross revenue. But the retailer's ad spend had not yet entered that zone.

At around the same time, many of the company's competitors had jumped on the bandwagon and also began to push a quality story in their advertising.

Frequency of Shopping At Waitrose
Press Ad aware vs. Non Press Ad aware – 2001

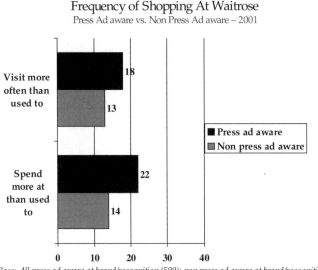

Base: All press ad aware at brand/recognition (599); non press ad aware at brand/recognition (2874)

Source: Consumer InSight Brand Tracking Study, January 2002

Figure 7.8

Marks & Spencer, for example, was about to launch its first advertising campaign for its food division; Sainsbury's had launched its Jamie Oliver TV campaign promoting its *Taste the Difference* range; and Tesco showed it had distanced itself from its "pile 'em high, sell it cheap" days by introducing its *Finest* range.

Waitrose needed to react and, in May 2001, aired its first TV commercial. The company had decided that, in order to convince consumers that it was a "main shop" supermarket, it needed to become more mainstream. It recognised that a television presence could:

- remind and reassure primary shoppers why they shop there;
- give secondary shoppers more reason to shop there;
- tell a wider audience about the "Waitrose difference" and protect the quality positioning against that of other supermarkets.

Like the press campaign, the objective was to enlighten consumers about Waitrose's commitment to bringing the highest quality food to its customers at a fair price. The provenance theme of the press campaign was taken onto television, with an added new dimension of music. The soundtrack of each commercial set against evocative photography worked together to depict the story of the product advertised, which, in turn, highlighted the retailer's commitment to bringing the highest quality food to its customers.

To set Waitrose apart from other supermarkets, each execution would illustrate a "killer fact", which demonstrated the Waitrose difference. More importantly, each ad would end with a caption of the product and price, highlighting how the company offers "quality food, honestly priced".

Rewarding results

As the campaign was intended to be a long-term brand building solution, its performance needed to be looked at over the long term. Early tracking results showed that the quality/price equation was being communicated, and that Waitrose was seen as being "particularly careful in selecting food for its shops" more than ever before. It was also a very visible campaign, for the amount of money spent: 70% of respondents who recognised the campaign correctly branded it as Waitrose, compared to an industry average of about 50%.

In addition, analysis showed that during the period of the campaign there was a 6.9% incremental uplift in the share of grocery spend, and an 18.7% incremental uplift in the share of shopping trips. This appeared to buck the received wisdom that short-term payback didn't usually cover the cost of advertising: an incremental sales increase attributed to the advertising more than paid for the first burst of TV advertising.

Marketing now permeates throughout the company, from boardroom to the shop floor. Through the creation of distinctive and consistent marketing communications, which continues today, with its agency, MCBD, Waitrose has been able to punch above its weight and be heard effectively.

All images appearing in this case study are reproduced by permission of Waitrose.

The Number 118 118: running away with the market

Snapshot: By giving the brand such a strong personality through the iconic use of two runners, The Number 118 118 grabbed leadership in a newly deregulated, fiercely competitive market.

Key insights

- The company's key insight was that no one *wanted* to learn a new number for directory assistance, so it was essential to make the process fun, engaging and entertaining to remember.
- The company quickly identified the critical role marketing communications would play in getting its brand to stand out in a new and crowded marketplace.
- It was determined to act as the market leader from the start – hence the name, The Number.
- The twin runners used as the emblem of 118 118 helped make the communications far more effective by becoming cult figures.

Summary

INFONXX is the largest independent directory assistance supplier in the world.

In the UK at the beginning of 2003 there were over twenty companies set to contest the race to take over the provision of directory enquiries services following the closure of 192, run by the incumbent provider (BT). Experience from other markets suggested only two would profitably survive – BT and one new entrant. INFONXX (parent company of The Number 118 118) was determined to be that single new entrant which would take on BT. So it set about creating and launching a new brand from scratch. This set a demanding brief for marketing communications.

The first step of this plan was to buy the "golden number" 118 118, which enabled the company to own the market generic ("118"). Having established a strong base of awareness through a high-profile advertising campaign six months ahead of 192's switch-off, the second stage was to develop a powerful personality for the brand which resonated strongly with the core target market of high users of directory enquiries.

While the success of the ads did lead to some temporary problems with service quality, due to overwhelming user numbers, in less than 12 months, The Number 118 118 had become the UK's leading provider of directory assistance, demolishing BT's 47-year dominance.

The beginning: deregulation creates a new market

Following the flagship privatisation of British Telecom, the UK had enjoyed one of the most deregulated and competitive telecoms markets in the world. Two decades later, however, there remained one minor anomaly – BT's monopoly of directory enquiry provision. With over two million calls to 192 every day charged at 40p per call from a landline, and with no competition, this was one of BT's remaining golden cash cows.

Directory enquiries had been provided by BT via the "192" service since the 1950s. It was, for many decades, a free service, although charging was introduced in the 1980s. The rationale for deregulation was to introduce competition, leading to lower prices and enhanced quality of service.

European legislation dictated that all European Union (EU) members had to deregulate directory enquiries, with a choice of services to be accessed via a common "118" prefix, followed by a further two to three digits. To ensure healthy competition, the legacy number would be switched off in all markets, following a brief period of "parallel running", where new services would co-exist with the incumbent.

The then regulator Oftel announced deregulation of the UK market at the end of 2001, with closure of 192 set for August 25th, 2003. This followed successful deregulation in countries such as Germany, Austria, Eire and Sweden.

US-based INFONXX followed these developments in Europe with great interest. INFONXX was, by this point, one of the leading providers of directory services to US wireless operators, with a strong track record of delivering quality services at low cost on a business-to-business, "white label" basis, allowing companies to brand the service themselves. It was now seeking to drive more profitable growth by developing a direct-to-consumer relationship, using the UK as a test market and foothold for European expansion.

Creating a crowded market

Oftel opted for open competition with allocation of 118 numbers by a lottery process. This meant that over 20 companies would now be competing to offer directory services, including:

- major fixed and mobile telecoms companies, such as BT, NTL, One.Tel, Thus, Cable&Wireless, Orange, Vodafone, O$_2$, T-Mobile;
- existing directory providers, such as Yell, Thompsons, Scoot;
- retailer/service brands, such as Tesco and British Gas;
- major European players, such as Conduit and Telegate – established providers of directory services in Eire and Germany respectively;
- a raft of smaller niche providers, such as Cheshire County Council, the Gay & Lesbian Directory, Welsh Directory Enquiries, and so on.

In short, the UK consumer was about to be hit with a dizzying number of new six-digit numbers: 118 118, 118 811, 118 888, 118 866, 118 500, 118 000, 118 800, 118 111, 118 247, 118 453, to name just a few. Marketing communications had the tough job of making one particular number stand out from the crowd.

Consumers wanted 192 with lower prices

Oftel consumer research from November 2000 showed that while UK consumers welcomed the *idea* of competition, they did not welcome the need to choose from a range of providers or having to abandon 192 in favour of a range of new six-digit numbers.

There was little active customer dissatisfaction with 192, despite research commissioned by INFONXX which suggested 192's accuracy levels were as low as 70%, compared to the US levels of upwards of 95%. In comparison to the US customer experience, calling 192 was also very terse and abrupt (a result of BT rewarding operators to keep calls below 25 seconds).

When asked by Oftel what improvements they might want to be made, the only response of any significance from consumers was "lower prices". But INFONXX's pricing strategy was such that at a headline level, its service would be priced at a relative premium to 192 – ruling out the obvious "low cost 192" communications strategy.

Harsh financial climate

This stemmed from the impact of the telecom and dot.com implosion, which meant that securing high levels of financing with long-term payback was extremely difficult. This, to a large extent, precluded the "land grab" strategy of spending large sums of advertising money upfront and offering low cost services, with payback over a five-year period based on market leadership.

Financing was instead to be based on business performance: the more calls generated and the more successful the business, the more financing would be made available for further investment. Marketing communications had to work in terms of call generation from day one, rather than just generating intermediate measures such as awareness and propensity.

Starting from scratch against well-established players

INFONXX's key competitors all had established UK/Eire-based call centre operations. BT was already taking the entire landline 192 market, and operationally its key task was to manage decline rather than manage growth. Conduit and Telegate were offering services to mobile operators in the UK on a white-label basis. Other new entrants, such as One.Tel and British Gas, had well-established call centre operations which could be switched over to handle directory enquiries.

INFONXX, on the other hand, had no UK-based call centres, and no significant excess capacity in its US and Philippines-based call centres. Management of growth was thus a key challenge for marketing communications: too few calls would lead to unacceptable return on capital; too many calls risked disappointing customers who then wouldn't call again in the future.

In addition, unlike most new product or service launches, the deregulated directory enquiry market was dominated by the events of one single day: "switch-off day". Experience from other markets suggested that only a tiny minority of consumers would switch from their engrained habit of dialling 192 to calling one of the new 118 numbers until it was absolutely necessary – i.e. when 192 no longer worked.

This meant traumatic overnight growth that was nigh on impossible to predict in advance, which was particularly challenging for a new entrant deciding on how many operators to employ. This also assumed that spending money on advertising early on would be money wasted. No-one was interested in directory enquiries anyway, so why on earth would they pay attention?

Marketing's role was therefore to ensure:

- that consumers readily remembered INFONXX's allocated 118 number ahead of those of its competitors;
- that this was based on a reason that was not grounded in price;
- steady and predictable growth in call volumes;
- the creation of a robust, cash-generative business ahead of switch-off.

First to mind is first in market

The guiding light for the marketing solution came from Ries & Trout's *22 Immutable Laws of Marketing*: "It's better to be first than it is to be better."

The belief was that first to mind would be first in market. INFONXX would be the first, and would act and behave as market leader from day one – acting as the only number, *the* number. Hence the brand name: The Number. This act would reposition the competition as "also-rans", rather than the "real deal".

As this strategy was being finalised, serendipity had it that the number "118 118" became available for purchase. This particular permutation of digits was originally allocated by the Oftel lottery to a small outfit called Leaf Telecom. While INFONXX already owned the "magic number" 118 811 (whose symmetry gave it particular memorability), the number 118 118 was clearly the definitive number in the category.

Fortunately, no other player saw the value of the number as much as INFONXX, and the bid for £2 million, taken straight out of the marketing budget, was accepted. This act enabled the company to own "118", or the market generic, the "new number" for 192 (just dial it twice). Combined with BT opting to promote 118 500 as its number, the company was also confident that by driving awareness of "118" it could prevent other players using the European "double digit" convention (11 88 XX) from gaining any traction in this market.

Figure 7.9

This would have the desired effect of eliminating the company's two most feared competitors – Conduit with 11 88 88 and Telegate with 11 88 66 – from even playing in the market, leaving a relatively clear playing field for The Number and BT. This led to the name, the number and the brand identity: The Number 118 118 logo (Figure 7.9).

The real challenge for marketing communications was to launch this brand in a way which would:

- generate real interest and engagement with a very low interest category;
- firmly embed the number in the mind of the target audience; and
- drive call volumes ahead of 192 switch-off.

INFONXX needed to convince investors that by going first it wouldn't simply be burning valuable advertising dollars too early. Its strategy was to communicate and deliver a brand and service which people would want to start engaging with and calling right away, rather than waiting until switch-off – something new and better, rather than a new number for the same old service.

The company called this directory *assistance*, as opposed to directory enquiries, to label it as a positive and helpful service which would help customers get through to the people, businesses or places they required. INFONXX's experience in the US showed that it was possible to deliver levels of service and customer satisfaction in a different league from that offered by 192.

Who's calling?

Quantitative research identified a clear target audience of high directory users, the 25% of the market who accounted for 89% of all directory calls. Further quantitative and qualitative research identified the core target as:

- 25–44;
- urban, primarily London and the Southeast but also Manchester, Birmingham, Leeds, etc.;
- professionals;
- having hectic work and/or social lives;
- advertising-literate.

The magic ingredient: brand personality

Having identified service as the key differentiator for marketing communications to focus upon, the company then set about building a powerful personality in order to create a brand, rather than just a six-digit number. The brand essence was defined as "Going the extra mile", with core values of passion, dedication, helpfulness and focus. The creative challenge was to find a way of executing this brand in a way that resonated with the core target audience.

It was clear from just a handful of focus groups that the advertising clichés used successfully in other markets – dancing numbers, jingles and so on – wouldn't really cut it. While it was essential to make number memorability absolutely central to communications, it was equally important that both the essence and the personality of the brand were communicated, using a fresh creative vehicle which uniquely resonated with the target audience.

The 118 118 runners

The special "twin" number clearly pointed to a pair of twins who represented the brand. After weeks of character development the agency, WCRS, was

Figure 7.10

inspired by a picture of US runner Steve "Pre" Prefontaine. His image was duplicated and doctored, and thus the 118 118 runners were born (Figure 7.10).

The campaign was developed and tested qualitatively and quantitatively, where it elicited a strong "love it or hate it" reaction. The 1970s theme resonated strongly with the target audience who had grown up during that period, and the honest British slapstick humour appealed to ad-literate consumers who were tired of irony and dark humour.

The runners first appeared in February 2002 on their own dedicated website: www.mysteryrunners.com. This contained photos, videos and interviews with a pair of "powerful, powerfully moustached men who quite literally refuse to stop". Links to the site were seeded in key Internet locations and weblogs, and in a matter of days, the site had generated hundreds of thousands of hits. Discussion sites suggested that many people thought this was a "serious" fan website, while others smelled a marketing scam going on but appreciated the sophistication of it.

The next phase was to create mass awareness of the 118 118 runners. An integrated multimedia campaign was launched across TV, outdoor and radio, featuring the runners and their soon-to-be famous catchphrase: "Got Your Number". The launch had the desired effect of generating manageable levels of call volumes, and also drew out one of the competitors, Conduit.

Playing the trump card

The gloves were now off and it was time to play the company's trump card: retiring the 192 number and replacing it with 118 118. Having established the icon and personality of the runners, a new elderly runner representing 192 was shown handing over to the more sprightly and energetic pair.

Along with mainstream media, the company wanted to use other ways to embed the image of the runners by making them into cult figures. This included significant investment in a range of activities, including real-life runners, washing lines with the logo, flyposters, ice cream vans, barber shop windows and viral/online activities. The runners were also cleverly placed at key events such as the Wimbledon tennis tournament, where they were viewed as genuine British eccentrics rather than a marketing ploy (a key part of the magic of the creative vehicle).

By August 2003, the runners had become a national icon and the brand developed significant status among opinion formers, particularly in media and marketing circles. This gave the brand a crucial point of leverage with journalists in the run-up to the switch-off of 192. Given that writing about this was necessary but hardly a thrilling subject, journalists inevitably wanted to write about the 118 118 runners. More importantly, to consumers this was now the only brand. The service was taking millions of calls every week.

Managing the post switch-off backlash

The switch-off was inevitably going to lead to a negative PR backlash. This was compounded by the unexpected implosion of BT's market share, which meant that overnight, the majority of calls switched from BT to new and relatively inexperienced operators. While all the new 118 entrants suffered service problems, 118 118's dominant brand and market position saw it taking the majority of the flak. To address this, marketing communications throughout October and November 2003 focused on service innovations.

For example, the company was the first to advertise a money-back offer for wrong numbers, and it also communicated some of the benefits of the service, such as the ability to have as many numbers as the caller wanted in one call or to locate their nearest restaurant without knowing its name or address.

These messages were delivered in an entertaining way in order to continue to build the brand's unique personality and approach to directory assistance. This helped the company weather an intense storm of negative PR, and arrested and reversed a temporary drop in call volumes and market share.

Breaking new ground

In less than 12 months, The Number 118 118 had become the UK's leading provider of directory assistance, demolishing BT's 47 year dominance. Marketing successfully drove call volumes steadily from a few thousand per day in March 2003 to over 400 000 per day by September of that year. While the unexpected success of the brand did lead to some temporary quality of service issues, the strength of the brand and continued marketing communications meant that market leadership was maintained, despite the bout of bad publicity (Figure 7.11).

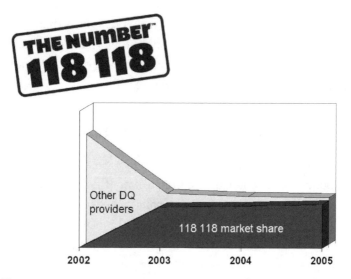

Figure 7.11

In addition, the company achieved the highest advertising awareness levels of any campaign on any budget in recent history. Being far the most talked-about and imitated campaign during the crucial period of June to August 2003 created a huge volume of "free" advertising. And, because the advertising was vastly more effective in generating awareness than the company's competitors, it gave strategic advantage in terms of return on media expenditure.

All images appearing in this case study are reproduced by permission of the Number (UK) Ltd.

TNT Sameday: making money from minimising stress

Snapshot: TNT developed a B2B marketing campaign that delivered significant results for a relatively small outlay.

Key insights

- TNT's research showed that focusing on taking the stress out of sending packages would resonate much more strongly with customers.
- This stood out against the traditional creative strategy in the sector that focused on promptness and efficiency.
- It highlights how a strong creative approach can have an impact in a business-to-business setting, as much as it does in consumer markets.

Summary

TNT Sameday is part of TNT Express Services, which itself is part of TNT, a world-leading provider of express delivery services, logistics supply chain solutions and mail services. The company reported €10.1 billion in revenues in 2005.

In the UK, TNT Sameday had identified two main objectives for the business during 2005: reactivation of lapsed customers and increased and consistent usage by existing customers. By mounting a well-targeted business-to-business campaign, and one which moved away from traditional marketing in the sector, TNT Sameday achieved impressive results.

Revenue increased substantially and return on investment (ROI) moved into quadruple figures, with the opening of 11 000 new trading accounts. This achievement was all the more remarkable given that nothing else changed in TNT Sameday's offering, service, prices or delivery. The effects can be purely attributed to the new marketing campaign.

Searching for the right solution

As part of TNT Express Services, TNT Sameday provides instant response, immediate collection and nationwide delivery in the shortest possible time.

On call 24 hours per day, 365 days per year, TNT Sameday offers exactly what it says – same-day package delivery across the UK via 40 local sales centres. This is a simple proposition, but one which has the inevitable downside of considerable competition from other providers. All players in the market basically offer the same service, with no real barriers to entry from providers, whether large or small.

Differentiation in the industry in terms of service had been negligible. However, the other leading brands, such as DHL and UPS, had benefited from considerable global brand advertising. In addition, customers tended to be promiscuous, with little or no brand loyalty, in a market that was, by definition, ad hoc and a "panic purchase". Among the less promiscuous, customers would often display loyalty to "local heroes" – small independent operators serving a local business community – because they saw them as more reliant on their specific custom and thus, hopefully, more reliable.

TNT Sameday's previous approach had been sales promotions in the form of incentivised mailings, with successful results and increased revenue. However, the sales growth tended to be short-term, with a relatively modest ROI.

Nor was it at all clear whether incentives drove sales growth or simply awareness. Analysis suggested that the sudden requirement for the service was the main driver and, provided awareness was top-of-mind, led to usage. Unfortunately, usage was unpredictable, and loyalty did not appear to be any higher as a result of the activity. In other words, customers with a sudden, very urgent need opted for the first company that came to mind, which was not necessarily TNT Sameday.

The company realised that it needed not only to make significant improvements in its sales loyalty from existing customers, but also to reactivate lapsed customers. Lapsed customers also exceeded existing customers by a factor of four.

The sales and marketing strategy focused on these two customer groups and aimed to increase weekly trading customers by an additional 300 every week by the end of 2005 – a sizeable target.

Gaining an understanding of customers

In formulating strategy, TNT Sameday segmented customers into three distinct groups:

- **Existing trading customers:** organisations that had traded with TNT Sameday in at least one week in the last 13 calendar weeks.
- **Lapsed customers:** organisations that had not traded with TNT Sameday within the last 13 weeks, but had traded previously.
- **Prospect customers:** organisations registered with a known requirement, but which had never traded.

Analysis revealed that approximately 50% of customers traded once during a typical 13-week period, showing the ad hoc nature of the market. To achieve its aim of increasing weekly trading, TNT Sameday focused on two principal objectives:

- to encourage trial consignments among lapsed customers and prospects;
- to encourage existing customers to continue to come to the company.

In line with previous marketing activity, TNT Sameday was clear that any new activity needed to be very creative and have a big impact, with an emphasis on the service being an essential one.

Taking a different creative approach

In December 2004, Rees Bradley Hepburn (RBH) was appointed to develop the creative strategy. Telephone in-depth interviews were conducted with a range of likely users in a variety of industries. The research was very revealing and led directly to the creative strategy adopted by RBH.

In considering the research findings, it soon became clear that the target audience was highly varied in make-up. The user could be anyone from a despatch clerk or secretary to a managing director. The gender split was also more likely to be 50:50 male/female, rather than the predominantly male audience previously assumed.

What united them, however, was the very pressing need to get a parcel or package out of the door and on its way as fast as possible. All the while the parcel remained on their desk it was a problem – and, specifically, their problem. This panic was only relieved once the consignment had been collected and entered into the delivery system. And then it was no longer their problem.

In TNT Sameday's own research among all three of the customer groups, the most consistently cited factors considered important to customers were

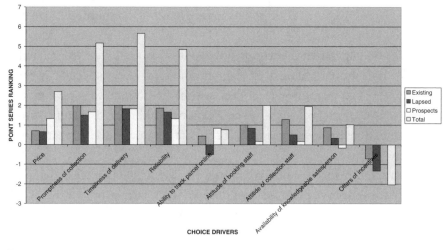

Figure 7.12

collection speed and timeliness of delivery (Figure 7.12). In terms of the market though, timeliness of delivery was a given, since large companies were presumed competent.

Creatively, this insight led to an interesting approach. Rather than focus on reliability or the unpleasant, stressful element of the need for TNT Sameday, the creative route developed highlighted the positive feelings engendered when TNT Sameday was underway with a delivery. Rather than reinforce a given ("we will deliver promptly") the emphasis was on the benefit of prompt collection, i.e. the moment the package has gone it ceases to be a problem. This led to the idea of "You can relax at work".

Departing from the norm

This creative strategy was a considerable departure from what TNT Sameday had previously been doing, i.e. reinforcing the promptness and efficiency of the service. To a great extent, this was now a hygiene factor and certainly claimed by all other operators in the market.

RBH's new creative direction enabled a wealth of ideas to be explored that encompassed how people could relax at work. It was deliberately designed not to focus on irrelevant service detail. Customers didn't care about this. They just wanted packages off their desks. TNT Sameday were able to engage at a different level entirely and create a brand identity that recognised how people behave at work. Ultimately, people wanted to minimise stress in their day.

It was also imperative that the creative route didn't require TNT Sameday to make operational changes to their business or link to specific service delivery, e.g. "we guarantee to collect within five minutes or your money back – so you can relax". Finally, the solution would need to stand out in a cluttered B2B mailing environment. It couldn't get lost on the desk and then be thrown away.

By considering the idea of relaxing at work, the RBH team created a series of highly cost-effective postcards and mailers which formed part of the "TNT and the Art of Stress Management" campaign. Each became a piece of helpful, yet somewhat tongue-in-cheek, advice from TNT on how to improve the recipients' sense of well-being and relaxation. The implication was that if TNT Sameday is used, you can spend far more time thinking about relaxation rather than worrying about a package being collected. The use of TNT Sameday's very vibrant orange colour identity helped the ad stand out (Figures 7.13 and 7.14).

Hitting the right targets

Each customer group was targeted differently. The existing customers received a postcard entitled "TNT and the Art of Stress Management", which acted as a humorous information piece to keep TNT Sameday top of mind and encourage usage when a short-notice delivery was required. A total of 106 555 postcards were mailed over a 23-week period in the first, second and third quarters of 2005.

The second mailing campaign ran in parallel and was aimed at:

- lapsed customers of TNT Sameday or those "known customers" that had never actually traded;
- customers of TNT Express who had never used the Sameday service.

This mailing offered an incentive in the form of a Kit Kat and a coffee mug, which was provided as part of the mail piece (Figure 7.15). Recipients were invited to try the Sameday service (thereby allowing them to take advantage of the gifts).

Figure 7.13

The lapsed customer group was mailed over 23 weeks in the first, second and third quarters of 2005, and a total of 27 809 packs were sent. The TNT Express customer campaign occurred over one week towards the end of the same phase.

Each of the mailings was followed up by TNT Sameday sales staff, and very accurate monitoring took place of all transactions. It was, therefore, possible to attribute revenue to specific elements of the campaign and to monitor ROI. Further activity took place in the fourth quarter of 2005, and the creative strategy was extended with additional postcards, trial incentives and also online activity.

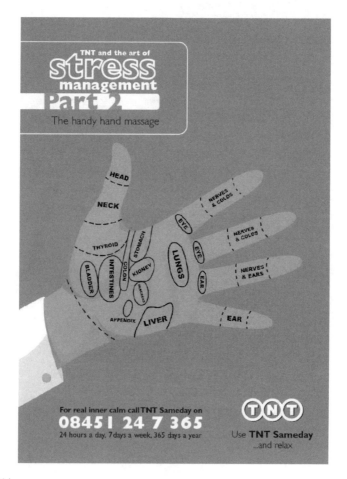

Figure 7.14

Figure 7.15

Explosive results

The results were astounding, particularly given the very low investment required to execute the campaigns. The results demonstrated spectacular effectiveness in terms of revenue generation, ROI and significant increases in the volume of transacted business (Figures 7.16 and 7.17). For example, by

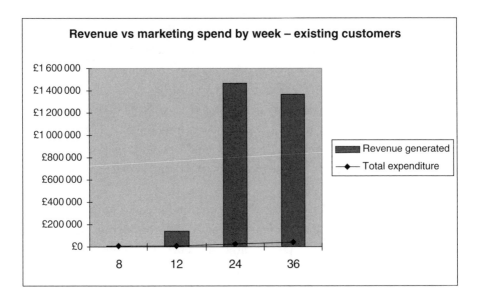

Figure 7.16

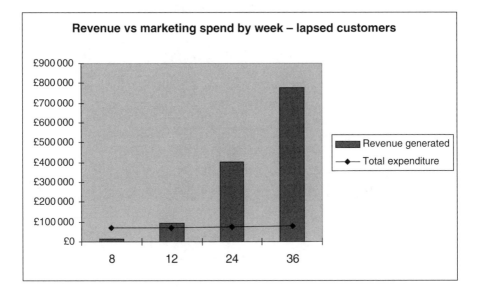

Figure 7.17

week 24 of the campaign, revenue had reached over £1.8 m, while expenditure at that stage was just £75 000. The campaign was far exceeding expectations in terms of revenue generation and ROI.

During 2005, the total investment by TNT Sameday on the whole campaign was £199 342. The total tracked incremental revenue for the period of 2005, during which time the campaign was running, was £6 187 912, giving a huge overall return on investment of 3004%.

The highest ROI figure recorded was 11 256% for a sequence of postcards mailed to existing customers during the fourth quarter of 2005. The lowest ROI recorded was 450% for a campaign to lapsed customers and customers who had never traded before (Figures 7.18 and 7.19).

The end of the overall campaign resulted in over 11 000 new trading accounts being created: in other words, new transactions undertaken. This corresponds to an average of 282 additional accounts per week of the campaign activity, which is close to exactly the business objective set of 300 at the beginning of the year.

Creative and original thinking was a powerful determinant in the success of the campaign. By using available research and considering the specific attitudes of those who made up the target audience, it was possible to create

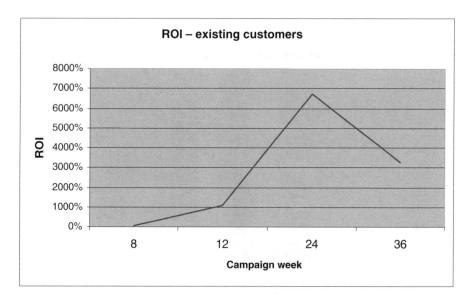

Figure 7.18

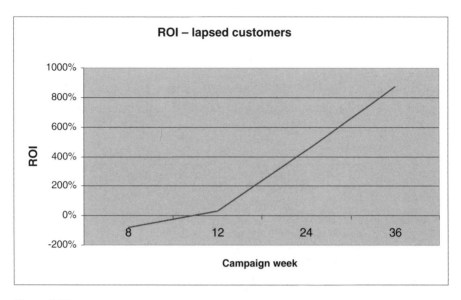

Figure 7.19

a campaign that was a first in the market. It was also unusual in the B2B arena of marketing communications.

TNT Sameday was also able to:

- improve the retention of existing customers and increase revenue;
- attract lapsed customers and increase revenue;
- attract customers who had never traded before and increase revenue;
- deliver phenomenal levels of ROI.

TNT has not only improved its continuing business performance but has continued to capitalise on the brand equity created through an imaginative solution. Its success is also proof that it is possible to achieve spectacular results without a spectacular marketing budget.

All images appearing in this case study are reproduced by permission of TNT.

Make Poverty History: campaigning to change the world

Snapshot: Despite a very small budget, Comic Relief and AMV BBDO created a compelling campaign which energised millions of people to lobby their governments to end poverty.

Key insights

- What turned out to be a huge and vastly influential campaign was done with almost no budget.
- Based on a simple but visionary idea, the communications initiative managed to unite a range of different charities and win the support of high profile individuals.
- Even more significantly, the campaign used the general public to get the message across to the world's most powerful leaders and force them to take action.

Summary

Make Poverty History was designed as a call to action for the world's governments to bring about the end of poverty in the developing world. A meeting between the leaders of the G8 countries, a review of the UN Millennium Development Goals and a World Trade Organisation summit was a combination of events that made 2005 an ideal time for the charity to act.

The communications challenge that faced Make Poverty History was to persuade the G8 leaders to deliver on three fronts: to double the aid budget set by the G8 countries to $100 billion (£54 billion) a year; to set new standards for trade justice, including rewriting the trade laws; and to cancel Third World debt.

The charity, together with ad agency AMV BBDO, identified that the most effective way of influencing the eight leaders would be to create a word-of-mouth effect that would draw the public to the cause. However, there were problems: not least, that the public did not believe it could effect any real change, coupled with a general air of charity fatigue.

The creative solution was to introduce a white charity band bearing the words "Make Poverty History". This simple message was communicated globally through PR, advertising, celebrity endorsements and special events.

The results were impressive. By July 2005, just seven months after its launch, 87% of the UK population had heard of Make Poverty History. The white wrist band was worn by eight million people, with one in three of those doing so under the age of 35. In the UK alone, nine million campaigning actions were undertaken, culminating in 250 000 people taking to the streets of Edinburgh ahead of the G8 summit. 57% of them had never campaigned before. And Live8 – an international event consisting of ten concerts that took place on the same day across the world – drew a global audience of 3.8 billion.

The pressure created by the communications strategy persuaded governments to act by doubling aid to all developing nations compared with 2004.

No more red noses

Make Poverty History began when film-maker Richard Curtis came to AMV BBDO to say he'd been involved in organising ten Red Nose Days now and felt that the moment had arrived to take the next, very difficult step.

Red Nose Day has raised millions over the past twenty years, as have hundreds of other charities. But there was still a feeling that the surface of the problem of extreme poverty had been barely scratched. So Comic Relief joined up with a coalition of charities to try to make 2005 the most important year ever in the fight against extreme poverty.

Over one billion people still have to survive on less than $1 a day. Not surprisingly, many of them don't manage it. The current rates see 50 000 people – 30 000 of them children – die every day due to poverty-related causes. That is 270 million people dead since 1990, roughly the population of the US. The sort of action that was now needed was beyond the scope of individuals. Only action by governments would make a real difference.

The right time

2005 was a unique year. Three forums were to gather in the second half of the year, all of them with the power to take the sort of decisions needed:

- In July, the leaders of the G8 countries were to sit down in the UK with a development agenda for the first time ever.
- In September, the progress of the UN Millennium Development Goals (a set of targets laid down in 2000 to eradicate poverty) would be reviewed.
- In December, the sixth World Trade Organisation meeting was to take place.

Such a combination of events would probably never be repeated within such a short timeframe. In anticipation of the special opportunity 2005 would offer, a powerful chain of non-governmental organisations (NGOs), international networks, trade unions and religious groups in 61 countries across the globe had already launched a Global Call to Action Against Poverty (GCAP). In the UK, 140 organisations had signed up to GCAP and were eager to take action on a national scale.

The aim was to get the G8 world leaders to commit to three decisive policies:

- Doubling the aid budget (from $50 billion a year to $100 billion a year) and improving the quality of aid.
- Setting new standards for trade justice, including rewriting trade laws so that people in developing countries can sell their produce without competing against subsidised produce from rich countries.
- Cancelling all Third World debt.

So this called for not one, but three messages to be communicated. Each one on its own was potentially complex to explain and worthy of hours of debate in its own right. How could they be unified?

Pinning down the audience

In theory, the target audience was a bit of a niche: just eight people. However, although eight people were the ultimate target audience for the message, an intermediary audience was necessary in order to influence these eight. That these eight people were world leaders who relied on public support to sustain their own positions gave the agency an opportunity. They needed convincing that the message really mattered.

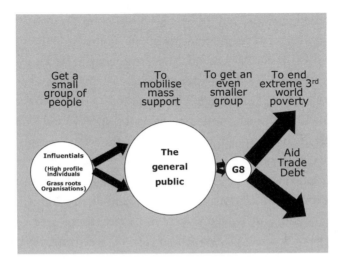

Figure 7.20

But there was another difficulty. Besides the potential complexity of the messages, there was no money for mainstream media. Mass participation was needed but mass media couldn't be afforded.

However, although there was no money there were people – lots of them – in the 140 or so organisations already signed up to GCAP, plus high-profile individuals such as Nelson Mandela, Bono and Sir Bob Geldof. So the decision was to use people as media to get the message across.

This was about more than creating a word-of-mouth effect. The charity and the agency aimed to harness 140 grassroots organisations and high profile individuals in order to recruit the general public to the cause, with the ultimate ambition of compelling the G8 leaders to act (true democracy in action). These people were called the "influentials" and their role in communications is shown in Figure 7.20.

Finding the right message

In terms of the message, the first challenge was to get the 140 charities and NGOs already signed up to GCAP to agree on one message. This was easier said than done when each organisation had a different set of priorities and potentially conflicting views. The partners in the project knew that if it could unite this group, it would have a stronger foundation on which to base the communications and develop an idea with the ability to unite people.

It was realised just what potential for greatness the public had. In 1985, Live Aid showed the world the extent of Ethiopia's famine and asked people to give money to help. People didn't need to think – they gave without question. This had been proven time and again by appeals and events such as Comic Relief. If the campaign could appeal to this side of people's nature, it stood a very good chance.

Having decided to use these influentials as "living" media, the agency now faced its next communications challenge. There were a lot of good intentions, but no commonly agreed direction. In fact, there were 140 different points of view. However, it was convinced of one thing. Whatever the message that was ultimately developed, the tone of it had to be positive and uplifting.

Overcoming charity fatigue

The real issue was that people didn't believe that they themselves could effect any significant change. They had seen that the millions raised by a succession of appeals had never cracked the core problem and were inclined to conclude that the problem was so big, and influenced by so many complex factors, that making any lasting difference was impossible.

After 20 years of giving, the images of suffering that everyone was hoping to stop were still on their screens. There was a lot of confusion about charity in general: people wondered, "Is the money getting through?"

On top of this, they were being asked to do something that most of them had never done: instead of giving money, their support was needed. Everyone had to be made to feel that they could be campaigners. The message needed to appeal to their appetite for greatness and make them feel that they could make a difference.

That called for a visionary thought, and something that conveyed the sense of standing on the precipice of history. It had to be something that was both emotive and capable of enrolling individuals to the cause – an invitation for people to be part of something historic.

Getting this right would be the key to making every person believe that change was possible and that what they did counted towards making it happen. The campaign had to celebrate the ultimate goal and people's involvement in achieving it, rather than just focusing on the G8 as the means of getting there. And by so doing, a picture could be painted of what the world could be like through collective endeavour: a positive picture that everyone would want to help create.

The big idea

In retrospect, the idea looks so obvious that it is hard to appreciate just what a breakthrough it was. It consisted of a band with three simple words: Make Poverty History (Figure 7.21). People wear black armbands to mourn death. This idea was to create a white band to symbolise its prevention: a sign of hope that positive change really could be achieved.

The statement "Make Poverty History" was clear, challenging and evocative. Most importantly, it had the potential to make people believe they could be part of something momentous. It gave the "living" media a message under which they could unite. And it gave people a goal towards which they could focus their own individual endeavours and efforts.

Marshalling the public

The plan had been to use an army of people to influence the eight most powerful national leaders in the world, who could save millions of lives lost everyday to extreme poverty. But neither Comic Relief nor AMV BBDO had any idea just how big it would become. Make Poverty History became the biggest civil movement the UK had ever seen. 540 organisations came together to create the UK's broadest coalition.

Figure 7.21

By July 2005, 87% of the UK population had heard of Make Poverty History, and in just seven months. (Compare this to 70% awareness of Walkers Crisps, which is the UK's largest grocery brand and has been established for over 50 years.)

According to the UK Prime Minister, Tony Blair, speaking in 2005: "Make Poverty History has been the most effective public pressure campaign ever." Other signs of success included:

- Eight million people in the UK alone wore a white band, while one in three were under the age of 35. The white band and the sentiment it embodied was adopted across the globe by all of the 85 countries that signed up to the GCAP.
- Nine million campaigning actions were taken in the UK by the living media, including emails, texts, letters, demonstrations and many more.
- 914 161 emails were sent to UK politicians, encouraging them to Make Poverty History.
- 250 000 took to the streets of Edinburgh to march against poverty ahead of the G8 summit. 57% of these had never taken any form of campaigning action before.
- The Trade Justice Vigil in April was the biggest ever protest to happen in a general election period, with 25 000 staying overnight in Whitehall.

Then there was Live8. It could be assumed that Live8 alone would have received enough attention and support to get the message across. And yes, it was a monumental event. But it only happened *after* the momentum of the Make Poverty History campaign persuaded Bob Geldof to change his mind and do what he swore he would never do post-Live Aid and put on another concert. Live8 was the biggest musical event the world has ever seen, and Make Poverty History was the premise behind it (Figure 7.22).

The concert was watched by 3.8 billion on July 2nd 2005, while ten concerts took place with 1250 musicians playing to the world's largest audience. But the audience wasn't just watching – it was lobbying.

Encouraging commitment

To the participants, the real measures of success, however, were that the Make Poverty History campaign helped the eight most powerful men in the world make the following commitments:

JULY

After bowing to public pressure as a result of support for Make Poverty History, Bob Geldof stages the biggest concert in history. The world watches.

JULY

The final push comes in Edinburgh on the weekend before the summit

The heat is turned up for the last time

The summit takes place and the spotlight of the world is on 8 men. They listen to us

Figure 7.22

- Aid to all developing nations was doubled compared to 2004, a commitment that will mean $50 bn a year by 2010.
- 100% cancellation of the outstanding debts of the 18 poorest countries in the world.
- All countries could achieve trade justice providing their economic plans and development policies met with G8 approval.

In addition, the white band and the sentiment has been adopted across the globe by all the countries signed up to GCAP, with the number of organisations pledging their support rising from 140 to over 540. Millions of bands are now being worn by people around the world.

There is another testament to the power of the message. It led to traditional media owners donating £3 million of free advertising space to the campaign. So, while the campaign was never destined to use conventional media, the media became part of the solution.

Finally, it has to be recognised that it was marketing which provided focus, at a time when all Comic Relief and AMV BBDO had was great ambition and loads of raw energy. Marketing defined a new role for communications: to recruit people as the media. It then helped develop a message to motivate them, while leaving them enough space to create their own way of contributing to the cause.

8

Creating loyal relationships

Introduction

Attracting loyalty from customers is, in a sense, the other side of brand revitalisation: holding on effectively to what you already have. Creating these deep relationships with a loyal and committed group of customers is the source of future cash flow. That is why it is surprising that so many companies still focus too much on acquisition rather than forming stronger bonds with existing customers.

It is hard, of course. The challenge is to create a brand vision or identity that recognises a brand as something greater than a set of attributes that can be imitated or surpassed. Both the case studies in this chapter achieved this.

"If we remember nothing else from these two case studies, we should note that loyalty is not the job of the promotions department. Real underlying loyalty is accomplished when brands deliver coherent, joined-up thinking across all customer contact points.

This will never be achieved if loyalty is treated as promotional points and prizes rather than relentless ongoing delivery of those core brand attributes which attracted the customer in the first place."

Mark Palmer, Marketing Director, Green & Black's

Toyota: using the power of *kaizen* to strengthen customer loyalty

Snapshot: The UK arm of Japanese carmaker Toyota used the company's philosophy of *kaizen*, or continuous improvement, to boost customer loyalty significantly.

Key insights

- When Toyota bought 100% of its UK subsidiary, it started transforming the culture from sales-led to marketing-led, employing the principles of *kaizen*.
- Integral to this was the implementation of an ambitious, comprehensive and centrally driven customer relationship management programme to deliver a "best in class" customer experience.

Summary

Toyota is Japan's leading vehicle manufacturer and one of the largest and most successful carmakers in the world.

The company recognised the need to make marketing a priority in the UK if it was to compete with rivals such as Volkswagen, Renault and Peugeot when it bought 100% of Toyota GB in 2000. In switching from a sales ethos to a more marketing-led strategy, one of the goals Toyota set was to outperform rivals in terms of customer loyalty and reduce the need to capture new customers.

Toyota's network of centres was initially rebranded to give customers a consistently excellent service. But there was also a powerful argument for a centrally driven programme to maintain more regular customer contact, given the average owner's purchase cycle of about 3.7 years and lengthening intervals between services. As the company had traditionally worked with its dealerships and not the end customer, the databases and customer communication channels were sporadic. Toyota undertook a systematic review of the entire organisation. A customer communications group was set up to review the look, tone and frequency of messages and the creation of a new brand identity.

This resulted in the development of a single customer marketing database to form the backbone of all Toyota communications, supported by a revamped website, customer magazine, customer experience surveys and the Toyota Club for premium customers. During a period in which both the overall car market and Toyota's benchmark competition hit a plateau, the brand's customer loyalty rose to 52% in 2004, making it the market leader in retained business. Sales of Toyota cars in the UK in 2004 reached 121 081, a 23% increase on 2001, while membership of the Toyota Club rose by 45%.

Setting ambitious goals

For their first thirty years in the UK, Toyota vehicles were sold, rather than marketed. Distribution was subcontracted to an importer whose ethos was more sales than marketing-driven, and for years, Japanese car imports were capped. As long as demand exceeded supply, "marketing" was hardly a priority.

Then, in 1992, the company began producing cars in the UK. What really transformed the company's ethos, however, was the purchase, in 2000, of 100% of Toyota GB by parent company Toyota Motor Corporation, with the goal of rivalling benchmark brands VW, Renault and Peugeot in sales and image.

Reaching this position would require a fundamental shift from a sales to a marketing mentality. The company knew that it would have to effect a step change in terms of Toyota's product, image and brand consideration. But it was also convinced that the foundations for the brand's growth would be stronger if the quality of the customer's ownership experience outperformed its benchmark competition.

The specific goals it set itself were:

- to deliver a "best in class" overall customer experience;
- to outperform benchmark brands in terms of customer loyalty, reducing the proportionate need to conquest new customers;
- to increase customer revenues dramatically, making the customer programme 100% self-funding.

To drive exceptional customer loyalty, the company knew that it had to have an equally ambitious vision: to deliver not merely customer satisfaction, but customer delight. In other words, it was time for *kaizen* – Toyota's phi-losophy of continuous improvement – to be applied meticulously to improv-ing the customer experience.

Connecting with customers

Customer "relationships" in the car business had two primary channels: centrally controlled broadcast advertising and the intermediated and variable dealer relationship. First, the company began to rebrand the entire Toyota centre network over the next few years to give customers a consistently excel-lent experience. But the level of contact that customers had with dealers was limited: the purchase cycle averaged 3.7 years and service intervals were lengthening.

There was thus a powerful argument for filling this gap with a centrally driven programme to maintain regular customer contact and deliver relevant and valued services. Toyota wanted to build affinity directly with customers while they owned a Toyota, not ignore them for 44 months until they were back in market again.

However, because the company had traditionally faced its dealers, not the end customer, it was not surprising to find the following eye-opening features:

- 21 different databases, but no central customer marketing database;
- 15 different customer telephone numbers with inconsistent service levels;
- no single manager in charge of customer communications;
- a wide range of departments communicating with customers;
- a chaotic range of customer communications material;
- after year one, the customer magazine went only to those who paid for it;
- a website designed for prospects, not for customers;
- low penetration of the Club Toyota service package;
- unimpressive sales of Toyota insurance;
- customer loyalty only slightly above average.

The company was determined that all of these issues would be addressed, but in careful sequence. It was going to be a lengthy journey, requiring dogged determination as well as vision. The solution was the development of a master plan which systematically reviewed company organisation, customer needs, infrastructure, communications and services: all geared to delivering "customer delight" directly from the Toyota brand centre.

Creating the customer-facing organisation

From day one, it was clear that delivering "customer delight" would require an overhaul of all customer-facing elements in the organisation. To manage, coordinate and drive this, a customer relationship marketing (CRM) manager was appointed, with a remit to include the customer database, contact centre, magazine, direct mail and the website, as well as overall management of other customer communications.

The company then set up a Customer Communications Group (CCG), chaired by the CRM manager, comprising all those with communications responsibilities. This group's brief was to review the look, voice, tone, frequency and relevance of all Toyota customer communications. This was followed by the development of a Toyota brand identity "bible", providing a comprehensive framework for the CRM manager and the communications group to unify all customer communications.

Gaining a deeper understanding

Toyota commissioned qualitative research, which told it clearly that customers wanted an ownership experience that was as good as the cars themselves, and for every interaction with the brand to work perfectly, from the buying experience right through the ownership experience. They rejected extrinsic "loyalty solutions" such as points or miles.

In addition, they wanted to be informed, recognised and valued. When they called the Toyota Customer Centre, they wanted the operator to have a record of their history with the brand, and to be empowered to resolve their issue first time. They valued additional customer services, but only those relevant to motoring and travel.

Establishing first principles

The company laid down three customer principles which would act as a guide to all dealings with customers.

Honesty – be clear and open with customers about our intentions.
Value – provide customers with value from the relationship.
Reciprocity – listen as well as talk, give as well as receive.

With these principles in mind, Toyota also agreed that communications should be regular (therefore expected) and be driven by individual customer knowledge (therefore relevant).

Streamlining the infrastructure

During the first 30 years of its existence, Toyota had spawned 21 different individual customer databases. Toyota Insurance, Toyota Warranty, Toyota Financial Services, Fleet, After-Sales, Customer Relations and Club Toyota – each of these silos had its own individual database.

So one of the earliest priorities was to put together a customer marketing database to keep in one place, and in one format, all the relevant information held on individual customers. The eventual goal was a database offering a full 360 degree customer view.

It was clear from day one that a single service-driven customer contact centre was essential (Figure 8.1). The winning supplier was given extensive staff training, test drive days and a working environment similar to a Toyota

Figure 8.1

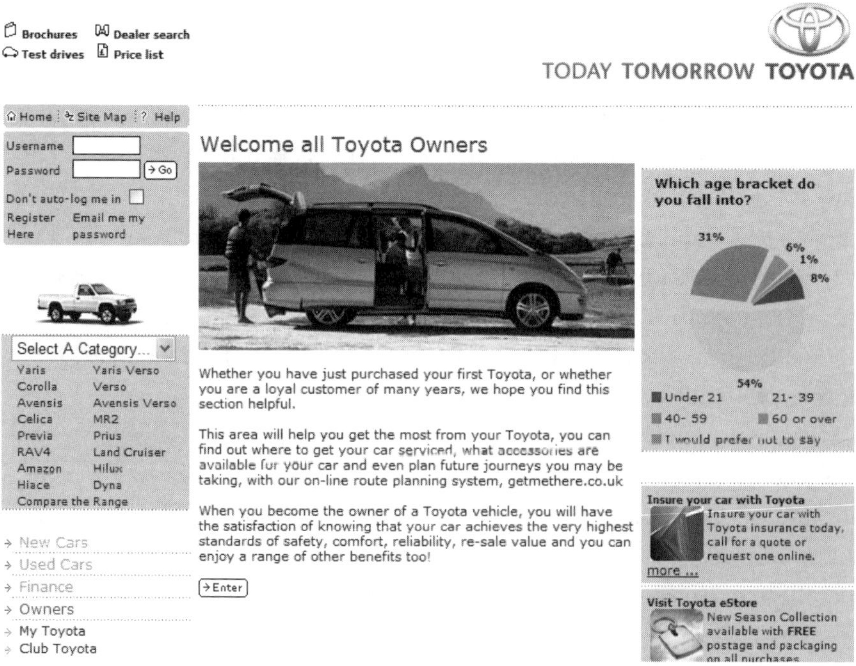

Brochures   Dealer search
Test drives   Price list

TODAY TOMORROW **TOYOTA**

Home   Site Map   Help

Username
Password   → Go
Don't auto-log me in ☐
Register   Email me my
Here   password

Select A Category... ▾

Yaris	Yaris Verso
Corolla	Verso
Avensis	Avensis Verso
Celica	MR2
Previa	Prius
RAV4	Land Cruiser
Amazon	Hilux
Hiace	Dyna
Compare the Range	

→ New Cars
→ Used Cars
→ Finance
→ Owners
→ My Toyota
→ Club Toyota

Welcome all Toyota Owners

Whether you have just purchased your first Toyota, or whether you are a loyal customer of many years, we hope you find this section helpful.

This area will help you get the most from your Toyota, you can find out where to get your car serviced, what accessories are available for your car and even plan future journeys you may be taking, with our on-line route planning system, getmethere.co.uk

When you become the owner of a Toyota vehicle, you will have the satisfaction of knowing that your car achieves the very highest standards of safety, comfort, reliability, re-sale value and you can enjoy a range of other benefits too!

→ Enter

Which age bracket do you fall into?

31%
6%
1%
8%
54%
■ Under 21   21- 39
■ 40- 59   ■ 60 or over
■ I would prefer not to say

Insure your car with Toyota
Insure your car with Toyota insurance today, call for a quote or request one online.
more ...

Visit Toyota eStore
New Season Collection available with FREE postage and packaging on all purchases

Figure 8.2

Centre. Customer-facing operators had to be encouraged to feel very much like "Toyota people", informed and empowered to help customers as much as possible, and encouraged to spend as much time as necessary resolving their issues.

The web was changed as well. The-then toyota.co.uk website had little customer content. It had been initially designed as an online brochure, to inform and interest prospective new car buyers. The new Toyota website was given an owner's section, allowing customers to renew their Club Toyota membership online, and triggering useful email reminders to customers when services, MOT, insurance and car tax renewals were due (Figure 8.2).

Strengthening the customer link

The Toyota Customer Magazine was the main customer communications vehicle. It used to be sent free to customers for their first year of ownership, but if they didn't renew their Club Toyota membership, Toyota stopped sending the magazine. The old magazine had a low circulation, was filled with irrelevant lifestyle articles, was not personalised and lacked calls to action. It mostly went to customers who had just bought a car.

It was slimmed down and had the content focused on Toyota news and travel. The circulation increased to 300 000, while it was delivered free four times a year to all the private customers with cars up to five years old. Each issue carried a Toyota range spread so that customers could see how easily they could change their car without changing their brand. In addition, crammed with calls to action, it was always sent with a personalised letter, with the content driven by individual customer knowledge.

Customer experience surveys became another important customer communication (Figure 8.3). These went to customers after they had bought a car, and after they had had their car serviced. But 75% of customers were failing to complete and return them because they looked intimidating and complicated. So they were redesigned to make them look easier and friendlier, rewritten in plain English and included photos. Response rates shot up from 25% to 55%. The feedback obtained created overall dealer customer experience scores, which were then used to identify specific areas for service improvement, while persistently poor scores triggered a holdback of dealer margins.

Figure 8.3

Joining the club

Club Toyota offered premium-level, pan-European RAC breakdown cover free for one year and then for £55, a fraction of the published price. Unlike other manufacturers' offers, it also provided a wide range of other motoring and travel-related benefits (Figure 8.4).

Toyota owners knew their cars didn't break down often, but RAC research told the company that 90% of calls to them were "customer-induced" – examples being flat batteries and tyres, lost keys and being locked out. So Club Toyota was marketed on the platform of "peace of mind".

In addition to European breakdown and recovery across 36 countries, Club Toyota customers could buy discounted vehicle insurance and inexpensive annual travel insurance. They could save 50% on RAC roadside assistance

Figure 8.4

for any non-Toyota vehicle they might also own, and £30 off driving lessons for any learner drivers in their household. Moreover, every issue of the customer magazine would have a spread featuring additional Club offers, benefits and services, thus encouraging readers who were not members to join.

Considerable efforts were made to increase the renewals rate, particularly as customers neared the end of their first complimentary year of ownership.

Achieving record results

Customer loyalty

Toyota achieved the customer loyalty goal defined at the programme outset.

- Over a period during which both the overall market and the company's benchmark competition had reached a plateau, Toyota's overall customer loyalty increased from 47% in 2001 (the base year) to 48% in 2002, to 49% in 2003 and to 52% in 2004, according to NOP's New Car Buyers' Survey, which covered 28 different brands, with a sample size of almost 40 000 customers.
- In that time, Toyota overtook Volkswagen (at 46%) and Peugeot (44%) and increased its lead over Renault (47%), thus achieving customer loyalty significantly higher than each of the three benchmark competitive brands it set out to beat.
- Toyota customer loyalty grew as premium-sector brands declined over this period. It was now outperforming Mercedes-Benz, BMW and Land Rover (all now down to 50%) and Jaguar (49%), as well as Audi (41%) (Figure 8.5).

Club Toyota membership and revenues

The company easily achieved its goal of a self-funding customer programme. In 2004, sales of Toyota cars reached 121 081, a 23% increase over 2001. It increased Club membership by 45% over the same period to 263 300 (Figure 8.6). 42% of Toyota owners with cars up to eight years old were now members.

Customer loyalty in the UK car market 2001–2004

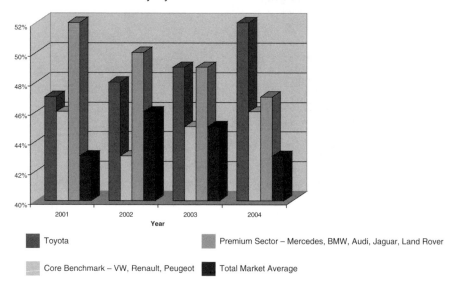

Figure 8.5

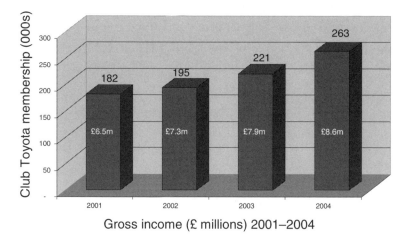

Gross income (£ millions) 2001–2004

Figure 8.6

Club Toyota revenues grew from £6.5 to £8.6 million over the period. The profits made from Club Toyota now paid for the entire customer marketing programme, including the contact centre, database management, the customer magazine, website and all customer communications.

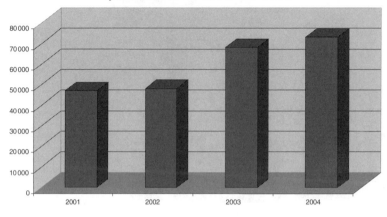

Figure 8.7

Toyota insurance sales

Toyota Insurance sold 72 900 policies in 2004, an increase of 55% over 2001, and way ahead of the original target of 40% by 2005 (Figure 8.7). Club Toyota was now the second biggest source of customers for Toyota Insurance after the dealer network. Every Club handbook had an insurance application form, and together with quarterly Club features in the customer magazine and on the website, helped to drive enquiries in this highly competitive market.

Customer advocacy

According to the UK's consumer magazine *Which?*, by 2004, Toyota enjoyed the highest level of customer advocacy in the UK.

All images appearing in this case study are reproduced by permission of Toyota.

O$_2$: taking the leap into loyalty

Snapshot: O$_2$ focused on cutting down the high levels of customer churn which characterise the mobile phone market by running a simple but highly effective integrated campaign aimed at existing customers.

Key insights

- O$_2$ used fresh thinking about its market to convince cynical customers that they really were important to the company and reduce defections.
- A non-traditional approach to media ensured that the right message got to the right people at the right time.
- The company involved staff to ensure this went beyond an ad campaign and underpinned its behaviour.

Summary

O$_2$ is a leading provider of mobile services, offering communications solutions to customers and companies in the UK and Ireland. It also has integrated fixed/mobile businesses in Germany, the Czech Republic (Telefónica O$_2$ Czech Republic) and the Isle of Man (Manx Telecom). It was acquired by Spanish-based telecommunications group Telefónica in 2005.

By 2005, the huge growth in the mobile market and emphasis on customer acquisitions, rather than retention, meant that churn was becoming a big issue for companies, particularly in the pre-pay sector. O$_2$ realised that it was time to act to boost loyalty among its more fickle customers.

The company decided to offer an inducement to them: 10% back on top-ups. The resulting campaign, in which the company rethought every point of contact, embraced a variety of touchpoints, including TV, SMS, interactive picture messaging, chat room seedings and brand experience days. The company worked hard to convince customers that this was a genuine reward for loyalty.

It worked. The company not only held onto its highest value customers, but churn was reduced to 29% in December 2005, from 37% the year before. There was also a marked shift in brand perception: a 20% uplift in prompted awareness across all channels over the campaign period, and an overall 32% uplift in spontaneous awareness. Among high-value customers, network consideration rose by 28% to lead the market.

Reaching a turning point

The O_2 consumer brand was launched into the hugely competitive mobile sector in the UK in May 2002. The brand entered a market that had enjoyed phenomenal growth in a very short period of time, and which, by 2005, accounted for nearly 2.5% of UK GDP – the same as the entire offshore oil and gas extraction industry, and more than several small countries.

The rapid growth had been fuelled by an intense focus on customer acquisition. However, as the market matured, there was a need for change:

- mobile phone penetration had hit saturation point, at around eight in ten of the population;
- parity in product and service had resulted in a "deal" culture to steal market share;
- this was reflected in unacceptably high churn figures of between 30–35% across the networks.

In fact, research showed that customer defection rates in the mobile telecoms sector stood at 33.4% in 2005, compared to 15.5% in 2003;

As the market exploded, all brands were chasing new customers to grow, rather than looking after their existing customers. On top of this, all operators had failed to create strong brand affinity and emotional attachment. They were not trusted or appreciated by their customers and there was very little loyalty,

The churn issue was even stronger in the pre-pay mobile sector. With no contract to lock them in, customers were free to move around. With more frequent and more tempting offers, they had quickly learned that they only got a good deal by switching or leaving. Being a loyal customer was a mug's game.

A change was needed. O_2 took the bold decision to address the churn issue, and switched the business emphasis firmly onto customer retention. The change towards a loyalty focus would be harder among pre-pay customers, who, unlike contract customers receiving attractive upgrade deals and preferential treatment, felt like second-class citizens – unrewarded and relegated to the back seats.

Research revealed a ray of hope: that O_2 customers wanted recognition and something in return for their loyalty (research also showed that nine in ten customers like to be rewarded) but there were two major barriers to communication cut-through:

- customers were highly suspicious of the small print in promotions;
- customers felt that promotions from different networks lacked differentiation, which meant they were very likely to be ignored.

The company thus faced a big challenge in the pre-pay market. Moreover, this was the most competitive year to date, with competitors easyMobile, Fresh and 3 introducing strong acquisition offerings, seeking to prise away O_2's customers. So how could the company cut through the mind-numbing plethora of deals and a cynical customer to demonstrate a genuine reward for loyalty?

Looking for loyalty

The solution was to create an integrated communications strategy based on the idea of "A world that revolves around you" (Figure 8.8).

Figure 8.8

Figure 8.9

In April 2005, O_2 became the first network to launch a strategy (much imitated since) clearly communicating to customers that their loyalty was recognised and rewarded. The communication was designed to put customers at the very heart of the organisation and ensure that all the propositions reflected the strategy in a relevant, tangible and beneficial way.

The first demonstration of the new "Loyalty rewarded" strategy was a reward campaign to O_2's most promiscuous Pay & Go customers, and was based on the message: "10% of your top-ups back" (Figure 8.9). Mindful of the increasing complexity and cynicism towards offers, simplicity had to be at the heart of communications, since the company was well aware that customers had limited interest in anything that is not very simple. So, not only did the 10% on top-ups have to be communicated simply, but it was vital that customers didn't see it as just a "big gesture" promise.

The company needed customers to make a small gesture of emotional commitment by actively opting-in to receive the 10% of top-ups back. In other words, they had to act.

Rethinking every point of contact

In a deal-rich marketplace, where customer confusion (and often lethargy) reigned, it was felt important to use new methods to cut through to custom-

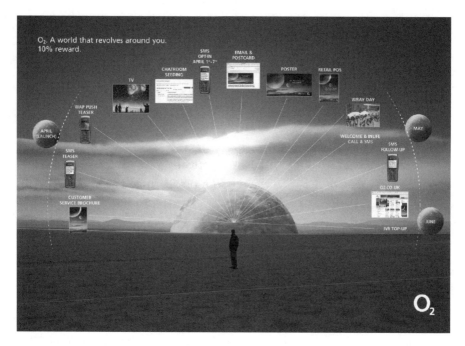

Figure 8.10

ers, encourage them to pay attention and actively opt in to the "10% back on top-ups" offer.

This was achieved by literally revolving around the customer and plotting non-traditional ways to talk to them at key points in their customer journey. That meant looking at the daily life of the customer and, with the company's marketing partners, planning media around them (Figure 8.10).

This included talking to them on their mobiles at different stages in their lifecycle: when they went looking for information online, when they called in to top-up, at home relaxing, in the O_2 stores, out and about with friends and in the street. The company ensured the messages truly revolved around them and their day, and the "10% back" wasn't just a big broadcast campaign: it was about them personally.

The company also employed chat room seeding to spread the word virally. This was a first and was used as another element in marketing to customers' daily lives. Key messages were seeded into chat rooms which fitted the profile of a pre-pay customer. The seeding enabled the company to talk to customers as "one of them", thus bolstering credibility of the offer.

A "World that revolves around you" (WRAY) brand experience day was set up, with the birth of the O_2 angels. For one day, O_2 customers were rewarded for their loyalty with random acts of kindness in an exclusive, branded customer space. Help was on hand from O_2 angels to sign up and deal with phone-related or general problems with life. It was an environment where they could relax and enjoy free massages, flowers, smoothies, and sip one of over 3000 cups of coffee.

O_2 angels were created for staff as well. Briefing packs and posters ensured everyone internally understood the proposition. O_2 angels at the call centres and head office performed random acts of kindness to staff, including shoe shining, car washes and fetching cups of tea and coffee to put them in the mindset of giving back to customers unconditionally.

Segmenting the customers

The O_2 Pay & Go customers were segmented based on value, so that the expenditure, timing and frequency of the messages could be prioritised. This included:

- First-to-know SMS for high-value customers. High-value customers – those most vulnerable to competitive poaching – were put to the front of the queue and contacted first, ensuring they were "first to know", through a teaser SMS.
- TV supported by SMS to drive action. The deployment of SMS coincided with the TV media schedule. The SMS messages were sent after TV ads in key programme breaks, where a high proportion of Pay & Go customers were watching, such as *Champions' League football* and *Desperate House-wives*, It was made clear there were no strings, no catches: the money was theirs.
- Interactive picture messaging (MMS) was sent to high-value data users. The message to known data users – those who send and receive picture messages – was brought to life through images and text with a text "reward" call to action.
- A WAP push to O_2 Active users. Innovative SMS messaging was used to link to the O_2 Active mobile Wap site. High-value O_2 Active users were directed to interactive pages on their mobile handsets, where the message could be driven home.

Getting the right results

A commitment to fresh thinking and non-traditional media resulted in the impressive success of this loyalty initiative. Importantly, O_2 Pay & Go customers made positive leaps in believing that O_2 had the very best intentions to "do right by its customers".

- Millions signed up, making a small gesture of emotional commitment. Just under half of O_2 Pay & Go customers actively texted or called into O_2 to receive their 10% rewards. This also gave the company valuable customer information in what can be the invisible Pay & Go market, where registration of details is not a requirement.
- A high proportion of the annual customer target was achieved in the first three weeks after launch.
- The company held onto its highest value customers.
- More customers stayed with O_2. Churn fell from 37% in December 2004 to 29% by the end of December 2005, which was seen as a huge achievement. 78% stated they would be more likely to stay with O_2 as a result of this campaign.
- Saved revenue from additional retained customers staying with the company ran into the millions.
- The fully integrated campaign achieved a very satisfactory gross return on investment.
- The SMS activity was highly effective in driving registrations among the highest value segment.

In addition, the simplicity of the message resonated with mobile users. Research showed that over one-third said their awareness of the campaign came from word-of-mouth. And 68% rated the rewards offered better than those they had heard/seen from competitive networks.

There was also a huge shift in positive brand perception (Figures 8.11, 8.12 and 8.13). The fully integrated campaign helped achieve a 20% uplift in prompted awareness across all channels over the campaign period, and an overall 32% uplift in spontaneous awareness. Among high-value customers, network consideration rose by 28% to lead the market.

The campaign also saw O_2 leapfrog the competition with huge uplifts to lead the market in brand statements "Looking after customers better" and

Brand image – Offer something different to other network providers

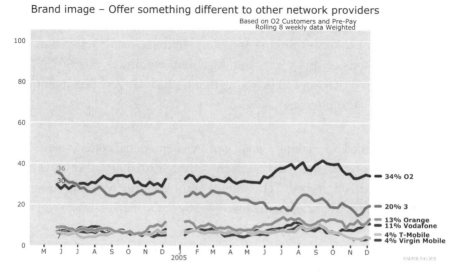

Figure 8.11

Brand image – Are brands that are setting the standards for the future

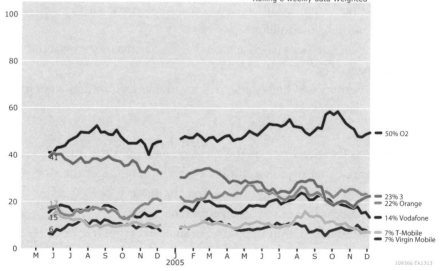

Figure 8.12

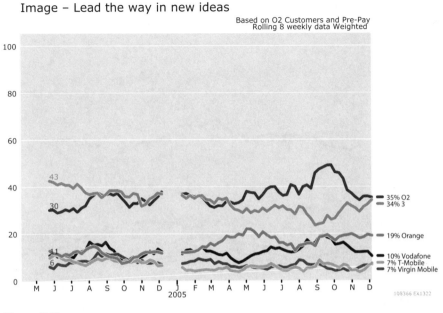

Figure 8.13

"Providing a good customer experience", while among the company's customers during the campaign period, there was a significant uplift in measures that indicated the increased regard that the customers felt for it (Figure 8.14).

Learning invaluable lessons

The company learned a number of important lessons.

- The first was the power of SMS to get customers to act. The total number of registrations during SMS stimulation activity increased three-fold compared to when TV aired alone. Registrations could be directly attributed back to the SMS stimulation activity because O_2 had the ability to track responses by time of day. It also learnt that the optimum time of day to deploy SMS and email to gain maximum response varied between value segments.
- The second was the benefit of spreading positive word-of-mouth through viral seeding of chat rooms. The viral seeding campaign succeeded in

Image – Look after their customers better

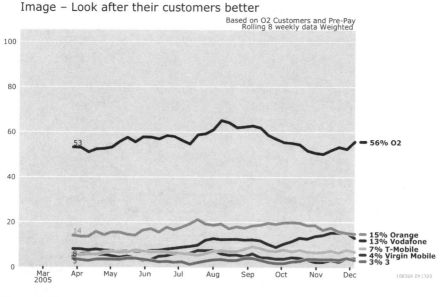

Figure 8.14

reaching 7.6 million people, and achieved the goal of having the brand stand out online. Analysis of chat room conversations confirmed that "Great value and rewards loyalty" was a key message by volume of conversation. The most positive messages were "Easy to sign-up" and "Better than the competition".

In other words, the campaign went beyond being a slick advertising phrase and convinced customers that it signified the whole company's attitude.

9

Crossing borders: international brand development

Introduction

Getting brands to travel successfully across borders is a tough challenge. It demands an approach that exploits the brand's core personality while also reflecting local nuances where necessary. The graveyard of international marketing is littered with brands which were leaders in their national markets but failed to make it in others.

What is noticeable about the case studies in this chapter is that they overcame this. All were based on a powerful idea that had worked very well in one market and which the companies, through careful research and consumer insights, believed could work in others.

"Getting brands to successfully cross borders is indeed one of marketing's great challenges. There is not one single formula for success – no silver bullet. The solutions vary. Sometimes the product formulation and packaging can be consistent, sometimes not. Sometimes the core benefit promise can be consistent, sometimes not. Sometimes the compelling relevant consumer insights work across countries, sometimes not. The same is true for the creative execution and the detailed marketing plan that reaches the target consumer.

So how do you do it? How do you successfully export a successful brand to new markets? What these case studies demonstrate is that you always need to put the consumer first. You need to understand where are the points of consistency between markets, and where are the points of divergence. Properly understanding the local consumer allows you to find out whether the benefit promise is attractive, whether the packaging works, whether the insights connect with consumers, whether the creative execution works.

Where they do, you can proceed. Where they don't, you need to be prepared to adapt, or find an alternative solution that does work across all markets. These companies accomplished this. They put the consumer first, and when you do, replicating the success is achievable."

Gary Coombe, General Manager, Procter & Gamble Fabric and
Homecare New Business Development

The Famous Grouse: a story of international brand migration

Snapshot: This long-established whisky brand conquered new markets around the world with an iconic campaign tailored to individual tastes.

Key insights

- The brand used humour to break free from generic whisky advertising.
- Developing a creative approach that resonated with consumers in widely differing markets helped The Famous Grouse to migrate abroad successfully.

Summary

The Edrington Group is Scotland's leading international premium spirits company. It owns and produces some of the best known brands in the world. This is supported by a number of specialist operations covering every facet of Scotch whisky, including distilling, blending and bottling.

One of its main brands is The Famous Grouse, the leading whisky. In the mid-1990s, the company decided to break away from the traditional approach of whisky, which put the emphasis on the glens and moors of Scotland. Instead, the brand's emblem "broke free" and became a quirky character in witty and unconventional ads.

The success of that approach led the company to consider taking the brand and the campaign to different countries. A clever analysis of the different stages of different markets meant that the ads could be adapted accordingly. The results were gratifying, with The Famous Grouse seeing a strong uplift in awareness and sales. Global growth was +16% year-on-year in 2005 from 2.8 million to 3.2 million cases.

Flying free of convention

One of the Edrington Group's main brands is the leading blended whisky, The Famous Grouse. In the whisky market, product credentials and heritage denote quality, and this essence stems from the past. The Famous Grouse was first blended in 1896 in Perth. From the beginning, it took the high ground with its distinctive nomenclature and premium blended whisky positioning, representing "quality in an age of change". It had always been different from other whiskies: after all, it was named after the game bird its drinkers came to shoot rather than the maker, Matthew Gloag (Figure 9.1). Its brand essence was "naturally unconventional".

The brand and its relationship with consumers had always been personified by the grouse icon, (Figure 9.2). However, beginning in 1996, there was a step change for both the bird and the brand, as the personality was given a significant boost by advertising on TV and 48-sheet posters for the first time. This campaign, developed by AMV BBDO, moved the icon firmly away from its historical habitat of the moors and the glens. This was essential, given that this approach had become generic to the promotion of whisky quality and thus was failing to give the brand its characteristic unconventionality, distinctiveness and differentiation. In other words, it was breaking free from the "whisky cage".

In the new presentations, the bird's actions were framed by a white background and it was given more space and energy for its character to expand. This new bird was a witty, dry, confident and likeable observer of the market.

Figure 9.1

Figure 9.2

Everyone could share his naturally unconventional, humorously quirky observations (Figure 9.3).

After its launch in the UK, the "Icon" campaign achieved the highest spontaneous and prompted ad awareness levels for a whisky brand ever recorded. Enjoyment reached an unprecedented 76%. This appealing and positive campaign rapidly generated a powerful UK brand equity which was distinct from other whiskies (Figure 9.4). It didn't take long for the company to begin to wonder whether and how far the brand and its creative approach could travel to other countries.

Leaving home

The campaign's migration was debated long and hard. It was insufficient to export UK Icon ads everywhere. "Naturally unconventional" meant building real, deeper, indigenous connections with different markets if the brand's sales potential was to be realised. In addition, the company was well aware that many creative ideas, even though effective, don't travel well. Their strength is so deeply grounded in insights particular to their indigenous market that they fail to connect abroad.

With water

On ice

Figure 9.3

After all, the company appreciated that consumers differ massively internationally. The Famous Grouse planned how it could gain consumer acceptance market by market. First, markets were segmented by life-stage: emerging, developing/mature and post-mature markets. Second, consumer insights were mined and identified by market type and "the wave theory" emerged. This was a real discovery, since it enabled the brand to create stronger, deeper relationships with consumers in quite different markets (Figure 9.5).

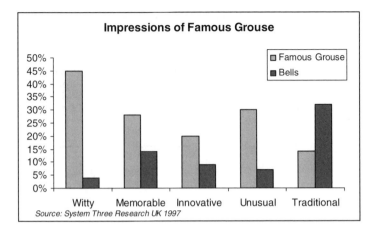

Figure 9.4

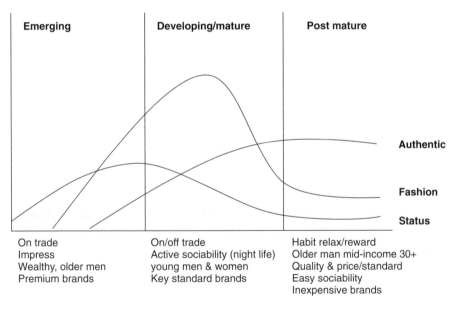

Figure 9.5

Three whisky market drivers were identified – authenticity, fashionability and status. It was a breakthrough in the migration plan. Drilling down into each of these drivers generated specific message dimensions which could be developed to plug the brand's core equity smoothly into differing consumer needs across markets (Figure 9.6).

Emerging market	Developing market	Mature market	Post mature market
Brand	**Brand**	**Brand**	**Brand**
Heritage	Quality	Sociability (deeper)	Sociability (deeper)
Provenance	Status	Relevance	Relevance
Quality	Fashion	Quality	Quality
Status	Sociability (older)	Accessibility	Contemporary
	Authenticity		New news
⟶	⟶	⟶	⟶

A smooth development adapted to market conditions from emerging to post maturity markets

Figure 9.6

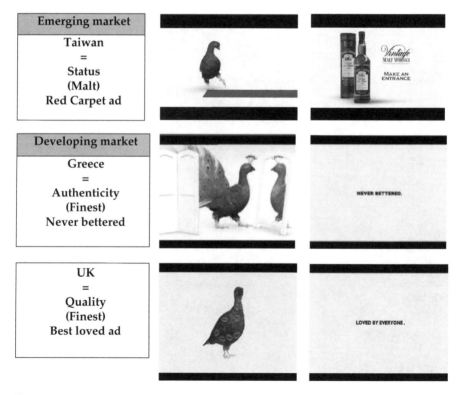

Figure 9.7

These examples demonstrate how the brand communications could be adapted to each market (Figure 9.7). The Famous Grouse personality was kept centre stage, while different messages could be developed to connect with each market's consumers. The brand's essence had international resonance and the Icon campaign embraced international markets with enthusiasm – the vehicle was flexible, production costs were low, and local agencies could easily adapt work. Beak-synch and translation accuracy were not an issue.

By 2005, The Famous Grouse brand was represented in a pool of some thirty pieces of print and TV advertising, each as true to the brand as it was to the markets it served.

A successful migration

The brand advertising was successful in achieving cut-through and being rated as memorable and liked (Tables 9.1, 9.2 and 9.3):

Table 9.1 *Brand advertising success in Taiwan*

Taiwan[a]	Brand driver perception index[b] 2005 vs. 2004	Prestigiousness index 2005 vs. 2004
Johnnie Walker Black	98	93
Matisse	104	102
The Macallan	95	97
The Famous Grouse Malt	**179**	**167**
2004/5 copy: Red Carpet/Goes Down Smoothly/On Ice: 12 yr old malt £1.2 m		

[a] Source: Ipsos Taiwan 2005
[b] Source: Ipsos; The Brand Perception index is an algorithm of five key measures – these vary according to the brand attributes desired in each country.

Table 9.2 *Brand advertising success in Greece*

Greece[c]	Brand driver perception index 2005 vs. 2001	Authentic index 2005 vs. 2001
Johnnie Walker Red	95	93
Cutty Sark	85	85
The Famous Grouse	**122**	**117**
Dewar's White Label	118	105
2005 copy: Never Bettered £400 k		

[c] Source: Ipsos Greece 2005

Table 9.3 *Brand advertising success in the UK*

UK[d]	Reputable	Fun	Brand driver perception index 2005
The Famous Grouse	253	152	171
Bells	68	42	164
Teachers	55	−26	94
Wm Grants	81	0	68
2005 copy: Red Carpet/On Ice/Best Loved £2 m			

[d] Source: Ipsos UK 2005

- it had the highest spontaneous and prompted advertising awareness of any Scotch whisky in the UK;
- it had the highest prompted advertising awareness of any Scotch whisky in Greece;
- in Taiwan, where the Icon campaign launched in September 2004:
  - spontaneous awareness increased ten-fold while competitors declined;
  - prompted awareness increased five-fold, while competitors declined;
  - prompted brand awareness tripled to 69% within three months of campaign launch, achieved with only a 21% share of voice;
- it had the highest enjoyment rating of any Scotch whisky in the UK and Greece;
- it had the highest brand attribution of any Scotch whisky in the UK (97%) and Greece (95%).

In the UK, *Marketing* magazine's Adwatch survey showed that the 2005 Famous Grouse Christmas campaign, with a spend of just £2 million, was in fourth place, putting it in the same league as big-spending UK retailers such as Marks & Spencer and Argos, and beating big-budget players such as the retail chains Sainsbury's, Boots and Woolworths.

In addition, international brand equity scores demonstrated not just the strength of the brand's equity but how it was able to adapt to markets at different stages of development.

- **Taiwan: emerging market dimension – status.** Taiwan had the highest ever brand equity scores after the Icon launch. The Famous Grouse performed above the market, particularly on the key dimension of "Prestige", where brand endorsement was almost double.

- **Greece: developing market dimension – authenticity.** Icon is an established campaign in Greece. In 2005, Greece achieved its highest brand equity scores ever. The brand continued to outperform the market, particularly on the key dimension of "authentic".
- **UK: post-mature market dimension – quality and sociability.** Not surprisingly, after ten years, the brand ruled the roost in the UK with the highest brand equity endorsement. Aligned with its quality and sociability dimensions, it continued as market leader for "reputation" and "fun".

In the broader world of alcohol brands, in autumn of 2005, The Famous Grouse was in the UK YouGov Brand Index top 10, keeping company with Guinness, Smirnoff and Stella Artois, and ahead of any other "brown spirit" competitor.

In the UK, the Icon campaign also delivered a significant longer-term benefit: the ability to maintain a price premium within a highly competitive market. Tracking showed over 51% of respondents thought that The Famous Grouse was "a brand worth paying more for".

Econometric modelling (discounting distribution/promotions, etc.) showed that The Famous Grouse enjoyed a significant price advantage over its competitors through the strength of its brand.

Driving the business

In the UK, The Famous Grouse was the only blended brand to grow market share in 2005, with 2% uplift in a stagnant whisky market where volume growth was minimal and declining relative to other categories of drink (Table 9.4).

Table 9.4 *Volume share in the UK*

Off-trade Volume Share[a]	Moving Annual Total 2004	MAT 2005	% change YOY
The Famous Grouse	10%	12%	+2%
Bells	13%	12%	−1%
Teachers	9%	7%	−2%

[a] Source: Nielsen Off-Trade Volume Market Share

Econometric modelling isolated the impact of the Icon campaign with incremental sales of £7.2m annually, a return on investment of 4:1 – a significant return in this category.

In Greece, econometric modelling isolated the impact of the Icon campaign on volume sales. It showed that it had net incremental sales of 12 416 units, accounting for 3.3% of revenue. Modelling also revealed that the Icon campaign was around 25% more effective in delivering incremental sales.

The campaign also had a marked impact in Taiwan. The Famous Grouse grew its malt volume from 35 000 cases to a staggering 210 000 cases, a sales uplift of +500%, while the category moved at a mere +75% (driven by Grouse). In the same period, its market share went from 8% to 30%, and weighted distribution from 6% to 65%.

A global success

The Icon campaign ran across 20 countries, with the business continuing to reap the rewards. By the end of 2005, according to Edrington internal data, for example:

- there had been global growth to over 3 million cases;
- of this, The Famous Grouse Finest grew at a significantly faster rate than the worldwide category growth of only 1–2%;
- the introduction of blended malt resulted in exponential growth, the most successful new product launch in the brand's history, primarily driven by the stunning successes in Taiwan.

Other sales highlights for 2004/5 year-on-year rises internationally included:

- The UK up 7%;
- Spain up 6%;
- Portugal up 7%;
- Bulgaria up 23%;
- Germany up 34%;
- Russia up 27%;
- USA* up 8%.

(Sources: ACNielsen March 05; *Adams liquor report 2004)

The brand has now successfully traveled to 100 countries, with international sales now representing the majority of the brand's sales revenue. The Famous Grouse is represented by a portfolio of nine products around the world.

All images appearing in this case study are reproduced by permission of Famous Grouse.

Olivio/Bertolli: selling the Mediterranean idyll

Snapshot: The emphasis on emotional engagement with the brand helped Unilever establish Olivio/Bertolli across European borders.

Key insights

- Unilever decided to think "big" rather than global in rolling the successful UK brand out across northern Europe, by emphasising converging attitudes to life rather than differing food tastes.
- By exploiting the idea of how people want to live, rather than how they want to eat, the company was able to produce consistent cross border campaigns that resonated with consumers in different countries.

Summary

Unilever is an international manufacturer of leading brands in food, home care and personal care. Its 2005 revenues were almost €40 billion.

In 1997, Unilever rolled out Olivio, the successful UK olive oil spread, into the rest of Europe. The company already had an olive oil product in Europe under the Bertolli brand name, so the spread was rolled out as Bertolli. However, the Olivio marketing mix was retained in terms of product formulation, pricing strategy and packaging approach. The question was whether the highly effective UK communications mix would translate effectively to other markets and work in what is the most parochial of categories.

The company decided that the solution lay in thinking "big" rather than global. Rather than focusing on the rational health benefits of the brand, the strategy used olive oil as a symbol of an entire way of life – the Mediterranean idyll – that was becoming increasingly desirable and aspirational. This meant targeting attitudes to life, which were converging across borders, rather than food, where attitudes are far more diverse. This led to a campaign that engaged consumers in the same way in Germany, Holland and Belgium.

The result was a growth in the brand of 150% in just four years, with Olivio/Bertolli becoming the fastest growing food brand in Europe in 2001. The marketing model also created a new approach in terms of managing the process of international marketing.

The beginning: finding a third way for international marketing

Food has always been seen as the most difficult category to internationalise, with different eating habits and traditions mitigating against the creation of a consistent international approach to marketing. Marketers have traditionally adopted one of two very different models:

- the "one size fits all" model, offering cost efficiencies but low consumer engagement;
- the "think local" model, allowing a bespoke but extremely expensive approach by region.

Global food marketing seemed caught in the traditional tensions between efficiency and effectiveness. However, as the marketing community was increasingly focused on achieving international synergies and genuinely global brand properties, neither of these offered a viable blueprint for the future. Unilever alone had pledged to cull its brands from 1600 to 400, with a view to developing a core portfolio of global "power" brands.

That meant marketers had to find an approach that was genuinely both efficient and effective, and one that was not just okay in all markets, but great in all markets. The company solved this dilemma by developing a third model: one which involved thinking big rather than global, by focusing on the way people want to live, rather than the way they want to eat.

Getting the brand to travel

Olivio was the first spread to contain olive oil. It was created in the UK by Unilever with a view to a possible roll-out to other markets. It grew strongly in the UK over several years, reaching more than a 2% share by the end of

Figure 9.8

1997. Its UK success was driven by a campaign that focused on older, healthy Mediterraneans, which built up genuine emotional resonance for the brand, setting it apart from own-label imitations which had dogged Olivio since launch, and stolen share (Figure 9.8).

This campaign generated a complete turnaround in Olivio's fortunes:

- targets were met ahead of schedule, achieving a record 182% growth between 1995–1997;
- share of olive oil spreads rose from 23.1% to 43.7% over the relaunch period;
- own-label users traded up to Olivio;
- the price premium over own-label increased from 37p in 1996 to 45p in 1997.

Given the success in the UK, plus a changing business climate focusing on international synergies, it was decided to roll out the Olivio mix across Europe. Unilever already had an olive oil presence under the Bertolli brand name and chose to introduce olive oil spreads as Bertolli, but retained the Olivio model in all other aspects of the mix, such as product formulation and pricing strategy. However, given the importance of communications as a sales driver in the UK, the company's key concern was whether the same campaign would work across markets.

The initial markets chosen apart from the UK were Belgium, Germany and Holland. The outlook for successfully developing a single international campaign was inauspicious. Received wisdom suggested that local differences would make developing one meaningful advertising campaign across four markets difficult, if not impossible. For instance, an analysis of food advertising across the world showed that Heinz had aired 33 different executions across 19 countries, Knorr 95 executions across 32 countries and Lipton 35 executions across 28 countries.

Finding a common idea

The company reckoned that the key to the successful international roll-out lay in the breakthrough thinking that lay behind the original UK strategy. Rooted in extensive analysis among opinion formers, it had unearthed a new trend. In reaction to the punitive health regimes of the 1980s, people were increasingly adopting a more holistic attitude, one which the company called "positive health".

Conjuring up images of happy, relaxed individuals enjoying life, the Mediterranean was seen as the cradle of "positive health". More importantly, olive oil was seen as the epitome of this Mediterranean lifestyle. So, rather than selling generic longevity, Olivio created a whole brand based on the Mediterranean idyll of enjoying a longer, fuller life.

By tapping into an idea about how people want to live, rather than how they want to eat, this campaign transcended everyday attitudes to food and health and connected with consumers at a higher level. Examining its other markets, the company discovered that, although differences in specific eating habits were manifold, common trends emerged at this level. Attitudes to food remained diverse, but attitudes to life were converging. Olivio's focus on higher-order benefits offered the key to extending the brand into other markets. Just as the Mediterranean dream bypassed everyday attitudes to food in the UK, it appeared to unite consumers across countries.

A report in 1996 found that the notion of balance was becoming increasingly important across Europe. When asked to define healthy eating, "balance/variety" was mentioned by 48% of the sample within key countries, making it the highest scoring definition in these markets. Moreover, *Health and the European Consumer, 1996* stated that while the actual level of olive oil penetration and usage varied, there was a common association of olive oil with the Mediterranean lifestyle and a shared belief in its benefits.

Client teams in other European countries were convinced that the appeal of positive Mediterranean health transcended local attitudes to food. They felt that the European markets were ripe for the message. Olivio/Bertolli had captured not just a health trend, but a macro-shift in the way consumers aspired to live.

This approach was an unconventional way of thinking about international advertising, as it did not start out as an international campaign. The immediate focus was to make it work in the UK. The secret of the campaign's success was that it thought "big" from the beginning: success in the UK required a major emotional connection to transcend the national nuances of price and product differentiation. Success in the rest of the world, on the other hand, demanded an emotional connection that would transcend local attitudes to food, health and yellow fats.

Crossing borders

Belgium was the first new market to receive the marketing mix, with the Bertolli spread launched in 1997. As in the UK, this launch created the olive oil spread sector. The media plan comprised substantial national investment in TV, split more or less evenly across the Flemish-speaking north and the French-speaking south of the country.

The Belgian team also extended the campaign idea into direct marketing, targeting the brand's core audience in March 1998 with *Gazetta*, a newsletter featuring information on healthy eating and the Mediterranean lifestyle, and drawing on imagery from one of the popular TV campaigns. Research showed there was 42% awareness of the mailing among the target audience, with 30% mentioning the link with the TV ad.

The result was the most successful launch in the category for ten years, reaching 5000 tonnes in less than three years.

This success accelerated the roll-out plans for other countries. Holland launched Bertolli spread in 1998 but without marketing support. But sales were disappointing. So, in 2000, Holland began to use two of the most popular television ads. The Dutch team was also active in supporting the brand in other forms of marketing promotions: images from the TV were used in stores in support of the olive oil parent brand, reinforcing the link between the two. There was also an online campaign which offered consumers a step-by-step guide to hosting dinner parties the Italian way, with recipe advice and invitations that could be printed off and sent to friends.

Finally, the German team relaunched its olive oil spread as Bertolli in June 2000, using the same two ads as Holland, the first in 2000, followed by the next in 2001. As Germany is a large market, and other media are disproportionately expensive, TV advertising was the main channel for marketing support.

Deepening the emotional connection

Views about how the campaign was working in the UK evolved over time. A 1998 review highlighted the opportunity to increase trial among younger consumers, who found the idea of Olivio aspirational but who had yet to try it. Then, in April 1999, Benecol spread was launched with a promise to reduce cholesterol. Unilever believed, however, that the role for Olivio was not to compete with this brand on a rational basis, but to deepen the emotional connection with consumers.

This evolution of the campaign had two objectives:

- draw in younger consumers by increasing relevance and "youthfulness";
- create even greater emotional engagement with Olivio by increased emphasis on full enjoyment of life.

The idea was that eating Olivio meant joining "Club 18–130". Ads showed the familiar elderly characters on holiday. This played on the Club 18–30 concept and introduced a youthful zest for life into the brand. Four TV executions were developed, along with print executions for 6-sheets and women's magazines. Packaging was revised, with the pack's aluminium seal urging consumers to join the club (Figure 9.9).

This approach helped deepen consumers' relationship with the brand and led to a significant increase in volume from younger consumers. In fact, under-35s accounted for 10.3% of total volume in 1998, rising to 16.2% in 2001. Penetration among this group in the UK rose by 5% year-on-year in the first year of "Club 18–130". The brand grew at the fastest rate since launch, rising from a 3.8% to 5.4% value share within three weeks. Belgium

Figure 9.9

also rolled out this campaign, where value share rose to 12% and volume share to 9% at the peak of the campaign.

There was now a clear model for campaign evolution. At launch, the brand would establish its proposition of enjoying a longer, fuller life, boosting trial among the core target market. Over time, it would evolve to embrace a broader view of the Mediterranean zest for life, deepening the relationship and drawing in younger consumers.

Savouring success

By the end of 2001 the brand had built critical mass in four markets and was achieving impressive results (Table 9.5 and Figure 9.10). It had reached a total volume of around 30 000 tonnes with combined sales worth around €100

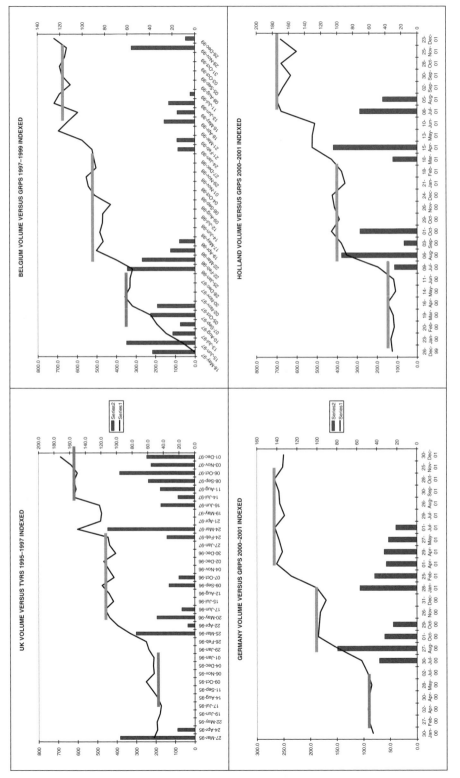

Figure 9.10

Table 9.5 *Impressive results in four markets*

	Penetration % (Total households)		Average weight of purchase (per HH)		Volume share % (Total market)	
	Pre	Post	Pre	Post	Pre	Post
UK	3.8	19.8	2.5	2.75	2	4.2
Belgium	17.2	22.3	2.4	3.3	0.2	7.3
Germany	4.6	8.2	1.2	1.8	1	2
Holland	2.8	5.3	1.2	1.8	0.1	1.4

million, making it the fastest growing Unilever brand in Europe in 2001. Germany and Holland led this brand growth, with an average 200% volume growth year-on-year since launch. The UK and Belgium grew more slowly as the markets matured, but, nevertheless, volume grew by 8.5% over a three-year period.

To see such sales growth build in such a markedly similar way across four different markets was extremely unusual. However, it proved the value of having a big idea on a global level that also enabled implementation on a local scale to deal with local sensitivities, but remained true to the core of the brand. It also led to considerable savings: the company estimated that this coordinated approach saved about £3 million.

Nicorette: fighting the right battles

Snapshot: Pfizer transformed the fortunes of Nicorette across very different markets by positioning it as a consumer, rather than a pharmaceutical, brand.

Key insights

- Pfizer realised that it had to look for the underlying human truths to get its brand to travel, since attitudes toward health and smoking differed so much. This meant turning it into a consumer brand.
- It personified the fight against cravings in the form of a memorable brand character.
- Giving it a high profile that resonated with consumers would encourage them to ask pharmacists for it by name, rather than asking for suggestions.

Summary

Pfizer is one of the world's leading research-based pharmaceutical companies. Its 2005 revenues were $51.3 billion.

Pfizer's Nicorette had been marketed to its natural pharmaceutical environment since its introduction in 1967. But by 2000, Pfizer was faced with the challenge of achieving aggressive international growth in the face of intensifying competition by developing it as a powerful international brand. That meant repositioning Nicorette by basing the strategy on a core insight: that while pharmaceutical brands don't travel, consumer brands based on fundamental human truths do.

It was a challenge to find an approach that resonated with consumers across borders, given the varied attitudes to giving up smoking in Europe. The company thus decided to treat Nicorette as a consumer brand and, instead of advertising a series of culturally specific attributes, the company tapped into a fundamental human truth: giving up smoking isn't a war, but a series of battles against each cigarette.

Nicorette could help someone give up one craving at a time. The resulting campaign used across media was centred around a 2.5 m high cigarette with arms, legs and a face, which personified the problem smokers face.

By ignoring the conventions of pharmaceutical brands, the company succeeded in developing a truly international brand. The campaign began in 2001, with Nicorette recording a 39% growth in volume sales by 2004. The creative idea travelled from six to 21 countries over two years and established the brand as the clear market leader.

The beginning: deciding the brand strategy

Nicorette began life in 1967. It was originally developed by the Swedish navy as a tobacco substitute for submariners. It was first licensed as a pharmaceutical product, and was made available to consumers in 1978. In 2000, the advertising agency AMV BBDO was appointed by what was then Pharmacia, and is now Pfizer, to establish Nicorette as the dominant player across Europe in the face of increasing and aggressive competition.

The strategy centred around one core insight: pharmaceutical brands don't travel across borders, but consumer brands built on fundamental human truths do. After all, attitudes towards health vary markedly across countries, which makes developing international pharmaceutical brands a problem. This is particularly true when it comes to smoking, and is exacerbated by regulation that varies across markets. A claim made in one country might not be approved in another.

The company realised that there would be limited international potential in trying to develop a platform based on culturally specific insights. It needed something built on a far more universal and fundamental human truth. It needed, in other words, a consumer brand.

Nicorette faced a number of business issues which, apart from the company's international aspirations, called for the development of a strong brand:

- **Increased competition**. Competitors had started to launch new products, like NiQuitin's clear patch, which presented serious challenges to the Nicorette business. The option of launching improved products to counter this threat was precluded by the lead times required for pharmaceutical development, especially given the regulatory environment. New product development could only come from a long-term solution. An immediate rebuttal was needed through smarter marketing of existing offerings.

- **Nico-confusion**. All the products in this category were based on nicotine replacements. Being pharmaceutical products, there are stringent regulations governing their names. As a consequence, all products sounded strikingly similar: Nicorette, NiQuitin, Nicotinell, Nicopatch, Nicopass. In addition, they were all based on the same science and boasted comparable efficacy levels. Not surprisingly, people saw little difference between the products.
- **The power of the pharmacist**. In many markets, the product sits behind the pharmacy counter. People who are uncertain which product they want are liable to be swayed by the pharmacist. If the company could get people to ask for the brand by name, pharmacists would rarely switch them to a competitive product.

Connecting with consumers

International aspirations meant the company also needed it to be a consumer brand, because the brands that cross borders successfully are consumer brands, based on deep insights and understanding of the target audience. The truly strong international brands, such as Nike, Pepsi and Apple, connect with people emotionally, not just rationally. Talking about efficacy and creating communications that addressed the "science of quitting" would not be a big enough or, in fact, branded enough idea.

Attitudes to health vary across countries and across the world. This is part of the reason there are so many small, local pharmaceutical brands. Attitudes to smoking also vary significantly across Europe. In some places, tobacco advertising is banned. In others, there are rigorous government-sponsored anti-smoking campaigns.

In 2004, smoking bans were already in force in public places in a number of European Union (EU) countries, and were being mooted in a number of others. While a general public acceptance of the dangers of smoking pervaded a large swathe of the continent, elsewhere the attitude was far more laissez-faire. Some territories even reported increases in both penetration and frequency of smoking.

With such varied attitudes towards the health risks of smoking, focusing on an "it's obvious you should give up" pharmaceutical solution didn't seem likely to resonate across Europe. What the company learned when it spoke to smokers confirmed that it needed to think of Nicorette not as a pharmaceutical, but as a consumer, brand.

For smokers, smoking was a lifestyle choice. Smoking and their brand of cigarettes were as much a part of who they were as the beer they drank or the car they drove. Smokers didn't think of themselves as sick, nor did they think of smoking as a disease. They didn't believe they needed medicine to help them give up.

What they did like, however, was a bit of aid or assistance. They didn't want anything patronising or didactic. They wanted something that felt like it was on their side. The real potential in this market was for a champion of smokers as consumers, and one that felt like it was for, rather than against, them.

Cross-border insights

Pfizer knew from desk research that most smokers made four to five attempts before successfully giving up. This was true of smokers everywhere. The breakthrough came from qualitative research. The company found that the struggle to give up smoking wasn't just about the headline of kicking the habit. Quitters didn't tend to focus on the idea that they were stopping smoking as much as they did on just not reaching for the next cigarette. It wasn't some great war that they found themselves immersed in, but a succession of individual battles against the next cigarette or craving.

The key was to focus on how Nicorette could help fight the battles with each individual cigarette by reducing the physical craving that makes quitting so hard. Every defeated craving is a victory and one more step towards being smoke-free.

This strategic insight led to the core thought for the advertising: "Beat cigarettes one at a time with Nicorette". This idea reflected smokers' reality and left them feeling empowered, with each cigarette they managed to beat a triumph in itself.

The creative device developed for all the advertising was "cravings man", a 2.5-metre cigarette with arms, legs and a face. He represented cravings – those urges that come over smokers as they are trying to quit. Each ad showed a smoker literally beating a craving as he appeared. This creative mechanic was an expression that travelled across borders, because it reflected an insight that applied to all smokers everywhere. It also had the flexibility to be taken through the line to online, PR and point-of-sale, which allowed the company to reinforce its message through a highly integrated communications campaign.

"Cravings man" was launched in the UK, Scandinavia and France, as the press advertisements from the UK and France show (Figures 9.11 and 9.12).

Figure 9.11

Figure 9.12

In the UK, tracking research confirmed that the creative vehicle was helping to build brand awareness. Econometric modelling showed these ads to be very successful, with one burst of the version "Karate" delivering a return of over £14 for every £1 spent.

All the world's a stage

The big challenge for 2003/4 was to roll out the strategy and creative device to an array of very different markets. These included southern Europe (where attitudes to smoking in general were a lot more relaxed than northern Europe) and eastern Europe, where there was little awareness of nicotine substitutes, let alone how they worked.

The strategy and creative idea thus had to earn their way across Europe. As a company, Pfizer didn't impose ideas centrally, but rather gave each market autonomy to develop the idea they felt most appropriate to their market. Each country was invited to pre-test the idea of "cravings man" using the Millward Brown LINK test methodology. The purpose of the test was to assess the suitability of the idea for a market, and, if suitable, to suggest ways in which the idea could be optimised for a market, as the example of the approach in the Baltic states illustrates (Figure 9.13).

The results of the pre-testing research were even more positive than the company had dared expect:

- **Czech Republic**. All three films ("Karate", "Killing Time" and "Café Girls") scored above the norm on every measure, a consistently higher benchmark than the norm for over-the-counter (OTC) drug commercials.
- **Italy**. "Karate" and "Holiday" were tested and received high scores. For both films, more than 65% of respondents said they couldn't fail to remember it was a Nicorette ad. Millward Brown described the results as some of the best the researchers had ever seen.
- **Germany**. Initial results were mixed for the two films tested, "Killing Time" and "Karate". While both executions were well-remembered, there was a reasonably high level of dislike of the perceived violence in the spot, and apathy toward the intended message. The company then tested a new ad, "Holiday", which had a simpler message. Both "Holiday" and "Karate" were also re-edited to minimise the perceived violence. Re-testing the films saw dramatically improved results.

The advertising continued to be successful in the developed markets. Since tracking started in the UK in 2002, advertising awareness in that market rose from 21% to 41%. The company also managed to open up a 25% gap between Nicorette and its competitors.

Sales soar

Across Europe, Pfizer saw 39% growth in volume sales over the course of the campaign, from 2001 to 2004. The category grew by 34% over the same

Figure 9.13

period, so the company was keeping ahead of a very dynamic market. Its share of market grew from 33.2% in the first quarter of 2004 to 42% in the third quarter.

In particular countries, the results were impressive:

• **UK**. The share grew from 28.4% to 38.7% between the first and third quarters of 2004.

- **Czech Republic**. According to IMS data, Nicorette volume grew 42% once the advertising began.
- **Estonia and Latvia**. Once the advertising started, volume grew by 361% in Estonia and 240% in Latvia.
- **Germany**. Despite an aggressive campaign from Nicotinell, Nicorette maintained market leadership and doubled its volume of patches.
- **Italy**. Growth was double that of the market, resulting in an 89% share.
- **Spain**. Nicorette was still number one, with growth ahead of that of the market.

All images appearing in this case study are reproduced by permission of Nicorette.

10

Internal marketing: engaging employees

Introduction

Winning the hearts and minds of employees would seem to be the first step in ensuring and improving good performance. After all, what is a company but its employees? This is becoming an even more pressing issue as levels of service are increasingly an important source of competitive differentiation.

The challenge for internal marketing is not only to get the right messages across, but to embed them in such a way that they both change and reinforce employee behaviour. It can't be a one-off effort. Otherwise it breeds disillusioned employees who have seen it all before.

"How many companies have you come across who launch a new vision or strategy or a set of new company values to their unsuspecting employees at a major event with a crescendo of activity, only to find that three months later, launch binders remain unopened on shelves, and the only evidence of employee involvement is the tea-stained branded mug by the photocopier?

To be successful, any internal marketing initiative must connect with employees at all levels in an exciting and engaging way. To become a topic of conversation at the coffee machine, it must communicate in a relevant and appropriate way, and talk in language that appeals to all. Consistency, scale and longevity will then motivate employees to change behaviours over time and take action to promote the cause as their own.

Both of these case studies, from Microsoft and Comet, demonstrate how effective internal marketing campaigns can be. Microsoft used a high profile topical character in communications and training materials to challenge employees to change behaviours and align behind their new company values, with outstanding results.

Comet needed employees to raise their game as they sought to change their service delivery and become more customer focused. They implemented innovative e-learning modules, communications and celebration events to put employees at the heart of their brand strategy.

Both case studies are excellent examples of the power of internal marketing."

Paul Philpott, Commercial Director, Toyota (GB) plc

Microsoft: winning the hearts and minds of employees

Snapshot: Microsoft's decision to use the award-winning *Office* star Ricky Gervais to get the message about the company's values across in a memorable and humorous manner proved highly effective.

Key insights

- Microsoft successfully employed a high profile comedian to ensure its new set of values made a real difference to company behaviour and performance.
- This overcame the scepticism that many internal marketing programmes engender.

Summary

Microsoft is the world's leading software company, with 2005 sales of almost $40 billion.

In 2003, the company decided that it wanted to concern itself not only with new technologies, but also its identity as a company and how it managed its business internally. To this end, it evolved its existing company values to embrace six primary attributes: passion, respect, accountability, integrity, self-criticism and eagerness.

The roll-out strategy to ensure this ethos was communicated to employees was defined in three stages. First, there was a campaign across the UK to generate positive feeling about the project. Second, a series of roadshows was held around the firm's UK offices to discuss the core values in depth. Third, a compulsory education programme was introduced to ensure all staff understood the proposition.

The creative for the "Office values" campaign centred on the David Brent character from BBC sitcom *The Office*. The humour of the character was used as an effective foil for the message Microsoft was trying to convey, attracting employees to the project. Buoyed by the involvement of Ricky Gervais, creator of *The Office*, a special 15-minute video of the sitcom was filmed, centred on the "Office values" philosophy.

This had an immediate impact with Microsoft employees, with feedback indicating high recognition levels for the main message of the campaign. It had such an impact that the initiative was picked up by the national press – something highly unusual for an internal marketing strategy.

Steering the company values

Microsoft used 2002–2003 to take stock of itself and its mission: to enable people and businesses throughout the world to realise their full potential in the face of both negative industry events (such as the demise of companies like Enron and Andersen) and the positive, onward growth of the PC marketplace worldwide – in which Microsoft would continue to play a bigger role with more responsibilities.

The company identified that its mission is not solely about building great technology, but also about who it is as a company and as individuals, how business is managed internally and how it works with partners and customers. Change on a global scale is never easy. Microsoft needed people who were creative, energetic, bright and absolutely committed to their mission.

It also recognised the positive impact on customer and partner loyalty if it adopted a core set of "instructions" that helped its people to deliver against customer expectations. Great people with great values automatically have passion for customers and partners and are accountable for achieving quality results.

To this end, Microsoft evolved its existing company values to better support its core brand proposition: "Realising Potential". The six evolved values were seen as mission-critical to the Microsoft brand, which underpins the value of the company. In addition, a values-based plan was put in place to help balance the drive of innovation and continued profit growth with the core "Value" propositions.

In April 2003, Microsoft CEO Steve Ballmer launched the company's six core values worldwide, declaring that "This is not a nice to have – it's a need to have." Together, the six values combined to form a behaviour standard that would set Microsoft apart for its customers, partners, investors, employees and potential employees.

As one of the main drivers of business success, Steve Ballmer instructed that the six core values be woven into every employee-related process at

Microsoft, from performance evaluations to dismissal policies. As such, all staff would undertake compulsory training on the values.

The six core values

- **Passion:** gain respect, build and maintain long-term relationships with customers.
- **Respectful and open:** share information and encourage others to express their viewpoints.
- **Accountable:** take responsibility for results achieved by yourself, your team and group, and create goals that benefit all stakeholders.
- **Integrity and honesty:** earn the trust of others. Communicate in a direct and truthful manner.
- **Self-critical:** seek opportunities and feedback for personal and pro-fessional development. View each experience as an opportunity for learning.
- **Eager to take on big challenges:** consider the critical issues. Take smart risks and accept the consequences that go with them.

Meeting tough objectives

The Microsoft team in the UK was quick to take on the challenge in the face of extremely aggressive values objectives, outlined globally as follows:

- 100% of staff to attend the up and coming values training sessions and be able to identify why values are important in the 2004 financial year.
- 100% of staff know the six values and can communicate them, within three months of launch.
- 100% of staff know where to go subsequent to training to secure further information.
- 100% of staff react positively to the values campaign.

A three-stage strategy was developed:

Phase 1: EXCITE. A Microsoft UK-wide campaign to generate positive feeling from staff about the project (June/July 2003).

Phase 2: INFORM. A series of roadshows around Microsoft UK offices to discuss the values in more depth (August 2003) plus a presentation at the company conference in September.
Phase 3: EDUCATE. Compulsory values education commences (September 2003 onwards).

This was going to be a big challenge. A dedicated Microsoft Roadshow Team had been set up in the UK in April 2003 to explain and evangelise the six Microsoft core values. Even though the values mandate came from the top down, there was very little, and often no, interest across the UK subdivisions of Microsoft to have this team visit them.

So the team clearly needed an innovative, radical solution to grip the entire audience (this had never been achieved before in an internal campaign – typically, internal campaigns had previously secured interest from very specific sectors of staff only).

This values initiative had to reach everyone – engage, excite and inform across *all* staff levels. The chosen route also had to provide a memorable platform from which to drip feed further communications during the following months.

Getting staff to pay attention

The David Brent character from the UK hit TV series *The Office* was always the first choice of Creative Direction, the agency working with Microsoft UK, to front this internal campaign for Microsoft. But, with a limited budget of just £50000 to spend on delivering the entire campaign from start to finish, the agency's negotiation skills were about to be tested. *The Office* and Ricky Gervais were at the peak of sitcom success, so this was indeed an exciting prospect.

Further, the agency knew the "David Brent" persona, adopting a personal spin on values, could provide the effective, humorous foil that it was looking for: a radical and memorable approach to the Microsoft values thinking and a twist on how full-time staff would be expected to (or rather not to) conduct themselves in the business.

So Creative Direction took the brief to Ricky Gervais and his co-writing partner Stephen Merchant. They were delighted to get involved with the project, and together they formulated an approach. Ricky and Stephen went on to write and star in the 15-minute video production – Gervais as David

Brent being interviewed by hapless Microsoft communications manager, Geoff Bowles (Merchant). A hilarious interview, centred around the whole values philosophy, ensued.

In addition, six posters were put up featuring David Brent's typical take on the six individual values – compared to what the values really stood for (Figures 10.1 to 10.6). These posters were so sought after that they were eventually auctioned for charity to internal staff.

Creating widespread excitement

Following final production of the "Office Values" video, a premiere opening-night screening event was held in Microsoft's auditorium in its Thames Valley Park headquarters in Reading. Attendance at the premiere was strictly

Figure 10.1

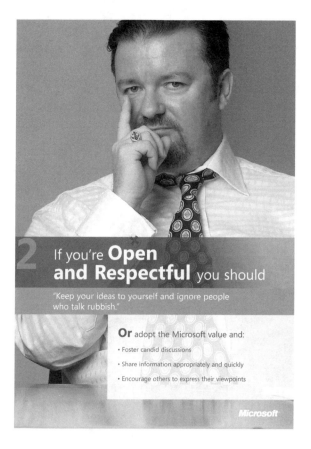

Figure 10.2

controlled via a "first come, seat allocated" competition launched on Microsoft's staff intranet.

The competition was communicated using UTV, Microsoft's internal TV
channel, Umail, Microsoft's internal email channel, campus posters, leaflets
and atrium banners, as well as through e-blasts and teaser voicemails to staff
smart phones.

The "Values" pages on the intranet site were updated and revised prior
to the competition going live, to provide a useful reference tool on the initiative. Once online, Microsoft people were asked six randomly selected
questions on the values. If they answered all six questions correctly, they
were immediately allocated a seat at the event (400 in total). The impact
was immediate – all seats were allocated within two hours of the competition
going live.

Figure 10.3

Keeping the message alive

The "Office Values" video thus became THE demand generation tool for the values roadshow team. The premiere screening had created the desired "buzz" around the business and now requests came flooding in from all around the UK for the team to visit and to show the video as part of their training session – even from ex-pats living as far abroad as the USA and South Africa. An online booking facility for the roadshow team went live on the values intranet site for other parts of the UK's business to book the team to attend departmental meetings and sessions.

The values roadshow team quickly built its session around the video, and created further support materials to reinforce the message. A booklet of the

Figure 10.4

script was created to be given to every attendee, as well as a pocket-sized card outlining Brent's guide to the six core values.

The video was used again at the Microsoft company conference in September.

Staff feedback

"Brent delivers an unconventional approach to our office values . . . truly unforgettable." Excerpt from *U..Magazine*, Microsoft's internal magazine.

"Often work-related info can be relayed badly – i.e., boring. Not so with this video. Very well thought-out and it conveyed the correct message. If only all presentations about the business were this fun, people might actually want to go to them."

Figure 10.5

Achieving measurable results

Directly due to the success of the "Office values" internal marketing campaign, the six core global values of Microsoft were now comprehensively retained across the board in the UK. At the end of September 2003, a quick sample of 100 Thames Valley-based employees (approximately 5% of the Thames Valley population) were selected randomly and questioned against the original campaign objectives to gauge the success of the campaign (Table 10.1).

The results speak for themselves:

• Between 23rd June and 10th July 2003, the campaign actively generated 1720 unique visits to the values website, which equates to approximately 86% of the Microsoft UK population in total.

Figure 10.6

Table 10.1 *Results of a poll taken in September 2003*

Campaign objective	Polled results (from 100 polled employees in the Thames Valley campus)
100% of staff attend the up and coming values training sessions and can identify why values are important in FY04	100% of sample correct
100% of staff know the six values and can communicate them, within three months of launch	100% of sample correct
100% of staff know where to go subsequent to training to secure further information	100% of sample correct
100% of staff react positively to the values campaign	100% of sample correct

- Retention of the core values has become a compulsory part of every Microsoft employee's annual performance evaluation, and one year on from the values compulsory training kick-off (September 2004), values retention levels were estimated at 80–90%.

To measure and monitor how the values initiative continued to make a difference throughout its business, Microsoft invested in a new "Customer and Partner Satisfaction Study". This study will be completed annually, with the first incorporating survey results from over 40 000 independent customer interviews. The results are fed into a bespoke customer responsiveness tool and will form an invaluable information resource to be applied to the design of Microsoft programs, products and business policies.

Following the outstanding success of the original creative solution, a second phase of the campaign was deployed in early 2004 to fast-track the adoption of the six core values into career development training.

Finally, because of the growing popularity of *The Office* in the US, Microsoft in the US was looking at adopting the UK approach as a roadshow tool to promote and evangelise its own values initiative.

All images appearing in this case study are reproduced by permission of Microsoft.

Comet: bringing the new vision to life

Snapshot: Comet successfully implemented a major internal communications strategy to get staff to embrace the new company vision of becoming more customer-focused.

Key insights

- Comet based its powerful new vision of becoming customer-focused, rather than price-driven, on an extensive internal marketing programme to make sure employees embodied the new vision in their behaviour.
- The programme wasn't just a one-off: continuous training has been put in place as a constant reinforcement.

Summary

Comet is the second largest electrical retailer in the UK and part of KESA Electricals, a pan-European group operating in seven European countries.

In 2005, the company decided that the way to differentiate itself from its competitors would be to realign the business around customers, rather than price, and make service the top priority. To do this, it needed to get all its staff to buy into this new vision as part of a total rebranding of the company. The goal was to increase sales and become the country's most trusted electrical specialist.

The resulting programme was extensive, and included new branding, comprehensive training and significant consumer research. The change in branding, including new uniforms, was coordinated to happen simultaneously across more than 250 stores, home delivery platforms and service centres, encompassing 10000 employees.

In addition, follow-up mechanisms were put in place to keep the vision alive, including board visits to the stores to listen to employees, reward systems and continuous training.

From price to customer focus

In August 2005, Comet realigned its business from a price-driven model to a customer service-driven model. The aim of this shift was to increase customer trust in the Comet brand and to instil a new code of behaviour for all staff. The realignment of the business model was extended to include a full rebranding of the company to differentiate Comet from its competitors. The entire project was called the new Comet "Vision".

There were three key objectives:

* educate staff about changes to the company and motivate them to embrace Comet's new vision;
* position Comet as Britain's most trusted electrical specialist;
* boost sales across all lines of business.

However, there were a number of challenges to overcome. First, the company operated in a price-driven sector where brand loyalty was relatively low. Changing perceptions about the brand would thus require considered and deliberate communication to both staff and customers. In addition, the communication of the new vision to both employees and consumers had to be carefully timed to ensure that both groups felt confident about the new Comet.

The company decided, as part of its strategy, to introduce a comprehensive training initiative for staff in order to communicate Comet's vision and changes prior to the launch date (18 August 2005). A communication programme would be implemented that provided opportunities for staff to give feedback on the changes and address any concerns with senior management.

Developing the vision

To support the launch of the "Vision", Comet rolled out a major rebranding programme which changed the red and white logo, similar to its competitors, to black and gold. The programme included new signage for over 250 sites and the Comet website. This programme ran through the summer, with head office signage being changed last to mark the campaign launch.

All sales and marketing materials were revised in line with the new branding, with new black and gold uniforms distributed to 8000 employees. All retail staff wore their uniform for the first time on 18th August to coincide with the launch.

While the rebranding provided a very visual indication of the vision, Comet also identified and introduced four key behaviours that would represent the core values of the new Comet and enable staff to understand and embrace the new business model:

- deep knowledge;
- care for every detail;
- passion for service;
- individual attitude.

These values were at the core of all training programmes that were implemented to support the launch of the vision (Figure 10.7).

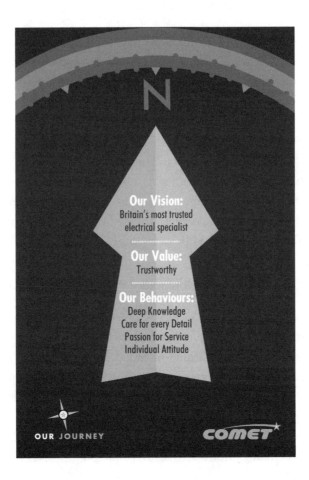

Figure 10.7

Communicating the change

The company then launched two initiatives designed to change the customer experience radically by improving staff knowledge. Recognising that staff motivation was key to a successful launch, and the biggest single factor in improving levels of customer trust, Comet invested 4500 man-days of training and briefing to explain the launch and generate excitement about the changes.

The first was called "Learn it, try it, prove it." This involved a comprehensive new training initiative to create 3000 colleague "product experts" and help sustain staff motivation to deliver the company's key behaviours. Developed after a period of intensive research and international consultation, the new training scheme was launched in early 2005 to ensure that colleagues were ready for the Vision when it launched in August. It was a process that empowered store managers and colleagues by putting training in their hands. At its core was a unique new e-learning system.

Learn it, try it, prove it

Stage one: "Learn it". Training rooms were set up in every store, with dedicated PCs and e-learning resources. An initial series of 25 bespoke, interactive product and category "modules" could be accessed at a convenient moment in the working day. The modules individually covered key product areas. Staff had to achieve an 80% score in the online test to graduate to the next phase.

Stages two and three: "Try it, prove it". A series of staggered role-playing exercises and real-life evaluations was carried out and measured by store managers according to strict criteria, enabling staff to graduate to "product knowledgeable" and "product expert" status.

The second initiative was based on significant consumer research and a mystery shopper programme to identify and understand the key moments of contact between staff and customers, and what impact these had on customer satisfaction, From this, it developed a fourteen-stage, deliberate customer journey for stores in consultation with its store managers, staff and customers.

This journey was a clear set of consistent behaviours, standards and actions for staff that covered all the key moments of customer contact, from how to greet customers when they walked into the store, to understanding their needs when they were browsing products, to helping them load their purchases into the car.

In preparation for the launch of the Vision, the programme was trialled and refined in thirty stores and successfully rolled out to all staff in the first half of 2005. The programme was communicated to staff through a series of in-store briefings and training sessions, and the roll-out was supported by detailed messaging packs, posters and the launch of a peer-to-peer recognition and reward scheme.

Ready for launch

The change in branding and uniforms was coordinated to happen simultaneously across more than 250 stores and service centres, with over 10 000 employees helping usher in the new era.

All Comet stores held celebrations designed to energise both staff and customers. Creating a fun, exciting atmosphere in every store, Comet used a wide range of communication channels to reinforce the message of change to staff and ensure the four key behaviours were sustained across the company. These included:

- Distributing DVDs and carrying out additional briefings carried out around the launch date to reinforce the Vision.
- Colourful posters and postcards containing the key behaviours were sent to all Comet locations.
- A commemorative issue of *Comet News* (Comet's internal communications magazine) was produced, with special sections on the build-up to the launch and the important role colleagues would play. A follow-up issue of the magazine was produced to include a special double-page pull out for staff, highlighting launch activities in different stores.
- Branded mugs, cookies, mouse mats and pens, which contained the four behaviours and poignant statements, were distributed to all staff.

• Toy Comet taxis linked to the ad campaign were distributed to staff for their children.

Maintaining the changes

Board lunches

Listening to staff is key to any successful communications plan, and colleague feedback was seen as an essential part of the execution of Comet's new vision. To ensure consistent open lines of communication, the board of directors planned to spend one day per month in a different store, service centre or home delivery platform across the business, inviting local colleagues to have lunch with them and discuss the company.

Colleagues were encouraged to prepare questions for the board, focusing on any concerns or suggestions they had, as well as any questions on the Vision. Comments were taken into consideration by the board when making decisions about the direction of the business.

e-Learning

Following on from the successful launch of e-learning, the company aim was to roll out a total of 46 e-learning modules in 2006. Information about this training scheme continues to be communicated to new recruits.

Comet stars

Leveraging the momentum and excitement generated around the launch, a peer-to-peer recognition scheme was developed to allow colleagues to reward each other's achievements in displaying and promoting the four key behaviours throughout the business. The scheme was designed to run for a finite time period of three months during Comet's peak period (this is the busiest time of the year for the company and runs from November through to early January).

Members of staff were encouraged to recognise colleagues who strongly displayed a particular behaviour and helped them in their job by awarding them a Comet star to be displayed at their work place. All the stars awarded were recorded at Comet's head office and those judged to be the top 100 stars were selected and presented with lapel badges.

The ten top stars would then be selected, with nine of the ten winners receiving an extra week's free holiday. The ultimate star would be awarded a trophy by the Managing Director and granted an extra week's free holiday as well as an extra week's pay.

Measuring success

Nearly 25 000 individual e-learning sessions had been completed by the beginning of 2006, with 80% of sales colleagues "product knowledgeable" in at least two product areas.

In addition, 8000 people across the UK were engaged in an ongoing independent mystery shopper programme to test every store on customer service competence.

Nearly 1500 Comet star nominations were received by head office. With over 10% of Comet's workforce receiving a star, the programme demonstrated high enthusiasm among colleagues, highlighting the company-wide success of the implementation of the four behaviours. Comet planned to run the scheme again in 2006, with enquiries already being received from colleagues about when that would be.

Consumer and colleague feedback to the new service-driven approach was unprecedented, which showed to what extent employees had embraced the new Vision and were consciously employing the four key behaviours. As a result, there was a 20% drop in levels of customer retail complaints and a 100% increase in customer compliment letters.

All images appearing in this case study are reproduced by permission of Comet.

11

Developing marketing capabilities

Introduction

Effective marketing can boost customer satisfaction, market share, profitability and employee enthusiasm. But this calls for more than traditional marketing strategies. It requires aligning the brand with corporate strategy and embedding brand values into both the company culture and the processes and systems through which it delivers its products and services.

Developing marketing capabilities goes right to the heart of how a company can become truly marketing-oriented. As both these case studies show, the results of this substantial effort and commitment can be very rewarding.

> "Nearly all businesses talk about customer focus, but it often takes ground-breaking work to catapult a marketing-led approach to the heart of a company. What is impressive about these case studies is the way in which they not only had a direct impact on the bottom line, but they also acted as a catalyst for a long-term culture shift in their businesses.
>
> Perhaps more than anything, they demonstrate the power of simple, consistent language that prioritises ideas and allows the whole organisation to focus on why it is different from the competition."

Tim Davie, Marketing Director, BBC

Whitbread: serving up a new recipe for marketing capability

Snapshot: Whitbread's determination to embed a marketing orientation across the company transformed the company's fortunes.

Key insights

- Whitbread is made up of a diverse portfolio of businesses. So, to ensure it was able to meet ambitious business goals, it put into place an equally ambitious programme to instil a marketing mindset across the business.
- Overseen by the marketing team and backed by the Chief Executive, the programme has been designed to turn brand ideas into brand action based on consumer insights.

Summary

Whitbread was founded as a brewer in 1742 and reinvented as a leisure business soon after 2000. As the UK's leading hospitality company, it attracts 10 million customers monthly, who are served anything from a cup of coffee to a gourmet meal, from a bed for the night to a tennis lesson. There are 67 000 colleagues across 1900 outlets.

Whitbread refocused its efforts on finding markets with potential for growth following its transformation from a brewer into a hospitality company. It reviewed its portfolio of brands in a bid to develop a market leader in every sector served. The brands were charged with showing strong consumer preference, creating relevant and noticeable improvements within a year and showing a rise in commercial performance within three years.

The scale of change required a bold approach which would ensure a single, unified message was coming from the company. To ensure consistency, a brand template was drawn up which connected the touchpoints each brand had with consumers to the values, promise and personality that Whitbread wanted to convey. Planning and development began in

March 2003, and pilot programmes launched in April, followed by master classes to give non-marketers the skills to understand and apply the complex marketing concepts.

The company estimated that over the next five years it would generate £20 million in incremental profits.

Setting new and challenging goals

In 2004, goals were set for the refocused business in order to double Whitbread company value by 2010:

- sustaining double-digit profit growth by finding markets with growth potential;
- managing a portfolio of successful brands with a number-one brand in every key market served (Figure 11.1);
- taking the company into the FTSE Top 50.

But the Chief Executive's "Winning Brands" challenge went further. Every brand had to have strong consumer preference, be built on deep customer insight and be managed by "talented, imaginative and rigorous leaders". It was great news for marketing that the Chief Executive recognised the power of brands and the need to understand and please customers. But it was also a huge challenge, since the marketing team knew it was not equipped to deliver.

Figure 11.1

Whitbread's brands were built more on operational strength than underlying consumer preference and differentiation. Leaders were talented operators, but not necessarily brand-builders. Consumer insights were "something marketers bang on about", not deep, shared and leveraged. Each brand was run as a self-contained business by a dedicated executive board with minimal shared marketing practices.

Marketing as a function was pigeon-holed ("they do new product development and communications") and sidelined. To find new markets and sustain organic growth, marketing had to engage everyone in generating real insights and delivering the best experience for the company's guests.

Programme goals were to develop world-class brand management capability evidenced by consumer-noticeable, relevant improvements within a year, and brand transformation with a hike in every brand's commercial performance within three years. The scale of change required was undoubtedly big. Whitbread called in strategic marketing consultancy Oxford Strategic Marketing to design the programme.

Finding the right solution

The main issue to be addressed was how to get from the theory of how to improve, to actually making a difference to brand performance, and to do this by getting nine businesses to change simultaneously and make a consumer-noticeable commercial difference. Also, and probably tougher, it had to be sustainable.

It was decided that what was called for was a seamless marketing capability and strategic planning process. The focus would be on what every business needed: proposition and insight. Real, practical output in the form of a brand template would be produced, not just "training". The end result would be strategic thrusts which plugged straight into annual strategic planning, guaranteeing immediate action in terms of investment priorities, people plans, property and innovation plans and aligned measures (Figure 11.2).

The company joined forces with strategic marketing consultancy Oxford Strategic Marketing to develop a comprehensive change programme to embed marketing practice into every aspect of the business.

The process was to start with the executive boards, not the marketers. The emphasis would be on gaining strong insights into each brand, and developing a new way to cascade this across all functions. And, while the plan would

Source: Oxford Strategic Marketing, 2004

Figure 11.2

Figure 11.3

encompass three years, the focus in the first year would be on people and aligned key performance indicators to reinforce change (Figure 11.3).

The resulting brand template was at the cutting edge of service brand management and crucial to the programme's success. The template was designed to do a number of things:

- give a sense of purpose;
- demonstrate the new skills attained;
- drive immediate action for brands delivered by people;
- institute measures of success;
- make the complex simple – but without being simplistic.

Getting started

The first phase of the initiative began in March 2003, and involved developing the brand template and skills-building material for non-marketers. In

April, a pilot was run at Costa Coffee, the company's leading coffee chain. Data packs were assembled filled with fact-based insights and propositions. The pilot proved that the approach worked, significantly improving training elements and, vitally, creating a powerful advocate for the process.

For the launch to the top 100 Whitbread executives, the Costa Managing Director was able to endorse the process and demonstrate the benefits: "*This has done more to change the way we think than any other initiative I or my team have participated in*". This was far more persuasive than having marketers "sell" the concept. Signing up to the programme by the other businesses was instant and unforced.

A class action

The skills and momentum of the programme were built on with a series of three "master classes", facilitated by Oxford Strategic Marketing, each of which was to produce real and useable output. The first was called "creating the Brand House ©". In a two-day session, each executive team generated their proposition for their "Brand House" ©, based on data and deep customer understanding so that the result was strong and believable. A five-step learning model gave non-marketers the skills and tools to understand and apply complex marketing concepts, such as insight, quickly.

The second master class focused on the consumer "Touchpoint Guidelines". Meeting a month later, and using the proposition (the "Brand House" ©) and the "ideal customer journey" developed between classes, each team then developed a set of 20–30 compelling statements which captured the ideal consumer experience of the brand across products, people/service, environment/atmosphere and communications. By prioritising the 25–30 Touchpoint Guidelines according to consumer need and impact, ability to differentiate and the quality of current delivery, the executive boards generated their strategic goals for 2004/5.

After the first two classes, individuals were charged with developing a "perfect state, world-class experience" for three to four transforming Touchpoint Guidelines in the four weeks before the final and third master class.

That final class, "moving to action" achieved the following objectives:

- final endorsement of strategic thrusts;
- sharing of "perfect state, world-class" for transforming touchpoints;

- what to communicate to whom and how to cascade skills, processes, tools and outputs;
- aligning key performance indicators (KPls) and measures.

Since the master classes, the company has communicated, cascaded and improved this winning brand capability by:

- tracking the impact of "Winning Brands";
- cascading a simple form of each brand's template and mission to agencies, property managers, food developers, front-line staff – in fact anyone delivering brands to guests;
- passing skills and template ownership to every new executive;
- running the "brand staircase": the year two follow-up to the master classes to ensure real brand differentiation;
- applying this new consumer marketing capability to the employer brand, so the company attracts and motivates the right people to deliver superbly;
- using the process and skills to engage every function in agreeing what the Whitbread Group should deliver for stakeholders: its people, suppliers, the communities it serves, the City and shareholders;
- extending "master classes" to international operations.

Measuring the results

The results were impressive in a number of areas. For example, the most compelling evidence of success in engaging employees came from the annual marketer survey run by *Marketing* magazine/Stopgap. Whitbread came from nowhere to rank third as the top employer, behind NatWest and Procter & Gamble, and also came seventh for marketing training. That this was attributed to the "Winning Brands" initiative was supported by internal data.

The group performance was also transformed across a wide range of measures:

- five continuous periods of double-digit growth;
- the company was in the top quartile of major UK companies for financial performance;
- among the highest "press favourability" scores;
- among the top 10 performing shares;

- jumped from 145th to 44th most admired UK company;
- received a request from *Harvard Business Review* to do a "Winning Brands" case study.

A key measure of success was to what extent the programme achieved specific goals. The first was strong consumer preferences. Brand tracking from September 2003 to the end of 2004 showed steady improvement across brands.

The second goal had been to build brands based on strong customer insight. Every business had now developed a unique consumer insight proven in consumer testing after the master class. For example, TGI Friday's insight for its "core" entertaining occasion was: *"I'm looking for that feeling and experience I got at parties I was given as a child"*. In qualitative research, consumers responded to that insight, as did TGI Friday's employees. It resulted in a successful initiative to make the restaurant the best experience for celebrations.

Because all the brand insights were produced not by marketers or agencies but by cross-functional teams, they drew on front-line experience of guests and could thus be believed by everyone in the business. In addition, they produced valuable insights in terms of both employees and other Whitbread stakeholders.

The final goal was to create talented, imaginative and rigorous leaders. One of the measures following the master classes was the number of real breakthroughs produced – these totalled over 60. Every team produced at least five real brand "a ha" moments (Figure 11.4).

Ambitious plans

All seven brand initiatives announced to the City by the Chief Executive in September 2004 came directly from "Winning Brands":

- expand Premier Travel Inn by 1500 rooms a year;
- integrate Brewsters into Brewers Fayre;
- convert Out & Out sites to Beefeater;
- expand David Lloyd Leisure in UK and Europe;
- significant expansion of Costa Coffee sites/international franchises;
- Marriott growth through management contracts;
- new TGI Friday's store format roll-out.

Figure 11.4

Redefining the culture

After only 19 months, the programme had achieved a transformation in marketing orientation. This was shown by the "before and after" signals, which were powerful and consistent:

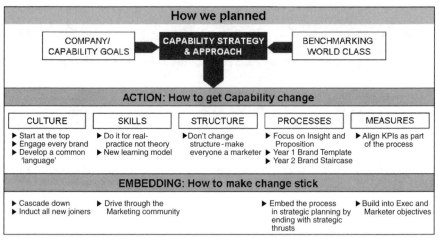

Source: Oxford Strategic Marketing, 2004

Figure 11.5

May 2003	December 2004
"Not another programme!"	"It's the way we at Whitbread manage our brands"
Strong, well-executed brands	Strong, differentiated, well-managed brands
Finance/operations led business	Priorities and investment decisions based on customer needs and insights, captured in the template
"Marketing does NPD and comms"	"We're all marketers"
Motivated and engaged people	People capable of recognising what matters to guests, and motivated and engaged to deliver it 100%
Marketing a cost	Marketing an investment

The programme cost around £400000 in development costs, materials and delivery. But a single initiative in a single brand covered those costs, and the company anticipated that over the next five years, it would generate £20 million incremental profit. It was voted the best initiative ever in November 2004 by the groups' top 100 managers (Figure 11.5).

All images appearing in this chapter are reproduced by permission of Oxford Strategic Marketing.

Vodafone: adopting a system for managing new ideas

Snapshot: Vodafone has put the customer at the heart of its business by developing a sophisticated system that makes idea generation both more efficient and more effective.

Key insights

- Vodafone has developed a highly detailed global diagnostic process for new product development that puts the customer's voice at the heart of the process.
- It is proving to be invaluable in helping the company make key decisions about its product portfolio.
- For large and complex companies, having a repeatable system for comparing and developing new ideas can be extremely effective.

Summary

The Vodafone Group provides a full range of mobile telecommunications services, including voice and data communications. Vodafone has equity interests in 27 countries and partner networks in a further 27 countries, with almost all the group's mobile subsidiaries operating principally under the brand name "Vodafone". Turnover for year end March 2006 was £29.4 billion.

A big issue for companies like Vodafone in the mobile phone market has been how to differentiate. New, breakthrough products are critical to win in this highly competitive sector. However, the industry has traditionally been technology-led, rather than customer-led. This has meant a pronounced lack of competitive differentiation.

Vodafone had come to realise that its traditional concept testing was not working hard enough. While hundreds of product concepts were tested, there was no standardised testing, no benchmarks and no way to compare one concept with another.

To overcome this, the Vodafone Global Insights team developed the Differentiation Potential System (DPS). This was an end-to-end system designed to put customer insight at the heart of product development. It was a complete business process to ensure that the voice of the customer was integrated into the way products were developed and priorities set.

By the end of 2005, the system was providing Vodafone with the common currency by which teams could measure the success of their product ideas. In addition, highly detailed diagnostics meant that further development on every individual product could be based on understanding customers. Even more significantly, it has changed the way the company does business by having a profound effect on the way Vodafone perceives and reacts to customer needs.

Setting the scene: rethinking the new product process

Sustainable differentiation has been a huge challenge in the highly competitive mobile telecoms market. All mobile operators have already been offering their customers a wealth of different products and services: voice, text, picture messaging, video calling, games, mobile Internet, and so on. For the customer, the options can be bewildering. Price/value promotions have played their part, but can't ultimately deliver sustainable differentiation. The market is awash with a huge array of different tariff options, bundles and offers. While these might be effective for a short period, offers can easily be replicated by the competition (and often are).

Vodafone has been keenly aware that "breakthrough" product concepts were critical to maintaining its position as the market-leading mobile operator across the globe. Customers' expectations in the mobile market move very fast, so it is critical to have a pipeline of new ideas and new products ready to deliver against their needs. And, within Vodafone, there has been no lack of new product ideas. At any one time, there can be upwards of 50 different products at various stages of development.

The question for the company was: how could it be sure it was putting development resources behind the best ideas with the greatest potential? It was critical to ensure that these important decisions were informed by the best information possible about what customers really wanted and what they would really use.

However, different methods of testing were making comparisons impossible. Each was using different metrics and methodologies. There was no way to make objective comparisons between one product idea and another. The lack of a historical database also meant ideas being reworked for no reason. With no way to track what ideas had been tested in the past, and how they performed, the organisation was wasting resources on unnecessary rework. And changing business objectives meant that there could be no single consistent measure of "success". As the organisation's focus shifted (e.g. from "acquisition" to "revenue per user" to "brand"), so did the measures of success.

To overcome this, Vodafone's Global Insight team set its sights on bringing all concept development research together into one system to promote consistency, simplicity and actionable results. Working in conjunction with strategic marketing consultancy Oxford Strategic Marketing and market research company Research International, a comprehensive global diagnostic tool and process was developed.

There were four key objectives of what was named the Differentiation Potential System (DPS):

- Provide one top-level measure of customer appeal for products and services at all stages of development by introducing a consistent, comparable "currency" by which all products and concepts could be measured.
- Provide diagnostics on every product concept – driven by customer insight – to help optimise the development process. This called for communicating customer insight in a way that was digestible for development teams, enabling them to apply what they learned to the products they created.
- Provide a way to reduce the complexity of many ideas researched with many customers in many markets, both in terms of the testing process to manage this, and the way in which results were reported.
- Make it easier to put the right resources against the best ideas and product concepts for the right reasons. Consistency in one common measurement approach, used across the globe, was critical to making this happen.

Creating a new system for measurement

First, a new and harmonised way of measuring product concept performance was developed: the "DPI Score". This combined a number of key product concept performance metrics into a single number. To measure these metrics properly, a great deal of preliminary research and analysis was conducted by Research International to identify the "killer questions" which had the greatest correlation with actual product performance and overall appeal.

The score effectively creates the common, consistent criteria which enable the swift comparison of any product concept with any other. This is critical in addressing the first objective for the new system: to establish one common currency by which all product concepts can be measured.

However, a single score was not enough. Vodafone worked with Oxford Strategic Marketing to design a "performance profile", which would be delivered for every concept. A good score is not a necessity, but an indicator of "a worthy concept". The performance profile measures every concept tested against the most important key performance indicators (KPIs) for Vodafone's business.

The full mix of metrics helps establish what role (if any) a product could play in the portfolio. Few (if any) products can deliver great results against every KPI. Different products need to play different roles in the portfolio. Some will help drive frequency of usage, while others will help drive brand preference, and so on.

Building a business process around research

The new system is not just about smart customer research, it is an end-to-end system, designed from the start to have a maximum impact on the business. Figure 11.6 shows a top-line overview of the different elements of the DPS process designed by Vodafone and Oxford Strategic Marketing. These consist of:

- idea generation;
- prepare and prioritise stimulus;
- fieldwork;
- analysis;
- action planning.

Management sponsorship and training for each stage ensures that the system is being embedded into the organisation. That means that insights generated by research will now be at the heart of how products are developed and prioritised.

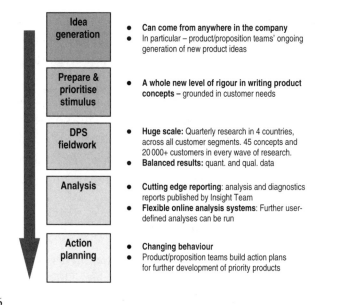

Figure 11.6

Centralising the process provides a "hub" for all development teams and eliminates the need for different testing on different products in different markets. The cycle is run four times a year. There is always an opportunity for any development team in Vodafone to submit their ideas and get detailed results back in just a few weeks. Better still, the system allows them to see the results for their own ideas in context with 45–50 other concepts run during the same wave of fieldwork, and also compared to the results for *every* concept *ever* run through the system (already over 130 by the end of 2005).

Anchoring ideas in customer needs

A structured approach to concept creation ensures that every new idea is anchored in customer needs. The new approach thus breaks down concepts into their constituent elements – need, benefit, features, etc. (the "raw material" for each concept). There are clear guidelines for what goes into each part. The approach enforces rigorous, customer-focused thinking.

Extensive training has established capability across the organisation, which enables non-marketing staff to regularly submit the elements of a well-structured concept. The company could not simply rely on a few market-ing-savvy individuals adept in concept-writing. It "demystified the art" and trained development teams, so they no longer need to go through the marketing department or an agency.

An online concept-submission system has reinforced the discipline. Users fill in all the key elements of a good concept, with online hints and tips available to build on the training. Every submission is crafted into a well-articulated product concept in customer language. An independent copywriter ensures consistency in quality, style and use of language.

Fieldwork on an international scale

In every wave of research, Research International manages concept testing with over 20000 customers across four countries. This mix of countries means that a sufficient range of different customer needs are collected to help predict likely reactions in most markets.

Every product concept is tested with every customer segment in every market, enabling Vodafone to see if its product targeting is right. In any wave of research, each of the 45–50 concepts will be seen by around 1200 customers. Every concept can be tested with a significant sample of each of Vodafone's strategic customer segments in every market. The company can thus immediately see the relative potential of any idea across segments and across markets.

Doing fieldwork online makes sure the process is fast and flexible, with research turned around in just three weeks. Customers are recruited from online panels, while Vodafone can also recruit "on the fly" during fieldwork and react to unexpected shifts in customer mix.

The research questionnaire is very focused. Every question is chosen to deliver against specific pre-planned analysis. Even though the company has collected comprehensive data on every concept, the questionnaire takes just 20 minutes to complete. Within this time, the company can capture information on the customer's profile, their usage of technology and all the critical KPIs of concept performance.

Because the research is totally consistent, it enables comparisons across all products, all segments and all markets. This is critical if the system is to establish a common currency and benchmarks to underpin the building of a massive database of results with both qualitative and quantitative data.

Reporting back

Vodafone, with Oxford Strategic Marketing, developed a suite of bespoke reporting tools which allow immediate comparison of every concept with every other. This has revolutionised the company's approach to portfolio planning, allowing Vodafone to answer a range of important questions such as:

- Which will drive high penetration of usage?
- Which will encourage highest frequency of usage?
- Which concepts are most likely to drive revenue?
- Which will encourage switching or loyalty?
- How does each compare with class benchmarks?

Further diagnostic tools have been designed to provide a detailed understanding of strengths, weaknesses and opportunity areas for each individual concept. The product development teams are now better informed than ever, because they can answer questions such as:

- Which customer segments does this concept appeal to?
- What's driving the appeal?
- When and how might they use this product?
- What impact might it have on Vodafone's business?

Within six months, the system was fully established as the single consistent global approach for testing new product concepts, and was helping Vodafone move from a technology-led to a customer-led organisation. By the end of 2005, the system had already built up such value and credibility among the insight, product and proposition teams, that the company found that people throughout the business were keen to submit even more ideas than there were research slots. That led to the company reviewing ways to improve the capacity and flexibility of the system.

Extending the toolkit

Beyond these bespoke tools, there is also a range of different analytic and reporting resources available to meet the needs of different internal stakeholders. These include:

- **Standard global reports for the whole business.** Quarterly reports, published by the Vodafone Group Insight Team, summarise results from the latest wave of research, with comparisons against all historical benchmarks. They are based on a standard set of customer-breaks and include commentary and interpretation of the data.
- **An online analyser for specific queries.** This is a flexible system to create a user's own customised charts, with search results for any concept past or present. It also contains plot results for any customer group in any country.
- **An interactive Excel database for detailed analysis.** This encompasses every data point for every concept by market and by customer segment. It is available for detailed analysis and understanding of what lies beneath the published results.
- **Action planning tools to help development teams.** These deliver all key data on one concept in a form that highlights key issues and opportunities, along with a structured approach for planning how to develop the idea further.

Transforming the business

Within a relatively short time, the company had become far more decisive about putting resources behind the best ideas and killing off the worst. Six key initiatives were halted or deprioritised as a direct result of the system's output. Again, this was a very tangible measure, demonstrating that the results had gained real "currency" in the organisation. Senior managers were genuinely using the system to guide them in some of their biggest decisions.

For example, the features of the "Vodafone Simply" handset (one of the best selling in the market – see the case study in Chapter 2) were changed based on the system's output. Even for a product which had already hit the market, the powerful diagnostic results were crucial in defining "release 2" of this highly successful handset.

All decisions on which products to include in the product roadmap now always incorporate the system as a critical input. It is used not only to help prioritise resources for one concept vs. another, but also to check that each individual product concept is genuinely delivering against a real customer need.

It has also revitalised the focus on customers' core need for communication. The mobile market continues to be drawn by the excitement of products delivering entertainment through mobiles. But the system has provided a great reality check, and is helping Vodafone renew its efforts to look again at what customers really want their mobile to do – to help them to communicate better.

Becoming much more efficient

The efficiency of the system has also meant that more concepts are being tested more rigorously than could ever have been achieved in the past. Centralising the concept testing process for the globe has delivered huge economies of scale as well. Funds and resources are no longer being wasted on ad hoc testing.

In addition, the system has been used to help build business models and inform financial planning. The system's range of metrics on potential penetration, usage and revenue from new products is proving invaluable to teams that need to estimate the business potential of new product ideas.

Furthermore, it is becoming a key input in the understanding of customer trends. Comparing the results over time allows the company to see how customers' needs from their mobile are changing. This is an important input for the innovation and idea generation process.

By the beginning of 2006, even Vodafone's local market operating companies were seeking to apply the approach. There is enormous potential for the system to spread its wings further, and for the techniques established at a global level to be used at a local level, especially for testing local variations of product concepts, or market-specific initiatives.

The company is confident that putting customer insight at the heart of new product development will result in a step change in the usage and adoption of Vodafone's future products, because the products which are being developed as a result of this comprehensive approach are better grounded in real customer needs than anything ever done in the past.

All images appearing in this case study are reproduced by permission of Vodafone.

12

Doing well by doing good

Introduction

Companies and their brands are under scrutiny as never before. Simply talking about cause-related marketing (CRM) or, increasingly, corporate social responsibility, is no longer enough in the face of rising consumer cynicism. Companies are under pressure to put into place programmes that are seen to make some sort of difference while having demonstrable benefits for both sides.

An important element of both of the case studies in this chapter is how involved the employees became. Doing the right thing can have an impact well beyond the initial goals.

"The old adage that managers are there to do things right but directors are there to do the right thing was never more applicable than to CSR. These two case studies – one a prompt and continuing response to a short-term disaster and the other an enduring association – show how CRM can echo the values of the company to the benefit of the shareholder, can cement employee loyalty and commitment and frankly do a great deal of good for the recipients: a three-way win."

Andrew Marsden, Category Director, Britvic

BT: partnering with the Disasters Emergency Committee for the tsunami appeal

Snapshot: BT's partnership with the Disasters Emergency Committee helped support hundreds of thousands of people affected by the tsunami, and boosted the company's reputation and social responsibility credentials.

Key insights

- BT's approach to corporate social responsibility highlights how developing a coherent and consistent strategy can benefit both sides of a partnership.
- It can also have a significant impact on both customer and employee perceptions.

Summary

BT is a leading provider of communications solutions serving customers throughout the world. Its principal activities include networked IT services, local, national and international telecoms services, and broadband and Internet products and services. Group revenue in 2005 was £18.6 billion.

One of the major aspects of the company's corporate social responsibility (CSR) programme is its relationship with the Disasters Emergency Committee (DEC), a consortium of 13 UK humanitarian agencies. The value of this partnership has been clearly demonstrated following the tsunami disaster in December 2004 in southeast Asia.

Thanks to BT's efforts, DEC was able to keep its donation website working, despite initially crashing because of the enormous number of calls. BT also supplied other forms of help, including sending skilled employees to the affected areas and helping DEC with its call centres. Over £350 million was raised (six times more than any other DEC appeal).

While not actively seeking PR coverage from the disaster, the company received record coverage worth over £7.5 million, reaching an audience of 43 million plus – the most positive press coverage BT has ever received on a single issue. The company estimates that CSR performance accounts for over 25% of the image and reputation element of customer satisfaction.

BT and corporate social responsibility

BT supports all major UK telethons, including Comic Relief, Children in Need and DEC appeals. It provides network management, telephony, call centres, volunteers, fundraising and PR. Using communications technology, BT can help raise millions of pounds through the telethons, doing so in the most efficient way possible through the telephone and online. Support of DEC is a key element of BT's CSR programme.

DEC, supported by BT since it was established, is a consortium of 13 UK humanitarian aid agencies. DEC disburses funds to member agencies best placed to deliver effective and timely relief to people most in need. BT's support of DEC is particularly important to the charity, as it is its only strategic corporate partner (Figures 12.1 and 12.2).

Figure 12.1

Figure 12.2

The key objectives of this partnership are to:

- help DEC raise millions;
- deliver strategic support;
- set up call centres within 72 hours and recruit 120+ telephone volunteers;
- enhance BT's reputation.

DEC relies on broadcasters to donate air time to promote appeals, usually during or immediately after news programming. As the appeals are reactive to disasters, this is sporadic and so DEC's profile is not as high as other telethons. However, since the tsunami appeal, DEC's profile has been hugely increased. For example, in December 2004/January 2005, the tsunami appeal raised an incredible £350 million.

BT has built systems to enable DEC to respond immediately to international disasters. The company is in constant contact with DEC providing technological and strategic advice, enabling appeals to run ever more efficiently.

Stakeholder research supports BT's strategy. In the autumn of 2005, for example, research found that 57% of stakeholders said they would like BT to donate products/services free to charitable causes. The three leading areas BT stakeholders believed most appropriate for BT to support are communication skills (36%), helplines (36%) and technology (34%), thus confirming BT's position in supporting telethons, and particularly DEC appeals.

BT internal audiences are also regularly updated. For example, in February 2005:

- *BT Today* (BT's internal monthly newspaper) gave over the whole paper to the tsunami appeal. This was sent to BT's 102 000 employees and 177 000 pensioners, and was placed in call centres, reaching tens of thousands more agency people.
- The intranet site included 35 items on the tsunami, with 94 551 hits in December/January 2005.
- *BT Today* produced a large follow-up feature in the February 2006 edition.
- The support of DEC was cited in both the BT and DEC annual reports.

In addition, BT has employed its PR agency, Harrison Cowley, to coordinate the media with DEC and offer issues management. BT's partnership with DEC won the Overall Excellence Award at the Third Sector Awards 2005, in addition to winning the category of corporate sponsorship – the campaign has also been awarded a Big Tick by Business in the Community. This led to features on the partnership within marketing and national media.

A quick response to the tsunami appeal

After the tsunami appeal was launched on December 30, BT Chairman Sir Christopher Bland rang leaders at the top 20 FTSE companies while on a personal engagement abroad to encourage them to contribute, pledging a donation of £500 000 from BT. In addition, more than £100 000 was raised via internal fundraising, including payroll giving.

BT traditionally handles pledges to DEC through the telephone. The BT call centre that takes DEC pledges is usually set up within 72 hours. However, the centre for the tsunami appeal was set up in record time, within 24 hours and, notably, over a holiday period. BT also provided 150 volunteers to take calls. As BT does not profit from appeals, the company gives back monies made from each call. Given the huge volume of calls for the tsunami appeal, this involved a sizeable donation (Figure 12.3).

Figure 12.3

On the morning of the appeal launch, thousands of people logged onto the DEC website to donate. The provider that managed the site could not handle the unprecedented response, and the site collapsed. BT stepped in following an urgent DEC request, and within 4.5 hours had delivered an alternative robust solution, thus preventing the potential loss of millions of pounds and hundreds of thousands of donors.

The cost of this e-donate platform, now a permanent solution for DEC, was more than £100 000, excluding the time of the technical team to set up and manage the system.

BT's contribution didn't end there, however. Two teams of BT engineers were despatched to the tsunami area, installing four satellite earth stations to provide voice and data communications. This opened vital communication channels for aid agencies, local people and for families and friends to make contact. Over 150 BT people were involved in this initiative, with a BT press officer sent to help with communications. The total cost of installing the satellite earth stations, including people and equipment, was £1.5 million.

Finally, due to the huge public interest in the tsunami, the DEC switchboard was jammed with calls. As the BT Tower call centre had been established, BT offered to reroute calls to volunteers who were briefed and supervised by DEC staff. Without this support, DEC would have had to pay agency staff to handle the calls.

More than the sum of its parts

There were a number of benefits to both parties from the appeal. For DEC:

- Over £350 million was raised (six times more than any other DEC appeal).
- Over 1.7 million calls were taken.
- The tsunami killed around 200 000 people and washed away the homes and livelihoods of millions. Monies raised saved the lives of tens of thousands and improved the lives of 3.6 million (DEC estimate). £112 million of the DEC fund provided clean drinking water, sanitation, shelter, food and medicine.
- The rebuilding that DEC agencies were undertaking with the cash raised was the equivalent of rebuilding both Birmingham and Glasgow from

scratch. More than £190 million was set to be spent in 2006, including building 20 000 new homes to house 100 000 people.
- The DEC site broke a Guinness World Record for the most money donated online in 24 hours. Between 30th and 31st December 2004, the DEC website received 166 936 donations, raising £10 676 836.

For BT:

- The appeal enabled it to showcase its information and communications technology capability to a mass market during an extremely high-profile event.
- Sir Christopher Bland persuaded numerous top 20 FTSE companies to pledge cash.
- While not actively seeking PR coverage from the disaster, the company received record coverage worth over £7.5 million, reaching an audience of 43 million plus – the most positive press coverage BT has ever received on a single issue.
- Awareness of BT working with the DEC, in a survey carried out by MORI (2005), increased to 34%, an increase of 21% from 2004.
- BT estimated that CSR performance accounted for over 25% of the image and reputation element of customer satisfaction. Further statistical analysis showed that a 1% improvement in the public's perception of CSR activities meant a 0.1% increase in the company's retail customer satisfaction figures. Customer satisfaction is at the heart of BT's business strategy.
- Opinion leader research in April 2005 cited BT's involvement as a positive story, countering the adverse publicity of rogue diallers, payphone maintenance and company break-up rumours.
- Employee research in January 2006 found that over 80% of BT employees were aware of BT's support for the DEC, an increase of more than 35% since the tsunami. Over 90% of BT employees felt more positive about working for BT because of its support.

The tsunami appeal had another, more widespread and longer-term impact: it provided the catalyst for the charity sector to realise the vast opportunities and benefits of receiving pledges online in addition to traditional methods.

BT's corporate values fit well with its work with DEC:

- **Trustworthy** – *"We approached BT to take over our online donations platform as a trusted partner,"* Brendan Gormley, CEO DEC.
- **Helpful** – *"The online team personify helpfulness. They were in constant communication identifying areas for improvement and making me aware of potential issues I could not have considered,"* Pat Willson, DEC.
- **Inspiring** – *"This is a Herculean effort and shows BT at its best, serving customers regardless,"* Ronan Miles, BT employee.
- **Straightforward** – *"All support planned, promised, communicated and delivered to a very exacting timeframe over the holiday period,"* Beth Courtier, Head of BT's Charity Programme.
- **Heart** – the Chairman personally endorsed this value in recognising the efforts of BT people.

Carrying on the good work

BT has continued to learn from helping with appeals, including Niger (August 2005) and the Asia quake appeal (October 2005), with robust and regular meetings to discuss successes and learning. For example, the donations website for the Asia appeal was set up in 1.5 hours, three hours faster than that of the tsunami. Volunteers for call centres also have increased as awareness rises. People that have left the business continue to volunteer, highlighting their commitment to the cause.

To help DEC with its targeting, the company further developed its online mechanism, and is now able to track donors by English regions and nations, as well as internationally. This has provided more management reporting information to support DEC's efforts, allowing it, for the first time, to write and thank donors online and requesting support for new appeals. As a result, donor retention can now be monitored.

BT Global Services has also agreed to support international disasters as a key element in its new CSR strategy, complementing the UK lead. It will be specifically coordinating BT personnel and communications technology to the area(s) affected. And, because DEC is a UK charity and therefore does not have international recognition, BT Global Services is planning to complement this UK activity by working with an international charity partner with an ongoing programme of fundraising and support.

Finally, the online platform has also enabled DEC to run appeals simultaneously. For example, the Niger and Asia quake appeals crossed over and people could donate to both simultaneously. The online platform was also being trialled by call centres with volunteers directly inputting data online from phone calls. This meant no paper records and a more efficient process.

All images appearing in this case study are reproduced by permission of BT.

Avon breast cancer crusade: keeping the partnership alive over a decade

Snapshot: The linking of cause-related marketing and company aims can be remarkably effective when there is such a good match between the cause and the brand.

Key insights

- Avon has found that the allegiance to a cause can become a hugely successful company/corporate initiative – a win for the cause, a win for the brand and a win for the consumer.
- In 2002 it celebrated its decade-long partnership by developing a highly effective programme.
- Having a cross-functional team overseeing all the various initiatives is important to ensure that activities are aligned with marketing and sales objectives.

Summary

Avon is a leading global beauty company, with over $8 billion in annual revenue. As the world's largest direct seller, Avon markets to women in well over 100 countries through over five million independent Avon sales representatives. Avon's product line includes cosmetics, fragrances and toiletries, as well as lingerie, jewellery and gifts.

In the UK, more than 160 000 independent sales representatives, mostly women, reach nearly one in three British women. As well as buying from an Avon Representative, whose key selling tool is a sales brochure updated every three weeks with new products and offers, customers can buy online at www.avon.uk.com. As women are at the heart of its vision and values, Avon regards it as vital to support the fight against breast cancer.

The Avon Breast Cancer Crusade, which began in 1992, was established as an ongoing programme with annual fundraising campaigns, generating funds for the research and awareness charity Breakthrough Breast Cancer. What started in the UK in 1992 inspired the company to establish the Avon Worldwide Fund for Women's Health in the USA, and a global roll-out of campaigns. By the beginning of 2006, through activities in more than 50 countries, $450 million had been raised globally for the breast cancer cause, including £12 million raised in the UK for UK breast cancer charities.

This case study details the UK's tenth anniversary activity in 2002, which surpassed all the key objectives. Fundraising through cause-related marketing over-achieved by 50% against target to reach £1.5 million, and was double the amount raised in 2001. Money was raised from royalties on the sales of lapel pins, a beanie Crusade bear and four key Avon brands spanning the make-up, fragrance, skincare and personal care categories.

Taking a pioneering approach

Having launched its Breast Cancer Crusade in 1992, Avon was one of the pioneers of cause-related marketing for the issue of breast cancer. With an obvious link between brand, corporate values, customer concern and issue, annual campaigns were highly successful.

Since the Crusade was established, corporate interest in cause-related marketing had increased steadily, creating a "noisy" marketplace for cause-related marketing activity between beauty brands and breast cancer, particularly in October's Breast Cancer Awareness Month (BCAM).

Maintaining Avon's strong leadership required new energy and creativity to hold the interest and support for the campaign internally, among customers, Avon Representatives and staff; and externally with opinion formers, media and the general public.

With a significant milestone of ten years of support for the single cause of breast cancer, Avon also wanted to reaffirm its commitment to long-term charity partner Breakthrough Breast Cancer, reinforcing its position as its number one corporate supporter.

Avon set challenging objectives for the anniversary year:

- Raise £1 million for Breakthrough, matching the funds raised in 1992, and representing an increase of approximately 25% over recent years' average annual fundraising.
- Add new impetus to a mature programme. Staff, Representatives and customers would need re-energising and motivating.

- Promote Avon's longevity of support and impact for the cause.
- Support Avon's beauty image principles: contemporary, fashionable and a beauty leader.

An integrated solution

The company developed a year-long, integrated programme of fundraising and awareness-building activities to encompass marketing, public relations and associate involvement across the business. It was planned and managed by the corporate public relations team, and operationally executed through the activities of a cross-functional, in-house working party.

The programme included creation and launch of an updated "anniversary" focus and identity, which clearly communicated the issue of breast cancer, the longevity of Avon's association with the issue and the passion Avon felt for the cause. This featured at every opportunity throughout the year (Figure 12.4).

The tenth anniversary identity was based on the underlying theme that encompassed the company's feelings about the ten-year milestone:

- passion for the cause;
- pride in the company's accomplishments;
- promise: a reaffirmation of the long-term commitment in the future, which would be used in communications as appropriate.

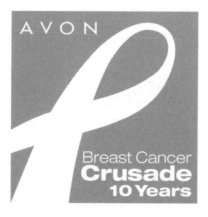

Figure 12.4

Figure 12.5

The common "P" in those three words was stylised to be reflected in a ribbon shape, synonymous with the breast cancer cause. A new logo was developed which incorporated this icon. The requirements were that it should be clean, clear, suitable for use across all audiences and media, and that it would communicate the issue, the campaign and the anniversary (Figure 12.5).

This identity was applied to marketing promotions, the website, staff communications and the products themselves. It became the focus for everything created and produced for the anniversary year. It was also important for this logo to be modified for a life beyond the anniversary year to maintain continuity in 2003.

Developing the right products

The company had been extremely successful in raising money through the sale of lapel pins at the low entry price point of £1, as a no-profit Avon item. Although still huge, Avon had seen a gradual trend of slight decline in pin sales since 1998.

The pins

Customer research in 2001 highlighted that the recent "badge-like" design of pins was less popular with Avon's core customer. To a lesser degree, there was also an indication of a collectors' market waiting to be exploited. This indicated the need for Avon to return to a more "jewellery-like" design for the pin, and the potential to offer more than one design of pin.

Figure 12.6

Avon took the ribbon icon as the basis of the design for an anniversary pin. For the first time, there would be a collection of pins, comprising three variants, with a phased introduction to give energy bursts through the year.

- silver tone, bearing Avon's charity partner symbol and representing passion for the cause (Figure 12.6);
- gold tone, with a "diamond" representing pride, to give a focus for Representatives at the mid-year peak of activity;
- pink enamel, to be introduced in Breast Cancer Awareness Month and bearing a kiss, reflecting Avon's promise to continue its support for the cause "until we reach the day when we can say we helped kiss goodbye to breast cancer" (which was the long-term theme of Avon's activities globally). This final pin would be launched with a matching Kiss Goodbye to Breast Cancer lipstick, as part of a global event.

They were each £1, with all profits to Breakthrough and of high quality manufacture, in line with Avon's regular fashion jewellery products.

The teddy bear

Research also indicated that customers would buy a giftable Crusade product at around £5, with a £2 charity contribution. A key product introduction was thus the Crusade bear, a cute teddy bear wearing a pink T-shirt, with the same "P" pink ribbon logo, picked up from the jewellery and logo design (Figure 12.7). The price was benchmarked against other leading "bean-filled" collectables. The quality was up to Avon's regular standard: higher than the

Figure 12.7

industry, especially in relation to children, despite being marketed as a gift, as opposed to a toy.

This bear became the focus for the website (Figure 12.8), where it was animated to give a hug and a kiss, creating interest and interactivity. Avon reinforced its commitment to fundraising by offering a donation when the bear was sent to a friend. A life-sized bear was also created to support PR and staff motivational activity, while limited edition motivational bears in different sizes, or dressed in bespoke T-shirts, were developed to motivate buy-in by top Representatives and sales managers (Figure 12.9). These had a huge "aah" factor, and were highly prized.

Creating stronger links with brands

Sales of the bear and pins were supplemented with quarterly merchandising offers in the brochure, which gave a royalty from each of four key Avon brands. All brochure promotions carried the tenth anniversary Crusade logo and a motivational statement for the cause.

In addition, the UK joined a global initiative offering a Kiss Goodbye to Breast Cancer lipstick for Breast Cancer Awareness Month. This campaign/product/cause theme was initiated in the UK in 1999 with great success in

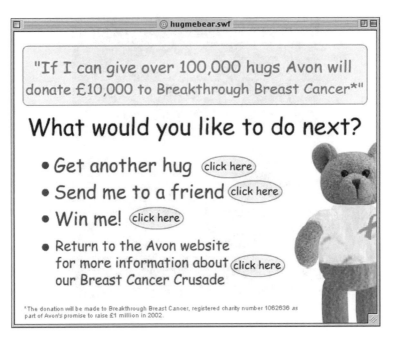

Figure 12.8

fundraising, PR and campaigning, and subsequently picked up globally as the "tag line" for Avon's US and global efforts for the cause.

A range of six lipsticks in globally relevant packaging and shades was developed and promoted around the world to mark Breast Cancer Awareness Month, and to give a final push to Avon's global goal of reaching $250 million raised by the end of 2002. These had exclusive, limited edition packaging and shades and were priced in the UK at £5, with £2 to Breakthrough.

The product offering and pricing and promotion throughout the anniversary year was designed to create high visibility and appeal to Avon's customers, address well-researched customer expectation and result in increased fundraising during the year, without detracting from aggressive sales and profit objectives for the business.

Spreading the word

There was an increased focus on brochures with a range of price points, products and promotions designed to address the research findings, while the

Figure 12.9

motivational statement of "by buying X you are helping to raise £1 million in 2002 towards Breakthrough Breast Cancer's vital research" was included in every promotion.

While advertising wasn't affordable for the tenth anniversary generally, the company sponsored Fashion Targets Breast Cancer. As lead sponsor, the company had its logo and "10-year partnership with Breakthrough" statement appear on all Fashion Targets Breast Cancer advertising. Product placement was also arranged by Avon for Target T-shirts in TV soaps (including Coronation Street, Brookside and Hollyoaks). This was highly motivational for Avon Representatives as well.

In addition, there was a comprehensive media relations campaign taking in women's consumer press, national, regional and broadcast media.

Gaining internal support

Getting Representatives involved was seen as critically important. There were a number of ways this was done.

- Regular space in *Link* magazine, produced exclusively for Representatives every three weeks, to highlight new products, special offers and business-building activities.
- A special Crusade anniversary booklet reviewing the past ten years, fostering pride in shared achievements and including endorsements from well-known people, including celebrities, HRH The Prince of Wales and the Prime Minister.
- Point-of-sale materials developed for those high-performing Representatives who developed further fundraising opportunities (e.g. selling pins in public places, posters, point-of-sale display boxes for pins, banners, etc.).
- While traditional value incentives were not deemed appropriate by Avon in the context of its Breast Cancer Crusade, support was recognised in symbolic ways (recognition certificates, visits to the Breakthrough Research Centre).
- Modest incentives were developed for 2002, e.g. to increase the overall level of buy-in for pins by a greater number of Representatives, so a 10 for 10 challenge offered Representatives a complimentary Pride pin as a thank-you from Avon when they purchased ten pins prior to customer introduction.

Beating all the targets

Raising the funds

Avon's £1 million target was exceeded by 50%, with total fundraising for the year of £1.5 million, which more than doubled 2001 fundraising of £639 000. Pin sales increased by 53% over 2001, and staff fundraising increased by 41%.

Supporting the brand

In addition, research trends, from a nationally representative sample of 1000 women, conducted via the NOP Omnibus Survey, showed the following highlights:

- Spontaneous awareness of Avon/Avon Breast Cancer Crusade as an event/ campaign that raises money for breast cancer increased from 3% in November 2001 to 10% in December 2002, while prompted awareness increased from 33% in April 2002 to 38% in December 2002.
- Awareness of the Crusade extended beyond Avon's current existing customer base, with 22% lapsed and 11% of non-Avon customers also being aware.
- Prompted awareness of Avon supporting a breast cancer charity was high. When women were prompted with a list of key companies that supported this cause, one-third of women cited Avon as the company most associated with supporting a breast cancer programme. The comparable figure in January 2001 was 26%, showing a 7% increase over the two-year period.
- During the same period, awareness of Avon/Avon Breast Cancer Crusade events was higher than other corporate activities supporting the same cause.

Adding new impetus

There were other indications of the impact of the programme.

- A letter of support was received from HRH Prince Charles, The Prince of Wales, and was published in *To show we care* – the anniversary commemorative booklet (Figure 12.10). He also recorded a video message of support/motivation during the year for staff and Representatives, which was used to add impetus to staff from August in readiness for BCAM.
- Supportive messages also came from the Prime Minister, Health Minister, various MPs and celebrities. They were published on the website, and used in PR activity as appropriate. An Early Day Motion supporting the Avon/ Breakthrough partnership and highlighting the need for more funding for research into the prevention of breast cancer was signed by almost 100 MPs.
- Breakthrough secured former Spice Girl Emma Bunton as the face of Fashion Targets Breast Cancer for the Avon brochure promotion of the Target products (Figure 12.11). Avon was strongly identified with the whole Fashion Targets Breast Cancer campaign, with the ten-year partnership branding on billboards and in press advertising, and all campaign events (including the launch to retailers, the British Fashion Week launch party and a fashion roadshow to six UK regional shopping centres).

Figure 12.10

Figure 12.11

- Media coverage increased by 66% over 2001, and included national, regional and consumer print media, radio and regional TV. S Magazine (published by the *Sunday Express*) was the media partner for the Avon Breast Cancer Crusade Awards, resulting in excellent coverage in S Magazine, *The Daily Express* and OK magazine.

Promoting longevity of the programme

In a general employee survey carried out every two years, of the 82% of staff who responded in 2001, 94% confirmed their pride in Avon's accomplishments – the highest positive score achieved across the whole survey. This confirmed the company's ambition that this was more than a cause-related marketing campaign. It was a totally integrated long-term company initiative that engaged customers, staff, the media, the public, politicians and celebrities.

Finally, the Avon Breast Cancer Crusade had helped to kick-start the launch of a brand new charity, and went on to raise one-third of the money needed to establish the Breakthrough Toby Robins Breast Cancer Research Centre, which opened in 1999. Money raised since the centre opened has helped fund recruitment of the scientific teams now employed there, and the vital research work they are undertaking.

All images appearing in this case study are reproduced by permission of Avon Cosmetics Ltd.

Appendix

The case studies in this book have won the following Marketing Society awards. The names of the original agencies involved (where applicable) are listed following each winner.

3	New Brand	2005
Agency: WCRS		
Avon	Cause-related Marketing	2003
BT	Cause-related Marketing	2006
Agency: Harrison Cowley		
Comet	Internal Marketing	2006
Comic Relief	Chairman's Special Prize	2006
Agency: AMV BBDO		
Famous Grouse	International Brand Development	2006
Agency: AMV BBDO		
Freeview	New Brand	2004
	Customer Insight	2004
Green & Black's	Marketing Achievement	2006
Agency: Brave		
Heinz Ketchup	Customer Insight	2005
Innocent	Marketing Achievement SME	2005
Microsoft	Internal Marketing	2005
Agency: Creative Direction		
O$_2$	Loyalty	2006
Agency: Archibald Ingall Stretton		
Pfizer Nicorette	International Brand Development	2005
Agency: AMV BBDO		
S A Brain	Brand Revitalisation	2006
Agency: Heavenly Marketing		

Sainsbury's	Marketing Communications	2006
Agency: AMV BBDO		
Silentnight Beds	Brand Development	2004
Specsavers	Brand Extension	2006
Stella Artois	Marketing Achievement	2004
Agency: Lowe		
Tesco	Marketing Achievement	2005
Agency: Lowe		
Tesco.com	Best Use of Channels to Market	2002/2003
Agency: EHS Brann		
The Independent	Brand Revitalisation	2005
Agency: Walsh Trott Chick Smith		
The Number	Marketing Communications	2004
Agency: WCRS		
The Times	Brand Development	2005
Agency: Rainey Kelly Campbell Roalfe/Y&R		
TNT	Marketing Achievement B2B	2006
Agency: Rees Bradley Hepbum		
Toyota Corolla	Brand Revitalisation	2003
Agency: Saatchi & Saatchi		
Toyota	Loyalty	2005
Agency: Miller Bainbridge and Partners		
Unilever Dove	Marketing Communications	2005
Unilever Lynx	Marketing Achievement	2003
Agency: Bartle Bogle Hegarty		
Unilever Olivio/Bertolli	International Brand Development	2003
Agency: Bartle Bogle Hegarty		
Vodafone Simply	Customer Insight	2006
Vodafone	Marketing Capabilities	2006
Consultancy: Oxford Strategic Marketing		
Waitrose	Marketing Communications	2002
Agency: Banks Hoggins O'shea FCB		
Walkers' Nobby's Nuts	New Brand	2006
Agency: AMV BBDO		
Whitbread	Marketing Capabilities	2005
Consultancy: Oxford Strategic Marketing		

Index

Index compiled by Terry Halliday, Indexing Specialists Ltd